Exploring the Emotional Life of the Mind

This highly innovative new book reconsiders the structure of basic emotions, the self and the mind. It clinically covers mental disorders, therapeutic interventions, defence mechanisms, consciousness and personality and results in a comprehensive discussion of human responses to the environmental crisis.

For openers, a novel psychodynamic model of happiness, sadness, fear and anger is presented that captures their object relational features. It offers a look through the eyes of these specific emotions and delineates how they influence the interaction with other persons. As regulation of the emotional state is the core task of the self, dysregulation can lead to mental disorders. Clinical cases of post-traumatic stress disorder, obsessive compulsive disorder and depression are discussed, using the model to outline the emotional turbulence underneath. Then, the interplay between emotions, the self and the mind is clarified. Finally, the elaborated theory is used to analyse personal responses to the environmental crisis and political strategies that capitalise on them.

This book will appeal to scholars, psychotherapists and psychiatrists with an interest in emotions and who wish to challenge their own implicit theory of emotion with an explicit new model. It will also be of interest for academic researchers and professionals in fields where emotional processes play a pivotal role.

Daniël Helderman has a background in therapeutic work as a clinical psychologist, psychotherapist and psychoanalyst. He teaches psychoanalytic theory at RINO Utrecht and RINO Amsterdam as well as supervising healthcare psychologists in the Royal Netherlands Army and speaking professionally on emotion-related issues. His ambition is to use psychodynamic insight to amplify environmental awareness and (inter)action.

"We work above all with feelings, so it is remarkable how undeveloped Freud's theory of emotion was. This book integrates everything we have learnt in the intervening century, in a new theory that clinicians will find immediately useful and practical."

Mark Solms, Research Chair of the IPA

"Living near a river, my parents told me to keep away from the maelstrom. I, however, invite you to dive into Daniël Helderman's Maelstrom model of basic emotions. He stirs up familiar psychodynamic concepts and connects them with contemporary insights into personality, mind and consciousness. This book is a stimulating read and might challenge you to reconsider your way of working with emotions and the self."

Dr. Frans Schalkwijk, psychoanalyst and professor
(of special education) at the University of Amsterdam, the Netherlands

Exploring the Emotional Life of the Mind

A Psychodynamic Theory of Emotions

Daniël Helderman

Routledge
Taylor & Francis Group

LONDON AND NEW YORK

First published 2021
by Routledge
2 Park Square, Milton Park, Abingdon, Oxon OX14 4RN

and by Routledge
52 Vanderbilt Avenue, New York, NY 10017

Routledge is an imprint of the Taylor & Francis Group, an informa business

© 2021 Daniël Helderman

British Library Cataloguing-in-Publication Data
A catalogue record for this book is available from the British Library

Library of Congress Cataloging-in-Publication Data
A catalog record for this book has been requested

ISBN: 978-0-367-19163-4 (hbk)
ISBN: 978-0-367-19166-5 (pbk)
ISBN: 978-0-429-20083-0 (ebk)

Typeset in Times New Roman
by Apex CoVantage, LLC

To Annegien and Elian, who move me beyond words

Motto

The edge of the whirl was represented by a broad belt of gleaming spray; but no particle of this slipped into the mouth of the terrific tunnel, whose interior, as far as the eye could fathom it, was a smooth, shining, and jet black wall of water, inclined to the horizon at an angle of some forty-five degrees, speeding dizzily round and round with a swaying and sweltering motion, and sending forth to the winds an appalling voice, half shriek, half roar, such as not even the mighty cataract of Niagara ever lifts up in its agony to Heaven.

Edgar Allan Poe, "A Descent into the Maelström", 1841

Contents

Outflow   **147**

Figures and tables

Figures

Table

Acknowledgements

Though most of the writing was done in splendid isolation, I am pleased to burst the bubble that it was a one-man job. There are more people than I can mention here who have helped me in ways I can't start to explain. Therefore, I first want to thank all of the "anonymous" people who are not on this list. My gratitude is unspoken but heartfelt.

Of course it brings me to the people who were willing to talk to me as their therapist. You have given me a chance to share my involvement and interest in the emotional world. I thank you also for your patience in finding out and explaining to me how things actually work. I want to apologise for the times when I wasn't able to listen, because of some inner conflict of my own or because of physical absence.

Certainly I can name the psychoanalyst who has helped me to understand myself better and live life more courageously. Utter thanks to Fred Wissink. Also thanks to Willem van Berkel, the outspoken coach who has helped me navigate through a career change. Over the years there have been many teachers and fellow students who have been guides and companions in the science of emotions and clinical work. I can only scratch the surface here, but explicitly thank my academic teachers Adriaan Tuiten, Jack van Honk and Cas Schaap. My fellow students who trained with me as healthcare psychologists and clinical psychologists made the work not only bearable but fun. It is heartbreaking that not everyone is here anymore, but the years spent together will remain with me.

Hanita, Hansa, Joey and Lisette not only trained with me as psychoanalysts, but they also came up with an unforgettable musical intermezzo at my wedding. I thank my psychoanalytic teachers Harry Stroeken, Gertie Bögels, Frank Kleijberg, Irene Mettrop, Jan Vandeputte, Ton Stufkens and Nelleke Nicolai, among many others. Also I have appreciated psychoanalytic supervision greatly, and I thank Pieter Niers and Antonie Ladan for that.

I would like to express my gratitude to a great variety of colleagues I have had over the years. I can testify to the notion that in the military, true camaraderie can be found. Some bonds are made for life, and some of them wear camouflage. Thanks to Paul, Willem, Karel, Marille, Sjef, Marea, Annemarie, Christine, Roderick, Joost, Liesbeth, Rene and many others. Also thanks to Eric Vermetten, who was my research supervisor at the time and helped me to write down the very first version of the Maelstrom model. When I left the army, I met very committed colleagues at the Altrecht Institute for Mental Health Care. Especially I would like to thank Suzette Boon and Desiree Tijdink for their team spirit and extraordinary expertise.

If it wasn't for the highly accomplished colleagues at the former Dutch Psychoanalytic Institute, I could never have made the transition to the treatment of children, adolescents and parents. Thank you all for having allowed me to become a junior once more. Filip, Catrien, Lisette, Muriel, Catherine, Cileke and Sonja: "De Maliestraat" lives on. A special thanks to Marcel Schmeets, who was one of the first to see potential in my (then still rudimentary) model of emotions.

Though I still have to regulate my own hyperarousal each time I teach, I find it fun and highly rewarding. Teaching is an advanced way of learning: students always come up with questions that I never thought of. Thanks to all the clever colleagues who train as clinical psychologists for children and youth in Utrecht or learn to use analytic drawing (Tekenanalyse) at the Pedagogisch Psychologisch Centrum Heemstede. A special thanks to Wanda Dondorp, who is one of the most creative and kind colleagues I know.

Supervision is one of the ways for me to stay connected with clinical practice right now. Thanks to Allison, Anouk, Hillebrant, Pauline, Rick and Wies for letting me be a part of your professional development.

Another clinical connection is my psychoanalytic intervision group. Many thanks to Frans, Catherine, Mark and Elke for being so open, interested and fun. Frans Schalkwijk especially has read and commented on several chapters. And more importantly, he has given me unsolicited and warm advice on how to become a writer.

My colleagues in the psychoanalytic reading group were the ones who motivated me to go public. Without the support of Claudia, Cileke, Hansa, Muriel, Freek and Jaap I would still be brooding in solitude. They are also the early adopters of the Maelstrom model and help me to notice deficiencies in my reasoning. I value it highly!

The one who gave me the final push to write a book is Mark Solms. He most generously listened to my ideas without having any professional relationship with me. That meeting on Sunday afternoon in Odijk was thrilling and truly mind-expanding. It was somewhat bizarre to hear him pick up on ideas so quickly that took me years to develop. Without his belief in me, I would never have dared to write this book: I really cherish the attentive support. Rosa Spagnolo has also been very kind to me in her interest and encouragement.

Without the trust and support that I received from the people at Routledge, this book would never have been finished. A special thanks to Russell George, Elliott Morsia and Payal Bharti.

Thanks to all friends who have endured my absent-mindedness and helped me to stay grounded. Astrid and Ramon, Ammo and Monique, Marc, Justin: thanks for your support and putting things into normal perspective! Also thanks to my family-in-law for being so caring and down to earth. Thanks Hans, Berthe, Marije, Janneke and Dick.

My dear brother Mike is the one to go to for intellectual and visual clarity. He very generously redrew all of the figures in this book in a professional way (though it is not his profession). Thanks Mike and Saskia.

My parents Ann and Aad always have lovingly believed in me and I know that it is not an easy thing to do. Thank you for enduring the concerns I gave you, for your love of life and for so much more.

I can't thank Annegien and Elian enough for being in my life. You are at the centre, around which everything else revolves.

Inflow

undertow

This book is about emotion and, as these things go, my fascination is both personal and professional. I have grown up in a warm and loving family, one whose history though is no stranger to psychological trauma. These traumatic events stem from the time before I was born, but my antennas quickly picked up on ripples of subcutaneous tension when particular issues were at hand. In those early years, these tensions seemed to circle around a centre that was as hollow as it was forceful. Later each of us learned to talk about what had happened and how it had affected us all. Eventually it has solidified my trust in sharing subjective truth. It is no coincidence that I have become a psychologist.

This book is also about finding meaningful words for what is felt but is unspoken. It is not about the recovery of facts per se, but about learning to speak from within. That is not an easy thing to do, because our emotions steer our subjective experience in an immediate preverbal manner. In principal our verbal thoughts come up for air out of this ongoing emotional undertow. But some emotional experiences defy words because they feel too conflicted, overwhelming, chocked up or shameful. Thinking and talking about emotions then feels like losing solid ground, like being taken by a fierce current that is beyond personal control. And some unspoken subjective experiences don't even make it to the level of identifiable emotions. Especially when children grow up in a situation that deprives them of safely getting to know their emotional inner world, they can have a hard time as adults to personally own their feelings. Though it can be evident that there is a lot going on inside, sensations and perceptions might lack the "simple" merging into understandable emotions.

Based on personal and professional experience, I present a model of basic emotions that can help to open up uncharted inner worlds. I use it as a therapeutic tool for finding words for what is going on inside. By delineating the preverbal mechanisms that govern happiness, sadness, fear and anger, I hope to capture what it is that these basic emotions are trying to say. I believe it to be a story of vital needs and wishes. Basic emotions drive us to fulfil vital needs and wishes in the outer world. When these needs are chronically unmet, they can become a disabling source of arousal. It makes it hard to make sense of the emotional turbulence that is seen at the surface.

I draw on my academic studies of biopsychology and clinical psychology and the pleasurable time spent in a psychophysiology lab. It was there that I was introduced to the science of hormone levels, subliminal perception, attentional bias and subjective experience. But I didn't apply for a PhD position; instead my appetite for studying emotions in live action drove me away from the university. So after a fellow student told me about his new job as a psychotherapist in the army, serving in the Netherlands and abroad, my letter of application was quickly sent. In the aftermath of the Yugoslav Wars ethnic conflicts didn't subside spontaneously, and a great international military effort was put into preserving peace. On many levels it made sense to be a part of that.

This book, *Exploring the Emotional Life of the Mind*, gives an account of what I have discovered about what is felt but unspoken. First I present the so-called Maelstrom model of emotions and discuss the clinical use in various cases.[1] The Royal Netherlands Army turned out to be more than an employer and enabled me to become a certified clinical psychologist. After that, I was fortunate to work in several civilian settings: a department for personality disorders (though I am still uncomfortable with that term), a department for chronic and complex traumatisation, the department for children and youth of the Dutch Psychoanalytical Institute and in my own private practice. I have learned from teachers, colleagues and supervisors, but most of all from the people who came to me for help. No one looks, let alone dives, into the maelstrom of emotion without anxiety. I am utterly grateful for all of the people who accepted me as a companion on such a journey.[2]

For reasons like that, and many more, I am also grateful to the psychoanalyst who has helped me on my personal path.

During clinical work, I brought my antenna for the rising and subsiding of emotional tension with me. With the focus on emotional tension (or arousal), one can learn a lot about its impact on social interaction. Though it is impossible to monitor all aspects of emotion in the real world the same way as one does in the laboratory, it has a huge advantage. The real world isn't limited to four walls, so one can observe emotional behaviour in complex interactions. These observations led to simple ideas that paved the way for the Maelstrom model of emotions. For instance, the idea struck me that emotions shift in time and space. Literally: "where and when" exert a great deal of influence on the kind of emotion that is experienced. Wondering what emotions are going on inside, one can learn a lot by thinking of the time and place people find themselves in. Basic arousal incites people into action, directed towards or away from the other. This *action tendency* (Frijda, 1986) manifests itself through the preparation of the body for movement. The tensioning of muscles, accelerated breathing, change in blood flow, even if the movement is inhibited, these telltale signs inform the attentive observer of an emotional shift within. And what comes across as a disadvantage at first can turn out to be fruitful. Not knowing what it is about, not knowing the story inside the head of the other, can help to focus on the workings of emotions in the here-and-now. Some movie directors really have a knack for portraying these kind of unverbalised interactions. Even when you turn off the sound of the movie, the story is still convincingly told.[3]

This idea shattered an assumption I didn't know I had. It dawned upon me that it is not merely the intensity of emotion that shifts in time and space – something like the further it gets, the weaker it feels – but it is the quality of the emotion. When a wasps enter the room, it surely attracts my fearful attention. But when the bugger decides to land on my arm, I strike mercilessly (even though I rationally know that I shouldn't). And like responding to a personal attack on my well-being, I will probably be angry while striking back. So it is the quality of emotions that steers our interaction with the other (whom I either love or hate). And changing the space in between is changing the sort of interaction that we might have.

Thinking along these lines also helped me to let go of the frame of positive and negative emotions, for I endorse Darwin's idea that all emotions serve an evolutionary purpose (Darwin, 2009, originally published in 1872). I state that it is not the evaluation of our emotional experience (as positive or negative) that helps us to make personal sense of the world, but principally it is the other way around. (We intrinsically evaluate the other through our emotional reactions.) It is my anger that opens up the possibility to represent the other as the bad guy, for it is my anger that links him to the prospect of stinging pain (in case of the wasp). I don't believe that it is a consequence of reflective rational thought that makes the other a bad guy in my mind, after which I get angry. Also I don't believe that the negative side of feeling angry causes me to avoid the wasp or avoid becoming angry myself. Anger signals that there is a need not being met (in this case a need to be safe and free from toxic pain), and anger makes me want to attack the other or to break free. In many situations, our learning processes are more determined through the intrinsic emotional evaluation of the interaction with the other than through the reflective evaluation of our emotional experiences.

Certainly I don't want to make a case against the importance of reflection. On the contrary, conscious thought helps us to treat our emotional experiences in more balanced ways. Without it, we treat our own subjective experiences in the same basic black-or-white emotional manner as we treat our friends or foes. Our emotional machinery steers us "towards or away from" our subjective experience in the inner world, just as they steer us "towards or away from" the other in the outer world. Generally speaking, people develop an aversive attitude towards their emotional experience when it is overwhelming, unacknowledged by others and undesirable to the self. Then the subjective inner world might appear as a dark undertow, wherein the sense of one's place in the world can get lost. Thoughtful reflection, especially within a caring relationship with the other, helps us to get to know ourselves. Healthy psychological development allows people to gradually explore their emotional inner world, so we can develop a safe sense of ownership and control.

So I came to conceive a model that includes these "live" impressions of the workings of emotions.[4] It delineates four basic emotions and their interrelatedness. I believe it to be new and clinically most useful, for it links preverbal arousal with basic emotions and the interaction between the self and the other. The model depicts how happiness, sadness, fear and anger serve as a quick response in order to meet vital internal needs in the outer world. These basic emotions move the self to influence the relation with the other through bridging the gap or providing space and through manipulation of the impact the other has on the self. Almost twelve years ago, I sketched this model and I have thought about it and used it ever since. It helps me to emotionally connect to people who have no words for their inner experience.[5] It helps to shed light on the emotional interplay in the here-and-now. I found it to be a useful tool when entering the emotionally charged sphere beneath the reflective surface. It doesn't provide clear-cut answers and it isn't a code for reading minds, but it helps to understand some of the intricate dynamics of the inner world.

Then three chapters follow on the therapeutic integration of emotional experiences and the regulation of stunted needs and desires. Clinical work is presented that exemplifies how the Maelstrom model can help focus on emotion and regulation for various psychological problems. I will try to shed some light on questions about nightmares (what is it about nightmares that makes the worst one the most susceptible to become repetitive?), about obsessive compulsive disorder (when one loses control of the need to feel in control) and about depression (why does depression so frequently involve a loss of the desire to move?). In Chapter 8, a link is made between the integration of emotional experience and personality organisation. Learned patterns of emotion regulation can become implicit and characteristic features of who we are. There I discuss the interrelatedness of emotions, the self and the mind, with a reformulation of three interrelated sections of consciousness.

More than twenty-five years have passed since I began to study psychology. Our natural environment is changing at an alarming rate and our foot- and fingerprints are all over it. Being in the midst of my midlife and having a beautiful son of ten years old, I will try to apply some clinical insights on the single most important problem of our times: how to deal effectively with the environmental crisis. In the final chapter I lay the groundwork for this effort.

Though these are serious topics, my aim is not to write a heavy book. I have warm feelings for the people and places[6] that help(ed) me to explore my own emotional inland sea. Also it is the crux of psychotherapy to help people relate to their inner world in such a way that they can experience the outer world more freely and fully. This book is an attempt to help navigate through our elusive emotional world, by mapping a small but important part of it. I hope that you will find this book has something to say about you too.

When someone comes for psychotherapy and asks the question "What on earth was I thinking?" out loud, I consider this to be a good starting point, fertile for gaining insight. But this point of view is certainly not self-evident; it is a huge developmental achievement. In order to reflect on yourself with open curiosity, one has to be able to recognise that the turmoil is not only on the outside but moreover within. And just like we know more about the surface of the moon than about life in the deep sea, exploring the latter might result in more unnerving encounters with the unknown. One has to be up for that.

And though I applaud the question, I state that it is fundamentally misleading. What people really want to know is what on earth they were *experiencing and feeling* besides thinking, though that seems to be an even more daunting question. In this highly subjective realm, wherein the body, the senses and social interaction mingle with emotions, dreams and words, the distinction between knowing and not knowing is blurry at best. In the inner world, reality is represented through the lens of personal subjective experience. Here we can find ourselves in apparently seamless crossovers; how we were, how we are and how we will be, in this place or in any other. And at the same time, we can also experience parts of this inner realm as completely isolated islands. Sometimes we encounter strange sides of ourselves that surprise or frighten us or that appear unknowable. But I found this to be a reassuring thought; there is no fate that condemns us to solitary blindness.

And the true heart of the matter is in the here-and-now. What is at stake is what we are feeling and experiencing *right now*, while we are searching for words to express ourselves in ongoing new ways. What is the source that sheds new light on past certainties? What do we want to do differently? Who is this new but strangely familiar person emerging from within?

By the way, if you personally never asked yourself "What on earth was I thinking?", what do you think that this means? Isn't it funny how sometimes, when you look at yourself from an unpremeditated perspective, your feelings get closer? And isn't it about time that you allow yourself a more playful inner space, expand your outer world and venture off the beaten track?

Notes

1 I view emotions as compounded, vital and basically unruly phenomena of body and mind. Difficulties in gaining conscious verbal control can make it hard to acknowledge them as part of the self. The importance of an empathic eye of a caring other cannot be overstressed. This will be a recurring theme throughout this book.

2 Not only have I anonymised personal information, I have also taken the liberty to combine elements out of different therapies. This was only done in order to illustrate the psychodynamics of therapeutic contact, while avoiding information being traceable to a single person. Several chapters are read and corrected by patients themselves. Many elements that were important in individual therapies are left out because they are not essential for making a point on emotion and regulation in this book. I hope that the atmosphere of these therapeutic vignettes is relatable for insiders as well as for outsiders.

3 This point of view is related to the psychoanalytic concept of "scenic understanding".

4 This is a different starting point than most other models, that use facial expression, verbal descriptions or neurological structures to discern various emotions.

5 And with animals for that matter. Personally I find anthropomorphic explanations of animal behaviour not seldom misplaced, but the de-animalisation of humanity is a far more common and alienating fallacy.

6 Thank you Scotland, for an unforgettable cycling tour.

Part I

What to think of something that is subjective, multifaceted and fluid

Chapter 1

Recurring themes in rivalling theories of emotion

During my first years as a military psychologist in the Royal Netherlands Army, I saw deployed soldiers who displayed more anger than fear. Men full of suppressed rage, occasional breakthroughs of aggressive impulses, sometimes at work but more often within the guarded sphere of their homes. Holding on to their body armour in personal relations and in a constricting love–hate relationship with themselves. As I was captivated by the brooding glance that subverted any expression of vulnerability, an enduring interest in the puzzling connection between anger and fear was born within me. The usual explanations – like: anger can be used to camouflage fear, the exhausted stress system makes someone agitated as well as irritable, the body reacts like it is still in a war zone – are useful for psychotherapy but didn't give me a satisfying answer to my more fundamental question. I suspected that some sort of underlying principle could be discovered and I searched for theoretical insight. Also I had an intuitive aversion to the distinction between positive and negative emotions, based on my belief that all emotions should be "psychologically owned" before labelling them desirable or unwanted. Back then I didn't have a clue though of alternative ways to think about basic emotions. Besides having my work as a therapist, I was fortunate to be trained as a clinical psychologist, gaining knowledge from different theoretical frames of reference. After completion I started training in psychoanalysis, being the most comprehensive body of psychological knowledge in my opinion. By now, seventeen years after I started my professional career, I want to present what I have found. I propose a new model for basic emotions, mapping not only anger and fear but happiness and sadness as well. In this chapter, I will delineate their underlying principles and some basic forms of emotion regulation.

Maybe you can imagine that my learning curve was bumpy to say the least. The more I learned, the more the perplexing nature of emotions baffled me. For instance, basic emotions provide us with a "quick and dirty" way (LeDoux, 1996) to orient ourselves in our surroundings and provide us with attentional focus, physical energy and external direction. What do I need to focus on? Where will I go to and what do I distance myself from? What will I hold on to and what will I let go of? These can be pressing questions that need an immediate answer, if you find yourself in a situation that is critical for your survival or the survival of your loved ones. A rational evaluation of the pros and cons of different reactions is a cognitive luxury that the natural world simply doesn't always permit. The primary reaction (of nature's choice) is an emotional one, in humans as well as other animals (Darwin, 2009, originally published in 1872). But how does a "quick and dirty" emotional system accomplish such a complicated feat? How does it make sense of a world that is diffuse and complex and prioritise inner motives that collide and diverge (Kris, 1985) in mysterious ways?

A vital model of emotions should shed at least a dim light on these various aspects. Fortunately, scientists from various disciplines are focussing their research on emotions and the way information is processed. Advanced brain imaging techniques make it possible to study former indecipherable connections between the mind and the brain (Solms & Turnbull, 2002). This rapid progress in the field of neuroscience doesn't go by unnoticed. Inspired by this scientific achievement, there is an upsurge of academic interest in the workings of unconscious processes (Dijksterhuis, 2007), though it has been the cornerstone of psychoanalytic thinking for more than a century. The opportunity now presents itself to combine insights from adjacent fields, from psychoanalysis, cognitive-behavioural therapy and the neurosciences, to name a few, and to do justice to the multifaceted character of emotions that transcends each separate perspective. I owe a lot to the rigorous scientific work done in these different fields and I feel obliged to apologise in advance for the way I make use of it. I will pick what I believe are the key components and will combine them in a new way in the Maelstrom model. I can't completely refute the critique that my behaviour resembles that of a shameless bear, who eats the spawn of the salmon and leaves the rest of the fish untouched. Hopefully there is some justification in the readability of this book. Precisely because of the multifaceted character of emotions, the possibilities to digress are endless. By sticking to the bare essentials of key concepts, I try to cover just enough ground to introduce a new theoretical connection between them. And if all goes well, you might subsequently experience a similar "Aha-Erlebnis" as I did, and the intuitive practicality of the model opens up new vistas for your personal and professional life.[1]

So now we can start with what I believe to be the key concepts for understanding basic emotions. I will take you through this possibly somewhat arbitrary-looking list as an introduction on seven-league boots. From a large array of theoretical concepts, these are the ones I found most instructive and I will link them to their scientific mothers and fathers. Then I will use them to build the Maelstrom model, adding some theory of my own. In Chapters 1, 2 and 3 a clinical case is presented, to illustrate the workings of the model as a therapeutic tool. Throughout the whole book, clinical material is written in italics.

Pleasure and displeasure

***

A non-commissioned officer enters my treatment room in uniform.[2] He is so formal in his choice of words that I immediately get the impression that he doesn't want to be here. His commanding officer has sent him to the military psychological unit after an incident with the police. He was pulled over after he took an illegal exit at the very last moment. The traffic fine he got made him furious and there was a heated scene at the side of the road. In my room, he rants on about the abundance of rules in the Netherlands and the bureaucratic "pencil licking" (in Dutch: pennenlikkerij) of the local police. Although he describes the scene as "awkward and inconvenient", he steers clear from every form of self-reflection. I get the impression that he thinks that by giving this account he is paying me more respect than I deserve. For him this whole exercise seems to be superfluous.

There is something intriguing going on here. If emotions serve an evolutionary purpose, how come this soldier is so conflicted in his affective attitude towards me? If there is such a thing as an emotional quick and dirty way to adapt to a personal situation, why does he burn his fingers so badly? And how can I understand that he seems to contemn me? Maybe he can't imagine gaining something of value for himself, so he just files complaints against others. But even if that is true, there are too many unanswered questions for a quick fix of his predicament. As I wrote earlier, not only did I start therapy with him, but I went looking for answers in the interlining of basic emotions.

***

The rapid ability to discern things that are good for you from things that are bad is a crucial element of our emotional equipment. Together with providing us with a rapid adaptive response, it forms the core activity of our basic emotional system. No wonder the polarity of positive–negative is a recurring theme in emotional theory.

Russell devised an influential model that categorises emotions along two axes (Russell, 1980; Posner, Russell & Peterson, 2005). On one axis, emotions are rated on a pleasure–displeasure continuum; the other axis specifies the level of emotional arousal.[3] In his line of reasoning, emotions distinguish themselves in their specific levels of valence and arousal. Joy, for example, consists of a strong activation of a pleasurable sensation together with a medium level of arousal. Other emotions are categorised along these axes as well, and this way a clear-cut two-dimensional model is constructed.

The simplicity of Russell's model is powerful, but it obscures a far-reaching assumption. Emotions are categorised by the way we label "the feel of the emotion" as pleasurable or unpleasurable. This division though can only be made from an observing viewpoint in the psyche, from a cognitively conscious recognition that "this feels good and that feels bad". Russell implicitly underscores his assumption that the prime function of emotions is to inform consciousness about the state of the inner world (that feels good or bad). And by being a part of the inner world, emotions logically should be classified as pleasurable or unpleasurable as well. I think that this claim needs some fine-tuning. First, it is far from decided what "the feel of each emotion" is. Because of the fact that we are multi-layered organisms and realistic situations rarely are not ambivalent, an emotion seldom comes alone. What an emotion feels like depends on a lot of things, such as personal history, actual context and subjective meaning. To feel sad is listed as unpleasurable, but it can be much worse if one is not able to feel sad at all. Being sad in some instances can feel good.[4] Above and beyond this, one can hardly claim that the prime function of an emotion is to inform consciousness of an inner state when one sees the intimate preverbal communication between a mother and her baby. When seeing a baby react to his available mother (as opposed to a stranger, for example), laughter or crying is a sure sign of his reaction to his environment. And this reaction has a direct and communicative function towards the one he is attached to (Stern, 1985). As a parent it is very hard to ignore cries of pain and anguish from your child, and they invoke an tendency to comfort and console. Also it is hard not to smile when you hear your baby giggle.(So, the positive and the negative side of emotions have a communicative and interactional function that colludes with the informational function about the state of the inner world towards consciousness) And this communicative and interactional function is very much dependent on the immediate context. Therefore, "the feel of the emotion" doesn't match the inner state completely but also is indicative of the subjective experience of the context. When emotions are not only about the inner state, they shouldn't be categorised in the way we categorise our bodily states. Maybe I can make a comparison here with taste, for which the continuum delicious–foul is relevant. The tastiness of food also has little to say about its sweetness, saltiness, bitterness or acidity. The underlying principles stay in the dark. It doesn't shed light on the reasons that something sweet sometimes tastes good but sometimes tastes really disgusting.

From psychoanalytic literature, I found the works of Melanie Klein to be illuminative for comprehending intense emotional states (Klein, 2002, originally published in 1952). In her study of the emotional life of the infant, she describes how the baby reacts differently towards the breast that feeds and the breast that frustrates. The feeding breast and the pleasurable fulfilling of an inner need (hunger) create the image of "a good breast" within the baby. The frustrating breast and the unsatisfied need create an inner image of "a bad breast". Dependent on the consistency (among others) of the "good breast image" the baby learns to react within a frame of trust ("the good is existent but can be lacking") or out of distrust ("I am confronted with badness and that is unbearable"). The latter experience causes intense feelings of hatred that are projected onto the breast. In an immature mix-up of feeling states, not the self but the breast is experienced as hateful and persecuting, causing it to be feared and attacked. In short these are the two basic positions that infuse the infant's (and adult's) emotional states. Klein calls them the depressive position (acknowledging the goodness as well as the possible absence of the other) and the paranoid-schizoid position (experiencing one's own hatred as persecuting). The splitting of the object (breasts or persons for that matter) in "all good or all bad" is an innate and elementary mechanism according to Klein. And it is a lifelong task to come to terms with one's own feelings of love and hatred within our most intimate relations.

There has been a longstanding debate in the psychoanalytic world about the ability of babies to make such an adaptive division between a good breast and a bad breast. Wasn't that reserved for the main seat of conscious control, the psychoanalytic concept of the ego? And isn't it a fallacy to assume that babies are born with rational thought and functional egos? I suggest that it is not thoughtful deliberation that achieves this distinction, but it is a consequence of the way we emotionally react to frustration and fulfilment, to pain and pleasure. For example, when the interaction with another stirs up anger in you, the other person is experienced as bad or at least is eligible to be filed under that category. Missing in the work of Klein is the specification of exactly this link, how the interaction of specific emotions create these fundamental categories of good and bad objects.[5] Probably this missing piece of theory is also the reason that the good–bad distinction is so closely linked to the object. While Russell claims that it is the emotion itself that should be categorised as pleasurable or unpleasurable, in Kleinian theory the good–bad distinction is experienced in close connection with the other, opening up the social dimension of emotions. Russell maps the subjective evaluation of the emotional inner world; Klein focusses on the subjective experience of the outer world.

I think that what these theoretical views lead up to is to connect the positive–negative distinction to the interaction between the emotional person and the involved other.[6] For it is the interaction that is experienced as good or bad, depending on the match (or mismatch) between inner needs and outer world. When I am hungry, feeding will give me pleasure. But when I am full, the sight and smell of food can make me nauseous and cranky. My emotions will vary in accordance with the interaction between the needs and wants of my inner world and what I meet in the outer world. The smell of fresh coffee in the morning puts a smile on my face. But the lingering odours of the greasy banquet from last night fill me with disgust and grumpiness and will lower my eyebrows. It is a surplus of this interactional viewpoint, shedding new light to the interconnectedness of basic emotions, which I will try to point out in the rest of this chapter.

Emotional parts of the evolutionary toolkit

If positive and negative subjective experiences with others are so closely intertwined with emotions, then what are these subjective experiences aiming for? And if bodily sensations of pleasure or pain, of basic emotions and positive and negative experiences with others are members of the same band, what sort of music are they playing? The answer to this question has been around for quite some time, and Darwin has come up with convincing arguments of the role emotions play in the survival and reproduction of animals and humans (Darwin, idem). Somehow, though, his theory has got bad PR. Maybe some of the resistance towards the evolutionary function of emotions come from religious beliefs that detest the idea that humans are animated through their "being a body" instead of through something higher and divine. I suspect an even more fundamental objection though. If we are animated through these vital emotional processes that are so hard to grasp cognitively, this puts us in a psychologically difficult position. Are we willing to declare ourselves dependent on processes that are so fleeting, not concrete and with which we are struggling to comprehend? It is hard to bear being less in control than the cognitive conscious part of our mind is striving for.[7] Somehow we are inclined to feel encroached upon our psychological integrity, fend off this unpleasant feeling and dismiss this humbling fact of life.

Robert Plutchick didn't give in to these inclinations. He was a psychologist who based his theory of emotions on solid evolutionary foundations (Plutchick, 1980). He stated that emotions arise when survival and reproduction – either literally or symbolically – are at stake. Also he pointed out that emotions give rise to adaptive behaviour, with each emotion eliciting a specific behavioural scenario that is adaptive in an evolutionary way. Goals that can be pursued are, for example, the gaining of resources, reattachment to a lost object, safety or the destruction of an obstacle. Plutchick described eight biologically based[8] basic emotions[9] that he theoretically paired into four antagonistic pairs. These are emotional pairs that are in a love–hate relationship of themselves; they can't live with or without each other. These conflicted partners are joy–sadness, trust–disgust, fear–anger and surprise–anticipation. All other emotions can be described as different types of combinations or mixtures of the basic ones, according to Plutchick. Shame, for instance, is thought to be composed of fear and disgust. Though emotions are not so clearly categorised as in Russell's model and some of Plutchick's emotion dyads seem outright arbitrary, his elaborate model appears to do more justice to the multifaceted reality of our emotional inner world. He also added a third axis, making his model three-dimensional, visualising gradations of intensity of each basic emotion. This clarifies the different names we use for different intensities of the same emotion (for instance, annoyance – hostility – anger – rage – fury). Clinically I find this addition very useful, and I will integrate this in the Maelstrom model in a modified way. Especially of interest is the transition of an emotion that can be consciously felt and thought of into an emotion that is physically and mentally overwhelming.

Jaak Panksepp has extensively studied the neural mechanisms of emotions in animals and humans (Panksepp, 1998). By teaming up with psychoanalysis, he also tried to bridge the gap between neural systems and functions on the one hand and unconscious and conscious levels of subjective experience on the other (Panksepp & Biven, 2012). He stated that emotions intrinsically help animals and humans alike to anticipate the future. We make use of an evolutionary emotional barometer, where positive subjective experience steers us towards survival and reproduction. This barometer is positioned in the deep subcortical parts of our brains. It resembles the quick and dirty way of emotional processing of environmental information according to Joseph LeDoux.[10] Panksepp meticulously describes seven primal (basic) emotional systems. These systems – he called them SEEKING, RAGE, FEAR, LUST, CARE, PANIC and PLAY – are the constituent parts of this barometer. These ubiquitous behaviours in animal life, alongside the well circumscribed neural systems that underpin it, make for a convincing argument in favour of the evolutionary foundation of emotions. It can be hard though to link all of these seven systems to a more subjective understanding of what we mean when we use the term "emotion". It isn't hard to recognise in oneself the basic urge to care for a child or to play joyfully, but subjectively these activities seem to have composite structures that exceed the level of complexity of basic fear, for example. Somehow these denominations seem more behavioural than emotional. One could ask the question of whether Panksepp's seven emotions, fundamental as they are, are equals among themselves. Or is there some organising principle to be found here as well?

There is an ongoing scientific debate on the best way to conceptualise emotions. Should we think about emotions as interrelated and focus on the variations of an underlying theme? This is the most fertile theoretical perspective according to Russell and others. Or should we consider each emotion as a category on its own? This is the point of view taken by Panksepp, who is able to link these categories with neural systems. Personally I don't see why both of these positions should contradict each other and why they cannot add value by providing us with "intra-emotional and inter-emotional" perspectives (see Zachar & Ellis, 2012). Panksepp's theory could benefit from a rethinking of the interconnectedness and underlying principles of emotions. I found his famous schematic overview of the excitatory and inhibitory influences of four primary emotions (SEEKING, PANIC, RAGE and FEAR) a bit peculiar (Panksepp, 1998). In his model, PANIC and FEAR only have excitatory influence on other emotions, while SEEKING and RAGE only inhibit other emotions. The psychotherapist in me considers this to be an oversimplification. On second thought, it might be understood as an evolutionary favour of the more proactive emotions (SEEKING and RAGE), because once they are felt, it is hard to change the mood. In terms of regulation, these emotions incite the person to take charge when vital needs are unmet.

Be that as it may, Panksepp's evolutionary and neuroscientific grounding of emotional theory is elementary. It surpasses the distinction between positive and negative emotions by stating that emotions are part of the evolutionary toolkit which is used to adapt the inner world to outer circumstances. This fact doesn't deny that emotions can have a positive or negative signalling function. It is just that the painful or unpleasant aspect of an emotion doesn't make it less adaptive. And the pleasurable aspect of an emotion doesn't mean that it is adaptive to strive for a maximisation of positive emotion in all circumstances. The ability to become emotional, quickly realising what feels wrong and what feels right – with its orchestration of attentional focus and physical energy – has evident evolutionary advantages. The range of emotions corresponds to a range of adaptive reactions in vitally important circumstances. And emotional flexibility under varying conditions is one of the telltale signs of mental health.

Inside and outside

intermediate position

Adding to the complexity of emotions – and maybe its most confusing and misunderstood element – is their intermediate position between the inner and the outer world. Emotions are the octopuses of mental life, with their tentacles stretching out towards the biological needs of the psychical body, the subjective experience of the inner world, the sensorial perception of the personal surroundings, the mental representation of the outer world, social signalling through facial expression and the preparation of a motor response. And this emotional octopus operates in all of these areas at the same time with lightning speed.[11] No wonder we struggle to track all its activities and get entangled when we consciously try to get our heads around it.

One has to be sort of a jack of all trades to study this particular octopus. Mark Solms is such a person, who unifies the most recent neuroscientific knowledge with the vast body of psychoanalytic theory within one mind. He coined the term "neuropsychoanalysis", which has become a cross-pollination of different academic fields. He thinks emotions to be closely connected to the inner state of a person (or other animal) and to the level of (in)congruence between what is present inside and what is biologically needed. Levels of oxygen, nutrients, and warmth for example drop in and out of viable parameters, giving rise to pleasurable and unpleasurable sensations. These sensations – that somehow are closely connected to emotions – incite the person to search and satisfy his inner needs in the outside world. Therefore, emotions play a key role in the "international relations" between the inner and the outer world. Basic emotions have a scripted response ready to be used and activate the motor system (among others). I suggest that a fertile way to look at this physical activation is to think of it as a tendency *to approach or to avoid* an object associated with desire or of distress.[12] I don't think that the distinction is clear-cut though; objects associated with pleasure don't always lead to emotional approach. And objects associated with distress don't always lead to emotional avoidance. It is an aspect that is somewhat lacking in literature, be it neuropsychoanalytic or otherwise. This is another aspect I try to illuminate with the Maelstrom model.

Solms describes emotions as related to the senses that are aimed inwards instead. More than information about outer objects, emotions provide us with information about the inner state of the body, according to Solms. Again – and a pattern emerges – I think we need to focus on how emotions provide us with information on the state of the inner body *in relation to* other persons (objects) in the outer world. Somehow it is very hard to maintain this binocular vision and resist the inclination to focus on the inner *or* the outer world. He clearly points out, though, that the state of the inner world is not one-dimensional. Various representations of the state of our body are mapped in the central part of our nervous system, the brain (for instance, a musculoskeletal map, a visceral map, etcetera). The ways in which these maps are integrated into a coherent, more or less conscious sense of who we are are certainly matter of debate. Solms ascribes a pivotal role for emotions in the integration and formation of consciousness. He claims (that it is an inherent function of emotions to raise conscious awareness) (Solms & Panksepp, 2015). An initial unconscious emotion starts off bodily and mental processes, raising awareness (and attracting and directing higher conscious control.) Panic in the voice of a crying child attracts and directs parental attention almost instantaneously. This situation can raise all sort of emotions in the parent (fear, hypervigilance, care, panic), and most parents will jump into action.

Metaphorically speaking, one could say that we are like spectators who try to discover the course and destination of a train by looking at railroad crossings and switches.[13] The train itself though, and all of its passengers, move too fast for the eyes to see. The train symbolises emotion here. Whether the starting point is inside or outside, if there is urgency in the need to reach a new inner endpoint through an outward journey, the train sets into motion. But then again, one could also say, depending on your inner viewpoint or the location of your sense of self, that we are passengers on our emotional trains. And conscious awareness doesn't spring from outside the train, but from the inside.[14] Yet another way of looking at emotions is that we consist of the multiplicity of trains themselves, travelling through a vast country that is also us and that we can never fully cover.[15] Dizzying indeed.

Energy and movement

But let's not get carried away now. Let's focus on the next aspect of emotions that has been clarified in different theoretical schools. According to Nico Frijda, emotions comprise a set of phenomena that involves the interaction between a (human) animal and his surroundings. Within this set of phenomena, unconscious states of psychological readiness can be found, as well as conscious intentions and feelings.[16] He coined the term "action readiness" as a central piece of his theory, addressing the preparation for movement and directed action (Frijda, 1986). A core function of emotion is to prepare the body for certain actions that fit the situation in which the emotion arises. Emotions muster energy for a quick and adaptive response in the personal environment.[17]

Long before Frijda, Sigmund Freud also thought it was viable to conceptualise the psyche as an energetic system (Freud, 1950 [1895–1896]). Though certainly acknowledging the importance of stimuli from the outside, Freud studied the inner origin and proceedings of psychic energy. He reserved a special category for the most fundamental inner sources of this (psychic energy and called them the drives.) This is the psychoanalytic well where aggression and sexuality spring from. Affect (as emotion was called) is defined as the reaction to an external stimulus, for which its subjective content is dependent from inner processes,

affect → via the external object → stimulates internal drives/energy seeking discharge

both conscious and unconscious ones. Affect urges someone to forget interactional alternatives and to take the shortest route to energetic discharge through motor action (Freud, idem). So it is through the workings of drive and affect that someone is "energised" and prepared for action.

The history of the search for what drives us as humans, what makes us move, is filled with lost memories, transformations and rediscoveries. This is true not only for humankind but also for each individual as well. We start living our lives in intense emotional bonds without the ability to give words to our experience. For this we are dependent on emotionally available caregivers, who do part of the emotional digestion of subjective experience for us and verbalise what we are going through. Without the right words, we are destined to "re-search and re-discover" the original imprint of our experience and react in primary ways. It leaves us speechless, faced by the questions of why we feel the way we do and what we intend to accomplish. This is another reason that I started thinking about only four basic emotions. I reckoned that it heightened my chance of success in finding the sort of movements in which they propel us. Fear, for instance, is almost unanimously associated with avoidance. And I don't believe that it is farfetched to assume that someone who is persistently avoiding something is motivated by fear (whether the emotion is recognised or not).

Seeking proximity or distance: to approach or to avoid

When an inner wish or need prompts an emotion that channels physical and mental energy in a prescribed manner, the subjective experience of the interaction with the other person changes. For the fulfilment of an inner wish or need, personal interaction is needed with the outside world. It is elementary, then, that the other person is close enough to make interaction possible. Emotions help us to find the right amount of interpersonal space to satisfy our needs. It depends on the need that is at stake, which is the right distance for fulfilling interaction. When a baby is hungry and crying, the mother's breast needs to be tangible and close enough for the baby to suckle. For a playful exchange of facial expressions, some larger distance is required. And when a noise is too loud, we flinch and back down. So emotions guide ourselves and others to adjust interpersonal space.

The consecutive zones covered by the senses are more important than the metric system for differentiating between various forms of interaction. Rather than in centimetres, one should envision space as divided in spheres of potential sensorial interaction.[19] These invisible boundaries are of crucial importance for shaping the way we feel. We prefer to reserve coming so close that you can taste and smell someone for people we love. Fear of contamination and disgust for the unfamiliar can hold us back from people we don't know. The next invisible sensorial boundary is arm's length, the zone wherein skin-to-skin contact is possible, both affectionate and violent. Intuitively, we define personal space as this zone of human touch. Imagine, for instance, "that colleague who always stands a little too close".

All through our lives we remain very sensitive towards these (invisible boundaries.) The visual field and hearing distance are the next emotional relevant zones. "Get out of my sight!", we shout out of anger. And it can be extremely frustrating when the telephone line drops dead when you speak with a loved one who is far away. The emotions that navigate you through these sensorial zones change colour when crossing an invisible line. This is because a quantitative change in interpersonal space leads to a qualitative change in interpersonal interaction. That is also what emotions are about.[19] Through sensing we become emotionally attentive; that's how emotions make sense.

(Emotions regulate interaction by urging us to approach or to avoid.)They instate an "interaction readiness" in us that leads us to take action. But something else is going on at the same time. Emotions give rise to facial expressions and distinctive vocalisations with (social signalling value.)Through these expressions, (others can be persuaded into taking action, to approach or to avoid.)The sudden cry of a baby will spur a parent to come near and pay close attention. It is a dual strategy aimed at the same directive:(to regulate internal states through changing proximity and interaction with vitally important others.)

Our main visual concept of distance is spatial, but we also experience distance in time. Movement in itself is the act of relocation in space and time. Maybe that is why it is so easy to experience time as a particular form of space. For moving objects, distance is better measured in time than in space. The now is here, the past and the future are (far) away. Emotionally we regulate distance consistently, no matter whether distance is spatial or temporal. That's because vital interaction takes place in the here-and-now. We need to be close in space and time to interact with whom or what we love. We require distance in space and time to feel safe from harm (in the here-and-now). There-and-when and there-and-then only gain emotional importance when we use memory or imagination. And when they do, we feel an inclination to approach or to avoid the mental image. The tendency to approach or to avoid the past or the future is an emotional reaction towards the images we have in mind.

Psychoanalysis has enriched us with a better understanding of internal ways to distance ourselves, to experience closeness and to regulate contact. Emotional regulation of proximity and distance can be applied to consciousness, with the unconscious as a foreign land far away. The concept of repression, for instance, can be thought of as creating distance towards a certain state of mind. Thoughts and feelings can be banned into the unconscious. This defence mechanism regulates the interaction between emotion and awareness in order to protect a valued self-image. Examples aren't hard to find. "No, I am not angry with you. That would mean that I am selfish and I am not." Or another: "No, I am not angry because you have nothing that means anything to me. You are more needy than I am." It's this kind of psychological trickery we use to bolster our sense of self, but that leaves us confused in our basic emotional reactions.

Yet another way in which we distance ourselves internally from unwanted emotions is to consider them as not part of *me* but part of *you*. Perhaps this trickery is even more confusing because our empathy enables us to feel emotions of another as well. This is the psychoanalytic defence mechanism of projection. "I am not angry, you are!" Now proximity is associated with the self, while distance is associated with the other. There is a whole lot more to say about these defence mechanisms, but I won't go into that now.[20] I just wanted to show how fundamental the dimension of proximity–distance is and how one can approach and avoid in both the outside as in the inner world.

Maybe this is the right place to be clear about a simplification that I have permitted myself up till now. Throughout this book, I will use the term "emotion" without drawing the contours of its definition in black and white. (Remember that I tend to visualise emotion as an octopus, with eight swirling tentacles and blazing changes in colour.) Especially when it comes to different levels of consciousness of an emotion, differentiation in designation can be helpful. Antonio Damasio (2010) distinguishes *affect, emotion* and *feeling*. Affect operates at a deep somatic level, giving rise to involuntary physical reactions, mediated on the level of the brainstem. Emotions are more composite structures, giving rise to action tendencies, subjected to emotional learning and capable of bridging the gap between bodily sensations and mental processing. Feelings are emotional states on a conscious level, closely attached to mental imagery and verbalisation and less prone to incite direct action. When I speak of emotion, I use the term in the sense that Damasio defines it. It's the composite, immediate and continuous, action- and consciousness-provoking, personal and social, intense mental phenomenon that somehow unifies body and mind or does the exact opposite and heralds internal conflict. Damasio's conceptualisation opens up a dynamic field in which emotions operate, not incompatible with the dynamics found in psychoanalysis. Emotions operate at the interplay between body and mind, between knowing and not-knowing and between deep-seated structures in the brain stem and that part of the neocortex we call the prefrontal lobe.

An implicit sense of control

Humans are social animals, and we are dependent on personal interaction with others all through our lives. We need others to fulfil our emotional needs and nurture, comfort and console us, especially regarding our gut reactions out of hunger, hurt or frustration. The emotional availability of caring adults who are capable of reflecting on their own emotions as well as on the subjective experience of the child is the potting soil for the development of a healthy sense of self (Schore, 1994; Fonagy, Gergely, Jurist & Target, 2002).

Babies are hard-wired to make contact with their caregivers (Stern, 1985). In the interactional dance between a child and his parents, subjective experiences lead up to expectations that are formative for a subjective perception of future relations. Are others capable of understanding me, of what is going on inside me and of what I need? Especially when I am not able to convey in words what it is that I need or want? Can I trust the other to be available, to be interested in what is going on inside me? When parental care is good enough (Winnicott, 1960) and when there are no other complicating factors, a child will develop an implicit sense of control, even when life itself starts in a state of complete dependency. There is no need to strive for perfection; parents don't have to be "the good breast" (in Kleinian terms) all the time. What is important is the active engagement of the parent in repairing the interactional dance when the child experiences breaches in contact as especially disturbing. It is the overwhelming intensity of the emotion that is aroused in the child that is the hallmark of the need to reestablish the connection. The gradual build-up of interactions with an emotional available "dancing partner" leads to the development of basic trust in the child. Basic trust enables the growing child to expand the space in which he feels safe, from close to his caregiver to greater distance. The mental sediment of early experiences of interactional predictability is an implicit sense of control in social interaction. The developing matrix of expectations gain reliability, and there is a gradual growth of secure attachment and of the self as the centre of emotional activity.

In healthy development, this sense of subjective control is closely tied to the interaction with loved ones. But when things go bad and there are insurmountable shortcomings of emotional reciprocity in early attachment, the sense of control goes adrift. This might happen, for instance, when parents themselves can't cope with the intense raw emotionality of infancy and restrict their involvement to instrumental behaviour. The sense of control can shift in two directions in search of a safe haven. The search for safety and predictability can shift from reciprocal interaction towards the seclusion of the personal inner world. This is the fundament of the avoidant style of attachment. Or it can shift towards attempting to control the concrete behaviour of the other, whose subjective intentions remain unfathomable. This is the basis of the ambivalent style of attachment. In these insecure patterns of attachment, basic trust is only to be found inside the self *or* in concrete actions of the other. The dancing part is hollowed out.

This junction reminds us of the distinction Julian Rotter made between an internal versus an external *locus of control* in 1966 (see Rotter, 1989). According to his social learning theory, people with a strong internal locus of control claim full responsibility for the fulfilment of needs, urges and desires. They are convinced that ultimately they are the only ones responsible for getting what they need. At the other end of the spectrum, we find people with a strong external locus of control. Those are the people who are convinced that they ultimately have relative little to say in their personal fate. Everything that is happening to them is the result of forces that are out of their personal reach. Rotter himself saw personality as inseparable from the interaction with the environment. Therefore, he strongly opposed medicalisation of pathological behaviour in fixed diagnoses and worked on the improvement of patients' ways of relating to their environment.

Yet in attachment theory, a pervasive blueprint is assumed. An unreliable pattern of parental emotional availability can lead to a lasting inclination for the sense of control to turn inwards or turn outwards. Both of these "psychological solutions" are labelled as insecure. When the sense of control is strongly localised internally, the relevance of the other is minimised and there is a subcutaneous tension and fear of intrusion; this is called an avoidant style of attachment (Ainsworth, Blehar, Waters & Wall, 1979). The expression of emotions is severely inhibited. But when the locus of control is external, adaptive concrete behaviour of others remain necessary to feel safe. One vigorously clings to others, persuading them emotionally to provide for elementary psychological needs while a constant fear of abandonment has to be suppressed. This is called an ambivalent (or anxious) style of attachment. Both of these forms of insecure attachment don't work very well in regulating the concealed or openly displayed arousal. Therefore, psychological tension can raise quickly and become volatile, either under the skin or in personal relations.

Psychoanalytic inquiry into the inner world of children shows that the redirected sense of control goes hand in hand with (un)conscious fantasies of power. The self and the other can be idealised or devaluated alternately. When emotional development is hindered, these redirections lead to a troublesome petrification of such fantasies. For instance, it is completely normal for a child to possess magic powers in the sphere of his imagination. There he can be omnipotent, a superhero, bigger and stronger than his own father. These kind of fantasies can serve as an antidote for a turbulent emotional inner world and a mysterious or unreliable outer world. It becomes problematic when the need for this fantastic fulcrum becomes so urgent that it interferes with reality and it shapes the way in which relations are perceived.[21] In the opposite version of this fantasy that is no less common, it is not the self but the other who is idealised. "My mom is the sweetest mother on the planet and my father is the strongest man alive." After all, it is very reassuring that you are blessed with omnipotent adults who happen to be your parents. In the schoolyard many battles are fought over this. Imbedded in an adult mind, this might direct the personality towards dependency, obedience and underground resistance.

As implicit as the sense of control is, so effortlessly we allocate it in space. The position of power and control is intuitively placed on top, high ranked. Lower positions are assigned to those who are supposed to obey and follow. The emotional significance of high and low is so self-evident (comparable to the significance of distance and proximity) that it is hard to see all of its manifestations. But once you see, they appear everywhere. For example, when a child looks up to his adored parents. Or when a religious person bows his head before the magnificence of God. How every soldier looks for higher ground in search of tactical advantage (except for the marines). How the top of the rock is reserved for the alpha animal. How emotional impulsivity is thought to come from the underbelly, while ideals can be lofty. When consciousness is considered to be the top of the iceberg, whereas the vast mass of the unconscious resides beneath the surface. There is a staggering abundance of associations between influence and height, though this is certainly unfair to the vast amount of bottom-up processes that influence our entire existence. Nevertheless, when we fall, we fall downwards. And when we are in the natural world, light comes from above.

Timothy Leary (1957) gave the dimension of above and below a central place in his model of interpersonal behaviour, also known as Leary's rose. His model is circumplex and consists of two axes. One of these axes assigns dominance to the above position and submission to the below position. This is called the power or status axis. The second axis quantifies togetherness versus opposition and is called the love axis. (Notice also the resemblance with the distinction of pleasure and displeasure, as discussed before.) These two axes are now commonly associated with the constructs of agency and communion (Horowitz, 2004). In psychoanalytical theory, two affiliated concepts have arisen. Sydney Blatt (1974) first developed a two-configuration model of depression, distinguishing anaclitic (social clinging) from introjective (self-critical) forms. Later on, he formulated a theory of personality based on two developmental lines. One line he called seperateness or self-definition, and the other line was called relatedness or attachment (Blatt & Blass, 1992). In my opinion, these theories reflect on the importance of the allocation of the sense of self, either towards the self or towards the other. Do I believe my sense of control is solely to be found in myself, or solely in the other?

Once again, we see a recurrence of themes in rivalling theories. Maybe the reader wonders why I am writing all this and whether I don't digress too much. When the Maelstrom model is constructed in the next chapter, the sense of control is included along with a notion of above and below. In the clinical examples that follow, the sense of control is alternately bound to the self and the other. I suggest that this is crucial for understanding different styles of emotion regulation. So let's move on by connecting the old dots in a new way.

Notes

1 The truth is that I suddenly sketched this model after an exhausting yet invigorating bike ride, trying for months to get my head around the underlying principles of happiness, sadness, fear and anger. Unconscious processing succeeded where my conscious efforts failed. After this sketchy discovery, it took me a complete psychoanalytic training and a decade of therapeutic work to grasp what I had found and to provide the model with clinical examples.

2 I could tell you that his first name was something like George, but the reality is that we never got on a first-name basis.

3 Russell claims that his model is based on two fundamental neurophysiological systems that correspond with the two axes. The use of neuroscientific arguments for substantiating psychological hypotheses is not without pitfalls though. First because neuroscience is a young and fast-progressing science, whose claims are less homonymous than the brain is visible. Second because the intricate gap in knowledge between neurophysiological and mental phenomena cannot be solved by stating that one of the two is more fundamental than the other. See for an illuminative explanation of the philosophical position of dual aspect monism: Solms and Turnbull (2002).

4 As well as being bad in other instances . . .

5 With the Maelstrom model, I try to fill some of the space where this link is missing.

6 In psychoanalytic theory, the terms subject and object are used respectively.

7 Freud delivered a blow to the collective narcissism of humankind when he stated that the ego is not master in his own house. See Freud, S. (1917). *A difficulty in the path of psycho-analysis*. Standard Edition, Vol. 17. London: Hogarth Press. We still seem to stagger and try to catch our breath, clinging to new possibilities of technological advancement as means to restore our sense of omnipotence.

8 Plutchick stated that emotions can be found in both humans and animals, underscoring the biological origin in both.

9 There is an ongoing scientific debate on the definition and exact number of basic emotions. The various theoretical demarcations are often based on different lines of research, ranging from the study of neural systems, transcultural facial expressions and linguistic entities. I do not pretend that I have anything to contribute to this discussion. I just assume that there is such a thing as a basic emotion. Happiness, sadness, fear and anger appear in all the different lists (but are not unique in this respect). See for a recent study that claims that there are only four basic emotions: Jack, R.E., Sun, W., Delis, I., Garrod, O.G. & Schyns, P.G. (2016). Four not six: Revealing culturally common facial expressions of emotion. *Journal of Experimental Psychology: General*, 145(6), 708–730.

10 And of System 1 functioning according to Daniel Kahneman. See Kahneman, D. (2012). *Thinking, fast and slow*. London: Penguin Books Ltd.

11 An elucidating and beautifully written book on "what is it like to be an octopus" is Godfrey-Smith, P. (2016). *Other minds: The octopus and the evolution of intelligent life*. London: William Collins. One of the intriguing topics of the book is a hypothetical dispersal of consciousness, divided between the central part of the nervous system and the octopus' arms, which have sensory input and motor output of their own. Somehow I found this to be a striking metaphor of emotions.

12 Melanie Klein would say that it is an elementary developmental task to integrate feelings of both love and hate towards the same person.

13 This is the perspective championed by William James. "[B]odily changes follow directly the perception of the exciting fact . . . and feeling of the same changes as they occur, is the emotion." See James, W. (1983). *The principles of psychology*. Cambridge: Harvard University Press. 449. (Originally published in 1890).

14 This is Solms' position.

15 Intuitively I consider this third position to come closest to "what it's like to be a sentient being".

16 Frijda stated this in a partly posthumous prepared article. Frijda, N.H. (2016). The evolutionary emergence of what we call "emotions". *Cognition and Emotion*, 30(4), 609–620.

17 It is my personal opinion that the term "action readiness" captures the essence of motor preparation very well, but that it would benefit from the inclusion of the interpersonal sphere wherein this action takes place. Therefore, I prefer the alternative term "interaction readiness". It expands the concept to include emotional behaviour that is functional because it serves as a social signal, such as the shedding of tears.

18 This might be a promising line of research in animal behaviour, comparing emotional behaviour of social animals with a wide variety of sensory and motor capabilities.

19 I have the impression that people who become sensory disabled lose more than a channel of information and communication. The calibration of their entire range of emotional reactions also seems to change. I believe that this impact surpasses the psychological reaction to a "singular" loss.

20 I will do so in Chapter 8.

21 This is the imprint for the grandiose version of narcissism. This form is especially persistent when it is consolidated by an uncontested (unconscious) belief that you are the only one who is capable of recognising who you truly are.

Chapter 2

Constructing the Maelstrom model and enjoying the view

Let's return to the non-commissioned officer first. Let's see what we find when we pay attention to the conceivable meaning of quick and dirty emotional reactions inside the therapy room. Which emotional interplay gives rise to his internal representation of our interaction and to his behaviour towards me? In other words: what sort of implicit interactional pattern drives our soldier to behave like he does? How do my intuitive impressions fit in? And how can I put them to good use?

***

Though I wear civilian clothes, I am aware that the non-commissioned officer knows that I outrank him. The idea bothers me that it is my military rank that earns his consent and that's the reason that he embarks on a conversation with me that for him is "dispensable". At the same time, it seems to be my only chance, by making it a conversation between two soldiers. His quick temper – appropriately called a short fuse – also mingles with his marriage. His wife has noticed that he picks fights more often after his last deployment. I use it as a point of entry to dwell on his subjective experience of the peacekeeping mission he completed. He gives a detailed and factual report of a transport, on which he was stopped at a road block by one of the warring parties. It took hours before he got permission to leave. Though he wasn't taken hostage in the strict sense of the word, his story evoked a brooding and grim atmosphere. Communication with the military base didn't run smoothly and he tells me that "things could very well have turned out very different". The link to the heated scene with the Dutch police is easily made. I take a gamble and ask him how he felt at the road block. The fuse is lit and he furiously comments on "the lack of professionalism of certain colleagues at the base". Apparently my interest in his personal well-being comes too soon and I ponder on the reasons that he feels such an urgent need to keep me at bay.

All sorts of hypotheses run through my head while I am listening to this soldier. I assume that the situation at the road block was very frightening and possibly he was in fear of his life. Maybe his experience was so intense that he lacks words to describe it. That would certainly be an obstacle for the integration of this experience in his personal life history. On top of that he is everything but eager to let me help him with that. Being pulled over by the police perhaps served as a trigger for an overwhelming fear, which he faces alone. These hypotheses create room inside me to listen to him non-judgmentally, while he rants on like his life depends on it. His fury raised by the alleged deficient professionalism of his colleagues appears to be an accusation against a lack of back-up, which was felt to be of vital importance at the road block. But what is going on between him and me in the therapy room? What kind of relational scenario am I part of, in his conscious and unconscious mind? I will come back to him in a short while.

***

The first axis: the association of the other with pleasure or displeasure

The first axis of the Maelstrom model maps the internal representation of an external object ("the other") by its association with pleasure (the satisfaction of needs, urges and desires) or with displeasure (frustration or pain). So the way in which this dimension is composed is a mixture of external and internal input. From the inside, we gather information about what we need through our emotional state, thereby establishing a frame of reference for imposing *valence* on the mental representation of the outside world.[1] The outside world presents us with others who are subjectively important and to whom we react emotional (otherwise we feel indifference and don't take notice or react). Their personal importance is measured by the degree of fulfilment or frustration of inner needs. When there is a strong match or mismatch, emotions arise in order to influence the interaction between the self and the other. In our mind and heart, we *associate* the other with fulfilment or frustration, good or bad, with pleasure or displeasure.[2]

Sometimes an inner need gets so thwarted that it hampers the discrimination of outer objects. The intense emotional turmoil then "attaches itself" easily to various others, like a pregnant cuckoo searching for a nest.[3] One could say that in these cases the expression of an emotion is derived from an inner need. But the other way around works as well. Sometimes we meet someone who surprises us, sweeps us off our feet or is really obnoxious. Then our emotional reaction doesn't seem to be born out of inner necessity that much, but seems to be solely invoked by the external other. The perceptive reader though will recognise different variations of interactional interplay.

The association of the other with notions of pleasure or displeasure is described by Freud (1915) as *Besetzung*, translated later as *cathexis*. It is an essential and easy-to-overlook concept when reflecting on emotional behaviour. But it is imperative if one is trying to avoid the pitfalls of thinking about emotions as "positive or negative" or of others as "good or bad" (as I have described in the previous chapter). For it is not the distinction between "positive and negative" emotions that leads us out of the conundrum of emotional conflict, nor is it the division of other humans as "good or bad". Truly helpful is the reflection on how your emotional activity shapes the way you perceive and form social relations.[4] It opens up vistas on new ways of relating other than the one that has the most unfiltered emotional urgency.

It is certainly not self-evident to know yourself. We all need caring and empathic others, our parents in the first place, to help us understand and get a grip on our inner turmoil and dwellings. Not only are we emotional beings with a cognitive capability to grasp our own intentions, we are also psychologically very well equipped to filter our emotional expressions. Human animals are uniquely equipped to confuse not only others but themselves as well. Humanity would have made a perfect typecast for the part of the sorcerer's apprentice in Walt Disney's *Fantasia*. (Mickey Mouse just beat us to the punch.) Across our lifespan we can encounter many obstacles that hinder us in getting acquainted with our emotional inner world, and sometimes we are the main part of the obstacle ourselves. Not only do we find it hard to recognise our own emotional state, but also it isn't always easy to take notice of our inner needs. And a large part of what we need in life is social.[5] We love to receive love but also love to give it. Somehow that last part gets out of sight in our Western individualistic day and age, wherein man is implicitly represented as a one-dimensional homo economicus.[6] Fortunately this can't refute the fact that it feels good to be good to and with others.

In a state of heightened emotional arousal, it is difficult to keep in mind that the association with pleasure or displeasure is just an association and not a given fact. When our feelings run high, we perceive the other as good or bad, as friend or foe. All that the other is, is reduced to what he is to us. We have to turn to Melanie Klein again for putting these phenomena in theoretical perspective (Klein, 2002, originally published in 1952). She describes how the perception of the other is fragmented under emotional pressure, turning the multifaceted real other into a subjective "part object". It is an intricate developmental achievement to be able to face one's own feelings of love and hate towards the same person. Melanie Klein states that it is imperative to come to terms with inevitable shortcomings in our search for pleasure. Yes, the other is good for me and gives me pleasure, but sometimes the other just isn't around. That doesn't have to mean that the other stops to be good. For it's the pleasure of interaction that is missing.

***

It seems fairly obvious on which side I am being mapped and tagged by the non-commissioned officer. Although he seems keen to follow military proto-col, his aversion towards me seeps through in small gestures. To him I am a source of displeasure. But for now I can only guess for the reasons this is so. Is it because I am wearing my civilian clothes that he deems me unprofes-sional, lining me up with the criticised colleagues on the base? Is it because I am ten years younger than him, giving him all the reasons not to put his trust in me? Does he experience his appointment with me as a kind of punishment for his heartfelt anger? Or does he see me as a psychologist who threatens to open up a door that he is desperately trying to keep shut?

***

The second axis: proximity and distance

The second axis represents the distance between the self and the other. This interpersonal distance determines the amount and sort of possible interaction. Think for instance how competitive and cooperative behaviours require the right amount of proximity or appropriate distance. Do I need to feel skin contact or should I stay out of reach? Is pleasurable interaction available or should I make a move? Is unpleasurable interaction imminent and should I better prepare for it? As I have described in the previous chapter, the same sort of emotions are aroused when dealing with others in the outer world as with dealing with represented objects in the inner world. This object can also be an unwanted feeling or an embarrassing experience.

The impact of proximity and distance on emotions are twofold. Emotions change both quantitatively as well as qualitatively when distance varies. The change in emotional intensity is probably the most intuitive appealing one, though I have come to believe that the change in the quality of emotion is more fundamental. For instance, fear gets more intense when a spider closes in on an arachnophobic. On second thought, one could ask the question whether it's the same kind of fear at varying distances. At a greater distance, it might be the thought about the hairy legs of the spider touching the skin that is horrific. But when a spider suddenly falls onto an arm, it might be the idea of poisonous fangs that turn fear into terror and other intense upheaval. The arachnophobic couldn't care less about this distinction: all second thoughts are thrown out the window as she is trying to distance herself from the eight-legged horror. Fortunately those among us who are not arachnophobics are now in the position to think it through.

I will give another example of how distance changes the emotion that is felt. I am happy when I see my friend coming and I am sad to see him go. The distance between my friend and me determines the sort of contact that we can have. Emotions change because they respond to the interactional situation and install an action readiness in me. My happiness leads me to my friend when he is in the vicinity, but it is my sadness that bridges the gap when I feel that he is too far away.

To approach and to avoid

Emotional impulses to approach or to avoid the other originally serve an evolutionary goal. We seek safety or try to eliminate a rival for instance. But a lot of our actual emotional behaviour stems from implicit scenarios or unconscious associations with basic emotions. Someone can jump out of his skin over a scratch on his car, while the evolutionary necessity of this behaviour is hard to find. It is only when you take notice of the subjective way in which meaning is given to a car free from scratches that some sort of logic can be found. The evolutionary purpose of emotions becomes most clear when we look at matters of life or death. This removes a lot of layers from the complexity of human interaction.

The evolutionary purpose of emotions is to energise and focus the individual to adapt to changing circumstances and to fulfil vital needs. Emotions stimulate to pursue pleasure (for that's the result of the fulfilment of vital needs) and to avoid displeasure and pain. Thereby they serve what Freud called the pleasure principle (Freud, 1911).[7] The counterpart of the pleasure principle is the reality principle, which enables the delay of immediate gratification in order to achieve more distant goals. The pleasure principle's activity however is instantaneous, tuned for immediate adaptation. We are very quick to turn to (or to avoid) someone (or something) that radiates pleasure (or pain).

Attacks on the association with pleasure and displeasure

The pleasure principle not only has feet; it has hands too. Not only do we walk towards or away from the other, we manipulate as well (that is, do things to the other to suit one's purpose; from the Latin words *manus* [hand] and *implens* [filling up]). For it is a mistake to assume that others who are associated with displeasure are always avoided. Anger also carries within itself the inclination to approach the other, to get your hands on him and teach him a lesson he won't forget. We become angry in order to eradicate the source of our displeasure and to remove what stands in our way. We vent our rage in order to detach the other from subjective displeasure. In extremis, this means that the only good enemy is a dead enemy, someone who can do harm no more. And on the love side of the spectrum, we don't always cling to the other who is associated with pleasure. We are also inclined to leave a potential fulfilling other when a gratifying relation is unattainable.[8] This is achieved by the disconnection of the other and the pleasurable association. The primary emotional way to do this is to devaluate the other. This makes evolutionary sense because it enables us to let go of unattainable fulfilment. Think for instance of an infant throwing away a toy that he can't use in the way that he wants to or a bottle that is empty.

This uncoupling of pleasure and displeasure can be accomplished by exerting physical force, literally taking the sting out of something. But at the same time, it is accompanied by an inner "handling". Something that is desirable but agonisingly unruly runs the risk of getting emotionally devaluated. "You mean nothing to me!" can be such a provocative declaration of independence. The association with pleasure is suppressed – not dismantled – because there will always be a memory trace left, adding layers of tension onto the subjective experience of interaction. This is a secret ingredient of most love–hate relationships. "Bikes are stupid", says the disappointed and jealous child when she sees her brother getting the bike she wanted for herself. The investment with pleasurable value is withdrawn, also known as *decathexis*. Further argumentation can be used to substantiate the unfiltered emotional reaction. The jealous sister might think: "This bike is worthless and only my spoiled brother thinks it's special. He is growing more annoying every day and that will make him very miserable someday. He is bound to be hit by a car." In this way, unfiltered basic emotions set a train in motion, picking up other emotions along the way (scorching envy in this case). Often there is an attack not only on associating the other with (dis)pleasure but also on "owning" emotions personally. The overwhelming intensity of the emotion – not contained by an emotionally available other – initiates a self-reinforcing mechanism that infuses subcutaneous turmoil (Bion, 1959).

A framework for happiness, sadness, fear and anger

The combination of the first two axes together with the (inter)action tendencies constitute a framework for basic emotions. Figure 2.1 depicts this elemental framework.

This is a framework for sorting immediate emotional reactions that vary continuously. Please note that the vertical arrows indicate a change of interpersonal space. These (inter)action tendencies energise "the legs" and can put them into motion. The horizontal interactional arrows are indicative for a more "manual" take on the other, defusing the association with pleasure or with displeasure. Together they represent an object relational view on Freud's pleasure principle.

These fast-shifting emotional positions can give rise to an abiding experience of a basic emotion, for which words can be used. I suggest that each of the four basic emotions of happiness, sadness, fear and anger can be linked to a quadrant in this framework. I invite the reader to link the four basic emotions to the quadrants before reading further.

***

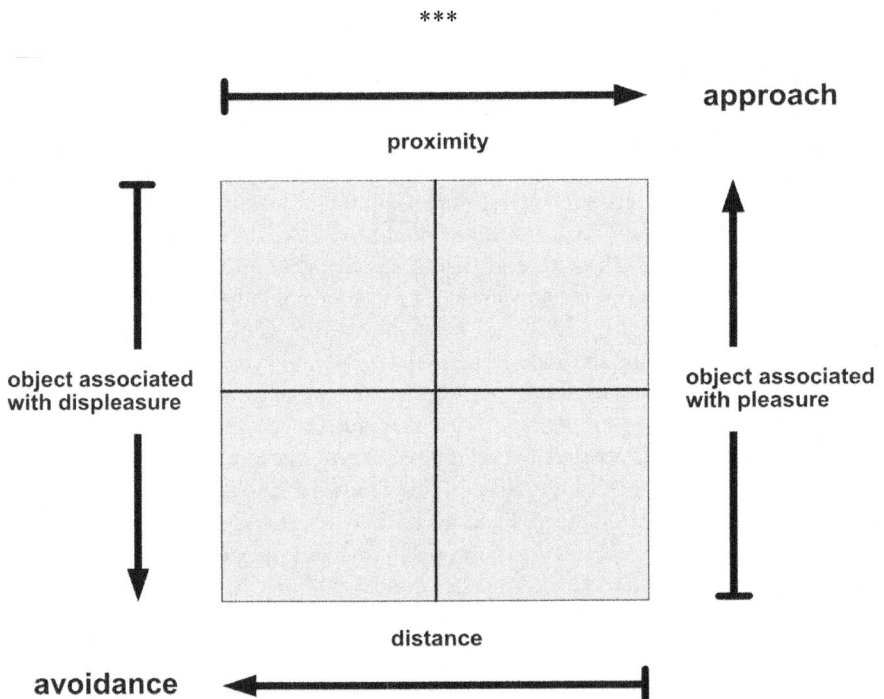

Figure 2.1 The motivating effect of the inner association of (dis)pleasure with proximity and distance.

This is how I fill in the blanks.

- The proximity of the other who is associated with pleasure makes us *happy*. We seek closeness to the ones we love. Happiness is about *approach*.
- Too great a distance to the other who is associated with (vital) pleasure makes us feel separation distress, which I believe is the precursor of *sadness*. We feel the need to bridge the gap and seek comfort and consolation. The expression of sadness is also dependent on the implicit assumption that one is not capable of closing the distance by him or herself.
- *Fear* is the alarm bell ringing when the other who is associated with displeasure is looming at some distance. The threat of proximity – and thereby unpleasurable interaction – spurs us into *avoidance*.
- Becoming up close and personal with the other who is associated with displeasure raises *anger*. (The expression of anger though is very much dependent on the solidity of the implicit conviction that you are able to stand your ground and make a fist.) The hated other stands in our way, has to be fought ("I will destroy you!") or forced to go away ("Get out of my sight!").[9]

The basic framework now looks something like Figure 2.2.

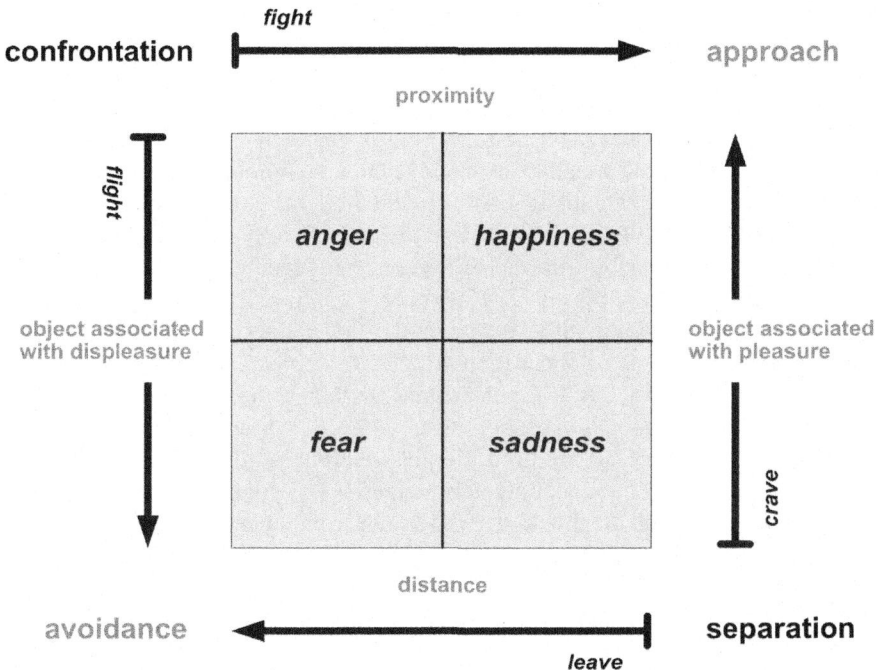

Figure 2.2 The interrelatedness of four basic emotions.

In support of my layout I want to make five points. First of all, some might find it counterintuitive to associate fear with distance. Isn't it when something creepy is near that we are frightened most? But let's take a wasp, for example, flying around in the room. Many of us will show a fearful alertness. This changes altogether when suddenly we find the wasp landing on our arm. The emotional representation of the wasp has rapidly changed from an annoying insect to a malicious attacker. The poisonous sting is much more painful than the humming is disturbing. And while we are "only" fearful when the wasp is flying around, we lash out and strike when he touches the skin (even though we know we shouldn't do so). "Bloody animal!" The line between fear and anger is thin indeed. To put it another way, somewhat more akin to Melanie Klein's notion of the paranoid-schizoid position: if anger can't exert itself, fear takes over. Fear is displeasure you can't get a grip on.[10]

Secondly, one could ponder on the question of whether anger goes hand in hand with approach as well as with avoidance. Depending on your personal experience, you will come up with different angry scenarios. In animal models of aggressive behaviour, however, a distinction is often made between *offensive attack* and *defensive rage*.[11] Offensive aggression is aimed at an intruder of a territory, a space that is identified as personal. The intruder is approached, attacked and put out of action. Defensive rage on the other hand is used in self-defence, for instance, when confronted with a dangerous predator. The display of teeth serves to scare the predator away, facilitating avoidance. So anger can be expressed in order to avoid a confrontation with an enemy but also to seek out a confrontation with an opponent. In both cases, it is anger we are talking about.[12]

And can we think of sadness as leading us to approach and/or avoid the other? Can sadness turn us towards the one we love but also turn us away? I think that's exactly the case, and I am not the first one who thought so. In his book from 1917 on mourning and melancholia, Freud described melancholia as an internal attempt to hold on to a relationship with a lost loved one, as if reunion is still possible. The mental representation of the unavailable other is *approached* as if real interaction is still feasible (against cognitive judgement). Such melancholic sadness can lead to psychological problems when it contributes to depressive feelings, but it can serve adaptive purposes as well, for instance, when reunion is still possible or when it invokes an empathic reaction in someone else. Freud's (outdated) notion of mourning was to break free from the lost relation with the loved one (in my words: *avoidance* of emotional mental interaction) by giving up the association with pleasure ("the libido should be withdrawn from attachment to the object"). Nowadays we acknowledge that mourning can be both adaptive and troublesome, for instance, when it hinders or support other attachments, be it existing or new attachments. From a clinical point of view, it is therefore very helpful to discern sadness that is aimed at reunion ("approach") from sadness that is aimed at detachment ("avoidance"). Mourning is about saying goodbye to a loved one, without losing your love.

This framework for basic emotions also shows that there are two ways that lead to the experience of fear. Fear can be about the impending interaction with a hostile other (the person, thing or inner experience that is associated with displeasure). This is fear in the face of danger that is embodied in an enemy. Another route to fear is formed by the threat of loss of a loved one. Here the vitally pleasurable interaction with the other runs the risk of being lost. This is fear not for a dangerous enemy, but fear for the loss of a safe haven. These two routes resemble two neurological networks described by Panksepp as the FEAR network and the PANIC/GRIEF network respectively (Panksepp & Biven, 2012).

Lastly, this framework maps two distinct ways to become happy. I think most people will agree that interactional happiness can be about the victory over an enemy or opponent but also about the (re)union with a loved one. These routes come together in a joyous junction, where happiness prevails.[13]

With the first two axes in place, I want to take some time now to investigate some of the characteristics of this two-dimensional framework before adding the third axis. So the construction of the 3D Maelstrom model is still some pages away. Let's enjoy the view while travelling.

Fight, freeze or flight and crave, grieve or leave

Figure 2.2 also depicts two interactional situations of imminent importance that are sure to raise stress levels to great heights. The first is the *confrontation* with danger (be it a person, thing or internal experience) that threatens to block the fulfilment of vital needs. This kind of confrontation triggers a behavioural defence mechanism that is known as the *fight, freeze or flight* reaction (Cannon, 1929). A cascade of neurophysiological reactions leads up to the hyperarousal of the autonomic nervous system. Changes in blood flow and muscle tension (among others) prepare the body for energetic action (*fight or flight*) or for immobility (*freeze*).

At least as emotionally stressful as the confrontation with danger is the *separation* of a loved one (or vitally important object or experience). Most dramatically this can be observed in young children, who are completely dependent on the presence and care of their parents. To do justice to the severity of this stress response and to distinguish it from the *fight, freeze or flight* reaction, I want to put forward a new term that captivates the behavioural defence mechanism that accompanies severe separation distress. My suggestion is to call it the *crave, grieve or leave* reaction. The immediate distress is expressed through intense crying, conveying a gripping mix of panic and desperate *craving*. When separation is experienced as a loss, *grieving* and sadness kick in.[14] Some children show clinging behaviour and stay upset (*crave* and *grieve*), while other children apparently calm down but hide within themselves in an aloof way (*leave*). This divergent behavioural pattern can be seen in children reacting to a physical separation from their mother in the Strange Situation test (Ainsworth, Blehar, Waters & Wall, 1979). Equally striking and perhaps even more gripping is to watch babies show the same distressing divergent pattern of *crave, grieve or leave* in reaction to two minutes of motionless mimicry of their mothers in the Still Face experiment (Tronick, 1989). In this experiment, mothers were physically present but emotionally unavailable because of their frozen face. Actual footage of this experiment is shocking to watch.[15] In both experiments children desperately try to re-engage their mothers into emotional co-regulation through a mixture of emotional lively approach (appealing to the mother to "join the dance") and interactional withdrawal (avoiding the subjective experience of the absent or absentminded mother). In the long run, the intensity of this kind of stress really is life-threatening. Children who were devoid of emotional interaction in the first and most sensitive period of their life were studied by René Spitz in 1952 in a Romanian orphanage (Spitz, 1965). He observed the most severe forms of psychological decompensation in these infants, which in some cases literally led to death.

Both confrontation and separation put humans (and other animals) in a difficult position. Emotionally we arrive at a T-junction from where we can "approach, sit still or avoid" the other, paving the way for future interaction. When this dilemma is intensely felt, it stops us in our tracks and produces an indecisiveness that prevents further action. Anger and sadness get tangled up, along with the emotional feel of the interaction with the other. This confusing indecisiveness can have severe consequences, for instance, when someone is caught up in an abusive relationship or in an emotional numbness after a personal loss.[16] These are complicated matters though and this is not the place to explore them further.

Four basic emotions acting in concert

The two-dimensional framework also illustrates how adjacent basic emotions relate to one another.

- Anger turns into happiness through victory.
- Fear turns into defensive anger through closing in, when a threat becomes a confrontation.
- The only thing that keeps sadness from changing into happiness is a blissful (re)union.
- Sadness walks alongside fear when separation leaves you feeling alone and unsafe.

It takes only one interactional step to change these neighbouring emotions into one another. It is because of this strong interrelatedness that often a mixture of these emotions can be felt, as in a smooth transition.

- We can cry "warm" tears, out of gratitude, compassion or happiness.
- Loneliness can make us sad and anxious.
- We can do harm to the ones we fear.
- We are capable of feeling pleasure in taking out our anger on someone.

In contrast with the adjacent basic emotions, the diagonal couples seem much less tolerant of each other. These emotions don't blend smoothly and seem to inhibit the intensity of the "opposite" emotion. Instead of a smooth transition, it is more likely to experience a sudden emotional shift, for instance, when fear turns into relief and happiness. We use this mechanism for tactical reasons when we make a joke to break the ice. Or – the other way around – movie directors can create an uncanny atmosphere by adding the soothing melody of a nursery rhyme to a scene of pseudo serene stillness in a horror movie. The mixture just doesn't feel right. Similarly, sadness can suddenly shift into anger and anger into sadness. The inhibiting influence these "opposite" basic emotions have on each other can be used defensively to avoid experiencing an unwanted emotion. "I hate you!" yells a scorned lover with tears in her eyes. But also, as a therapist I have seen many persons who were very frustrated about their tendency to cry when they were actually trying to express their anger.

***

With these notions of basic emotions in the back of our minds, let's look at the possible subjective experience of the soldier again. He is on the defence to say the least regarding psychotherapy. For him our talk is completely dispensable, and I get the notion that I shouldn't go near him. His ranting about the arrest by the police implicitly tells me that I shouldn't make his life any more difficult and I should really let him go. If I insist on a therapeutic conversation, I will be silently accused of the same sort of "pencil licking" he attributes to the cop who arrested him. Associations with unbridled bureaucracy and homosexuality pop up inside my head, most likely precisely the two things that this masculine soldier doesn't want to be associated with.

Despite his correct formal behaviour, I get the impression that meeting me is beneath his dignity. Possibly he implicitly robbed me from my professional abilities and devalued me. But he is way too much of a soldier to show this in public. The easy way out is not to have a conversation at all. Second best is a conversation in a military setting, a talk between an officer and a noncommissioned officer. Behaving professionally might also be a way to steer clear from becoming personal.

His description of the situation at the road block is very grim and the collegial backup didn't provide him with a sense of safety. Vicariously, unspoken fearful feelings of abandonment are aroused within me. When I asked him about his personal experience, the intensity of his rage surprised me. Maybe I got too close to an experience that he can't or won't talk about. Maybe it was too soon. He vents his anger on his colleagues, keeping me out of range (even though I am the one who puts the screws on him). Nonetheless, he is keeping me at bay and doesn't speak of his personal emotions at the road block. Possibly the non-commissioned officer "uses" his anger to suppress other emotions. It's very important not to rush into therapy and take the time to work on a base for cooperation that inspires confidence and is trustworthy.

This is essential for helping him cope with the emotional upheaval that might come about when he decides to open up and become vulnerable. During all this, I suspect that I have to avoid making any comments on homosexuality or on writing my report (that is his medical file).

***

A comparison. Someone walks through the room while reading and stubs his toe. The searing pain amounts to intense displeasure searching for an object. This would be the immediate stage of "feeling without an object". When the table leg is found, the emotional reaction is focussed on the table ("displeasure and proximity"). Many tables are hit after being run into. This phenomenon can also occur within the therapeutic relationship. Often there is a rise of resistance (and of an aversive attitude towards the therapist) when emotional pain suddenly becomes close and conscious.

From basic emotions to self-referential emotions: the self-image as the other

Hopefully the picture is getting clear that "others" who are associated with (dis) pleasure can be "objects" residing in the in the outer world as well as in the inner world. The emotional processing of information from the outer world follows the same basic rules as the emotional processing of information from the inner world. In fact, it is the mental representation that is getting processed. In the course of early development the differentiation between self and other is established. This enables the child not only to express more distinct emotions but also to see the self as separate from the other. Basic self-perception comes into being and with it the ability to look at the self if it were the other. The self is represented within the mind, for a great deal by means of the way we feel about ourselves. Somewhere between eighteen and twenty-four months most children show an intensification of emotions that point at rudimentary self-evaluation (Schalkwijk, 2015). The newly found perspective on the self keeps up with the expression of *shame and guilt* versus *pride and hubris*. Through these self-referential emotions, the self-image and reflections on personal behaviour are intimately linked with pleasure and displeasure.

***

It is not unlikely that the non-commissioned officer experiences suppressed forms of shame. At this moment, I don't have a clue what sort of self-evaluation could be the possible source of this presumed shame, but it would certainly fit with my impression of him as defensive. When his self-image is internally associated with displeasure, then I – as an inquisitive therapist – am a threat. The harmful self-image would become more realistic when I treat him as a failing soldier. A shameful state of mind would certainly use this as ammunition to deepen the shame and strengthen the defences.

It would reduce him even more as an unpleasurable "part-object" (Klein, idem). There is no doubt that he prefers to shun me and if a conversation is unavoidable, then he prefers to talk about his factual experiences instead of his subjective emotions.

*** *

In short, shame can be thought of as a frontal self-devaluating attack on the emotional centre of the self, which provokes a specific set of reactions. Donald Nathanson (1994) described two dimensions underlying the specific reactions to shame. These dimensions are combined in his model "compass of shame". On the first dimension, reactions are sorted out that either represent an attack or a flight. The second dimension specifies the target of these reactions, whether the attack/flight is aimed at the other or at the self. Nathanson's model is very practical for it helps to recognise various ways in which shame can express itself. This is very helpful if one is trying to lower defences and to make contact with someone who suffers from an afflicted self-image.

With this small detour on the topic of shame, I am trying to show that more complex self-referential emotions also adhere to the fundamental mechanisms that govern basic emotions. The way we feel about ourselves is added as an extra ingredient and processed in the same way we emotionally react to others in the outside world. The case of the soldier also seems to point in the direction of internal conflict in this department. The self-image is reduced to a part-object, a primitive representation of which its main characteristic is the association with pleasure or displeasure. In the development of the psyche, shame is more intensely felt when the ability to reflect on the self has grown, but the mentalising emotion regulating capabilities are still immature.[17] (I will expand on this issue in Chapter 4, where I will address the question of why shame is such an excruciatingly painful emotion.) The self-devaluating attack caused by shame is basically absolute. Because of the vital distinction between pleasure and displeasure, the self is experienced as *all good* or *all bad*.

Self-referential emotions can lead up to devaluation of the sense of self but also to idealisation. Then the sense of self is excessively invested with pleasurable feelings, which is very endearing to see in toddlers who are falling in love with themselves and the world. As parents, we feel the inclination to rejoice and defer the reality check, preserving a solid base for a positive self-esteem. We also find it inspiring to see someone feel good about him or herself, who is clearly human and not perfect in any "absolute" sense. But when this base is not so solid, it takes a lifelong effort to be content with oneself. Forced attempts might lead to excessive pride and hubris, which is one of the great themes of classic Greek tragedies. Frustrations then change very quickly into psychological injuries. When one is excessively prone to experience frustrations as attacks on the self, and as a result the emotional reciprocity between self and other is rejected, we speak of narcissistic problems. Such a narcissistic injury can be thought of as the painful separation from a pleasurable self-image, which is confronted in a "black-or-white manner". Some cling to the idealised image of the self (the "crave and fight" arrows in the Maelstrom model) and ignore reality, opposing the other who is made responsible for the injury. This often leads to arguments and fights. Others might "surrender" (the "leave and flight" arrows in the model) and implicitly forfeit the positive image of the self altogether. Someone who is dealing with narcissistic problems usually is also troubled by looming feelings of worthlessness and depression.

Rising arousal and the distinction between informative and overwhelming emotions

Basic emotions set up body and mind to take interactional initiative to fulfil needs and wishes that are vital to the survival of the individual and of the species.[18] Basic emotions automatically raise physical tension and mental attention in preparation of an adaptive response. In order to fight or flight, to crave or leave, one has to be able to move and to know which way to go. Rising arousal therefore can be seen as the central characteristic of the intensity of basic emotions. Levels of arousal fluctuate in accordance with the subjective perception of the interactional situation and these are synchronised to the exact second.

The idea that arousal is a general measure for the intensity of basic emotion is often criticised using the case of sadness. Isn't it true that sadness drains our energy and destroys the desire to move? I suggest that in this case *emotion* and *feeling* get confused, in the way that Damasio uses these terms in his 2010 book. For feelings are emotions that are partly consciously processed, adding mental imagery and verbal thought to the mix. When a baby cries in reaction to the separation from his mother, the emotional state innervates the baby and the mother to bridge the gap between them. But it is only when a conscious notion is added – the notion that separation is permanent and in fact is a loss – that crying can turn into the reclusive sadness that is associated with mourning.[19] It is an emotional reaction in the aftermath of the immediate rising levels of separation distress (Panksepp & Biven, 2012). Why move, when reunion is impossible? Without further ado, I endorse the idea that arousal can be seen as the measure of immediate emotional intensity. The powerlessness that can arise in the wake of separation is not caused by sadness alone.

Following Plutchick (1980), I want to incorporate a measure for the intensity of basic emotions within the model. I will use the level of arousal as indicative of the ability to *reflect* on the interaction between self and other. Besides this, the level of arousal is also indicative of the ability to make a clear distinction between self and other. Moderate levels of arousal produce *informative* emotions, which energise body and mind while someone is still able to use his internal state as a conversational argument. As a therapist, I would welcome a patient's comment such as "Your being late really annoys me, and I wonder whether it is your intention to frustrate me" as a sign of healthy emotional regulation. But when the inner tension gets too high, the subjective need to take action becomes precarious and acute. Reflection and conversation fall further behind. *Hyperarousal* (as well as the *hypoarousal* it can give rise to)[20] is characteristic for *overwhelming* emotion and has a detrimental impact on the cognitive processing of the interactional situation. Body and mind are in a state of evolutionary emergency, so act now and think later!

Language is endowed with different words for emotions of varying intensity, intuitively marking levels of reflective functioning. Our four basic emotions can be named as follows.

- Happiness (*arousal*) – euphoria (*hyperarousal*)
- Sadness – despair
- Fear – terror
- Anger – rage

On this note, I want to introduce the third axis of the Maelstrom model, which is closely related to the level of psychological arousal.

The third axis: the implicit sense of control

A built-in emotional mechanism that adapts quickly to evolutionary needs and frustrations imposes its own requirements on the psyche. In order to adapt to novel situations for which there is no unequivocal emotional response, one has to make use of other mental faculties as well. The ability to reason and to reflect on the emotional states of self and others has great evolutionary advantages.[21] But it is really a developmental achievement to get to know the workings of your inner emotional world. The main route towards this desirable state of affairs is to grow up with parents who are emotionally available and attuned to the inner world of childhood. Unfortunately, for a considerable amount of children this is not the case. Then the reflection on one's own emotional state remains strongly influenced by the attentional focus of the immediate emotional state that one is in. When angry, the focus is on an external opponent and not on the intricacies of thwarted frustrations. Therefore, the regulation of emotions is a prerequisite of optimal cognitive processing. It is really helpful if you are able to distinguish between your own swift and emotional associations and your elaborate and argumentative logic.[22] This developmental achievement is akin to the psychoanalytic notion of maturation of ego functions.

So a healthy regulation of emotions not only requires the "psychological owning" of one's emotions but also the ability to reflect on them and to inhibit them or consciously endorse them. According to Solms and Turnbull (2002), the ability to say "no" to one's emotional demands fundamentally contributes to a firm sense of self. The *implicit sense of control* is tightly bound up with the regulation of emotions. When regulation is fragile, emotions tend to become overwhelming. Emotional hyperarousal disrupts mental processing and diminishes the sense of control. Then emotions own you instead of the other way around. Interpersonal behaviour can become tenacious, though emotions can change rapidly each second. The sense of self can lose coherence because primary emotional reactions take over and subjugate reflective functioning. "You are driving me mad and I can't stand this anymore!" yells someone who is emotionally upset. When the regulation of emotions stays on track, the implicit sense of control is unaltered. This enables someone to admit being powerless and not in control, without losing the internal and implicit sense of control. One can give words to the subjective experience of powerlessness, while staying in the director's seat.

To put it differently, the implicit sense of control determines when the arousal of informative emotion turns into the hyperarousal of overwhelming emotion. When the sense of control is fragile, emotions are hard to regulate and arousal turns quickly into hyperarousal. But if the sense of control is firm, one is more tolerant of experiencing intense emotions without losing personal grip. The arousal level can become high, but not hyper. And maybe there is no absolute difference in the level of arousal, but the processing of emotional tension is more flexibly canalised and better regulated.

One could say that the regulation of emotions is dependent of the *tolerance of arousal*. A proportional correlation with the implicit sense of control can be visualised as in Figure 2.3.

I really want to stress that the implicit sense of control is *not* based on the ability to cognitively restrict the experience of emotions. The latter produces a superficial sense of control at best and is not very resilient against pervasive unconscious forces. The firmness of the implicit sense of control is a result of the acquired ability to (co-) regulate emotions within the interaction with the other. The blueprint for this ability is formed within attachment relationships in the first couple of years of life.

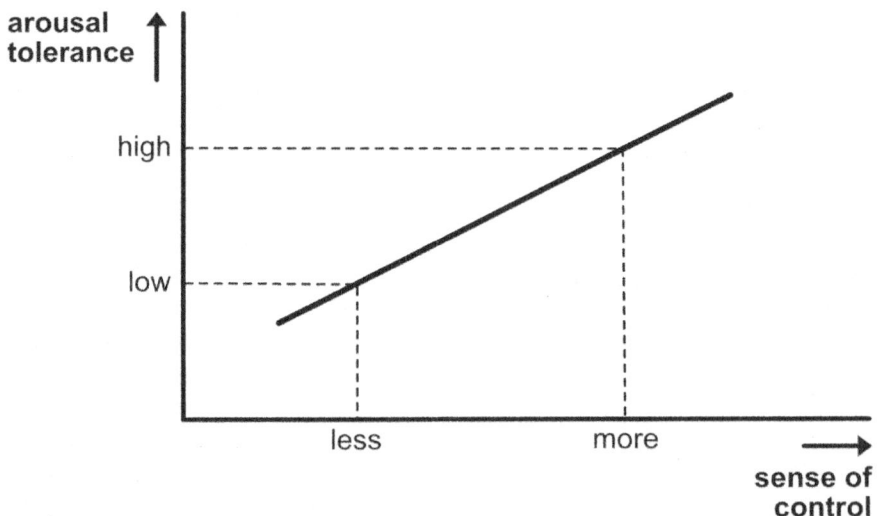

Figure 2.3 A hypothetical correlation between arousal tolerance and sense of control.

Optimal emotional development enables a child to mentalise, to think about feelings and to feel about thoughts. A child is very much dependent on the mentalising abilities of the parents for this. A parent should display a reasonable level of sensitivity to distinguish moments wherein help is needed to co-regulate emotions (when the child is overwhelmed) from moments wherein the child is given freedom and permission to explore his interactional world in his own pace and tempo. In this way, a healthy and flexible balance can be reached between self-regulation and interactional regulation, when the other is involved in regulation (Beebe & Lachmann, 2002). Long-lasting shortcomings in emotional availability of the primary caretakers endanger this healthy development. Some children constrict themselves to self-regulation, wherein the reality of physical and emotional immaturity is denied and replaced by fantasy, displaying out-of-place precocious behaviour. The implicit sense of control is then excessively positioned within the self. Other children focus pre-eminently on the regulation by the other and display clinging and controlling behaviour. The implicit sense of control is then excessively positioned within the other. In both unfavourable cases, the sense of control remains fragile because of the lack of internalised trust in co-regulation. The implicit conviction that one is personably able to find help if help is needed is missing.

The 3D Maelstrom model

When the correlation between the implicit sense of control and the tolerance of arousal is added to the 2D framework of basic emotions, a three-dimensional model comes into existence. This 3D model has the shape of a vortex and is called the 3D Maelstrom model (Figure 2.4).

Perhaps this 3D layout doesn't speak directly for itself, though the image of a vortex appeals to one's imagination. It visualises the intuitive association of a lack of control in the deep, narrowing the space where one is free from overwhelming terror, despair or rage. People often fear the swirling current of their own emotions that threatens to engulf them. At the bottom, we find the "emotional turbulence" that Wilfred Bion wrote about in 1977.[23] At the top, the implicit sense of control is firm and one is not easily swept away by strong emotions. The water is relatively tranquil there.

The image of the vortex is often used in literary works as a descent into the unknown world of the unconscious. Freud makes a reference to Friedrich Schiller's ballad "The Diver", wherein a young man takes a second and fatal dive into a swirling vortex to satisfy the curiosity of the king and to marry his daughter.[24] But perhaps the most famous story of a vortex is "A Descent into the Maelström" by Edgar Allan Poe (1841). Within this story, a young man with grey hair gives his account of how he was able to survive the relentless suction of the Maelström by trusting his own judgement and choosing a small piece of the wreckage instead of a big one to hold on to. In my opinion, it is also a metaphor for the false safety provided by clinging to the obvious and large part of your personal vessel, be it

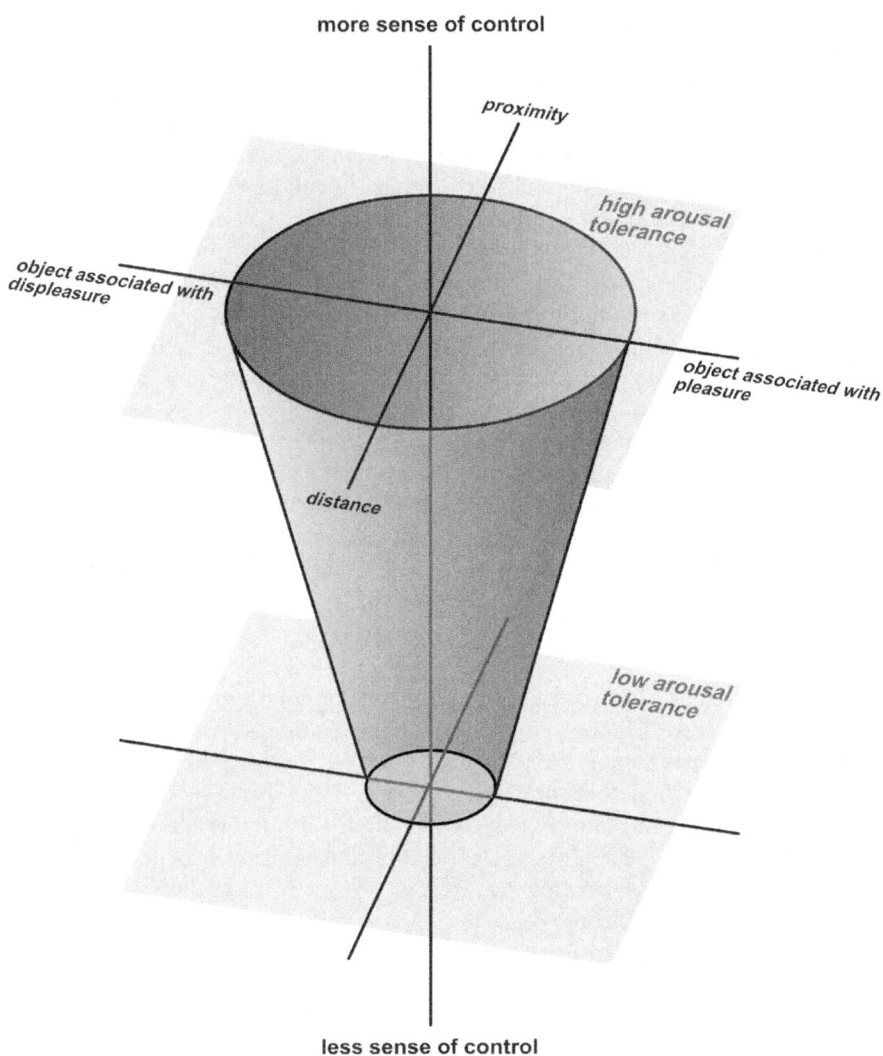

Figure 2.4 The Maelstrom model: a 3D model of the interrelatedness and intensity of four basic emotions.

the self or the other. The less conspicuous harmonisation of emotional interaction is the better way to go.

Rodolfo Llinás, professor of neuroscience at the New York University School of Medicine, wrote a book beautifully titled *I of the Vortex: From Neurons to Self* (2001). Based on his studies of the life of the sea squirt, he suggests that the nervous system is devised to make predictions that allow moving animals to wander safely through their environment. Animals need to anticipate the consequences

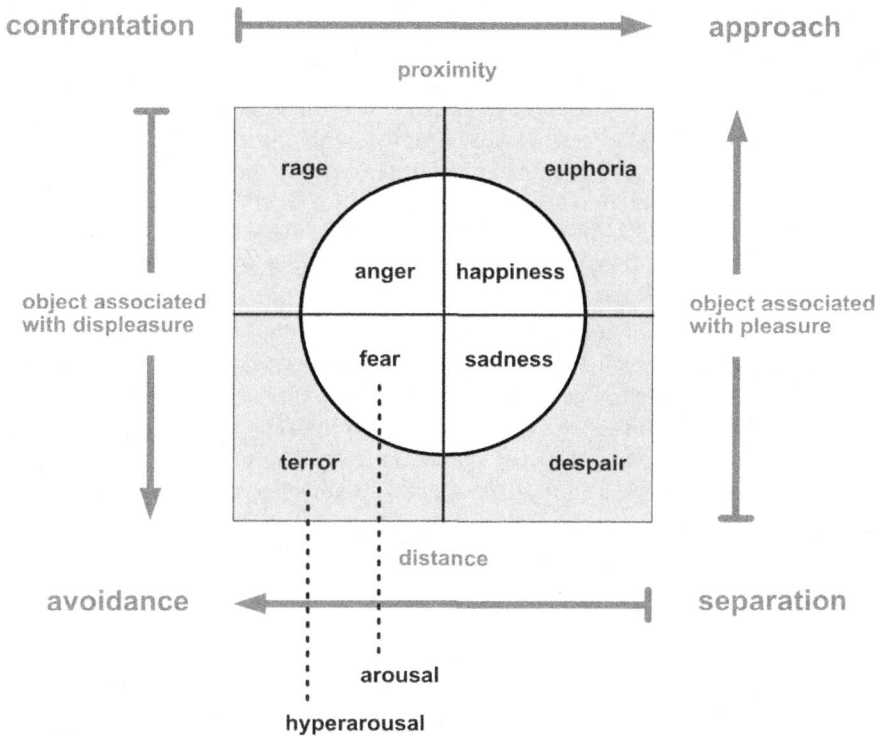

Figure 2.5 Intensity and naming of four basic emotions.

of each movement on the basis of sensory information. According to Llinás, prediction is the ultimate function of the brain, where the coordination of sensory information and motor activity takes place. The place of the self in the human mind could correspond with the centralisation of prediction. In line with Llinás, I stress the vital importance of movement and focus on the way it regulates interaction and evolutionary needs and wishes. The similarity of the image of a vortex is striking, considering that we took different paths to reach our conclusions.

Figure 2.5 depicts a cross-section of the 3D Maelstrom model and shows gradations of intensity of basic emotions.

Intense emotions, splitting and the corrosion of the sense of control

From the day of birth, a baby experiences emotionally satisfying and frustrating interactions with the mother. Ronald Fairbairn (1963) has described how these exciting and frustrating experiences lead up to split off representations of the mother that are repressed by the ego (and become unconscious). Though he suggests that there is an (idealised) core representation of the mother that is conscious, there is also an unconscious image of an exciting mother and an unconscious image of a frustrating mother. Feelings of love and hate are bound up with these split and repressed representations. I suggest that it is the perception of the mother *in a particular emotional state of the baby* that is incorporated in implicit memory. The intensity of the emotion is a measure of the vital urgency of the situation, and therefore it gets preferential treatment in the admission to the relational blueprint.

When an adult is emotionally overwhelmed and reflective lucidity is temporarily missing, the normal ambivalent impression of the other is split and (according to Fairbairn) repressed. The other (that can also be the self) isn't experienced as a multifaceted person, but is *all good* or *all bad*. In an emotionally overheated head, people are reduced to being "part-objects". I suggest that it is the shift in attentional focus caused by intense emotional arousal that is responsible for perceiving the other in a restricted way. Intense emotions instigate splitting by limiting the attentional focus to those parts of the other that either give or frustrate pleasure. This can be interpreted by the overwhelmed person that the other is the cause of the intense emotion. "I am furious because you are such a bastard!" The (inter) action tendency is also aimed at the interaction with the other, after all. It can be hard though to correct a misinterpretation. It might very well be that the other is perceived as a bastard *just because you are furious.*

Powerful emotions and splitting can occur in overwhelming situations in which one has no control. Powerlessness and helplessness increase emotional vulnerability. This doesn't imply though that power and control are a safeguard against emotional impulsivity. Unfortunately a powerful position doesn't protect someone from confusing mental matters. In clinical practice, we see a lot of people who have experienced an *internal loss of control.* Prolonged periods of intense emotional pressure tend to leave their mark on the implicit sense of control, especially for children who go through sensitive periods. The tolerance of arousal diminishes, leading up to heightened irritability and vulnerability for overstimulation. Someone is easily caught off guard. It also makes it harder to "psychologically own" emotions, to consider emotional experiences as something that belongs to you instead of something alien, unmentionable, unpredictable or hostile towards the self. Without mental representation of personal emotional states, the sense of control gets corroded. And nothing is a greater obstacle for finding a fulfilling relationship than to be a stranger for yourself.

Notes

1 This is in line with Bion's explanation that we can only know ("K") the other by how we feel (love or hate, "L" or "H") about them. Bion, W.R. (1962). *Learning from experience*. London: William Heinemann.
2 In cognitive-behavioural therapy, the assignment of affective value is also considered highly important. See Brewin, C.R. (2006). Understanding cognitive behaviour therapy: A retrieval competition account. *Behaviour Research and Therapy*, 44, 765–784.

Brewin states that changes in the *attentional bias for positive or negative cues* of the object are crucial for understanding the principles of cognitive therapy. He considers the object to have both positive and negative aspects, but emphasises the relevance of selective attention to one of them. This, he states, is crucial in the cognitive understanding of the development of psychopathology. He describes the attentional balance between positive or negative aspects of objects as *retrieval competition*.

3 This is the basic mechanism for what psychoanalysts call "transference". Emotionally conflicted relational scenarios tend to manifest and repeat themselves in the therapeutic relationship. Professional training and a continuing focus on intersubjective reflection help the psychoanalyst to recognise such scenarios. Instead of reacting in a primary and emotional way that "fits" the scenario, the psychoanalyst will use his subjective emotions to find words for describing this implicit relational scenario. (For example: "You really need a listening ear, so my being late today really upsets you. The idea that I did this intentionally would really be infuriating. Perhaps that's the reason that you don't feel like talking today to a fraud like me?") To do this in such a way and to find the right moment so that the other can actually hear what is being said takes genuine concern and professional craftsmanship that sometimes resembles an art. Personally, I stumble far more often than I get it "right".

4 "Gnothi seauton" or "Know thyself". This famous Greek aphorism seems as modern today as it was two thousand years ago.

5 A heart-wrenching example of the importance of touch and social bonding can be found in Harry Harlow's work with rhesus monkeys. In his series of studies, a clear preference can be observed in baby monkeys after separation from their mothers, for a robot with a terry cloth "skin" above a robot of steel wire that feeds the monkey. Touch is especially important for establishing feelings of safety and attachment and is of equal fundamental importance for psychological development as the availability of food. Harlow, H. (1959). Love in infant monkeys. *Scientific American*, 200(6), 68–74.

6 See, for an eloquent account of the detrimental impact of neoliberalism on the notion of humans as social beings, Verhaeghe, P. (2012). *Identiteit*. Amsterdam: De Bezige Bij. It is a cultural myth that pleasure is really "all about me" and that it is only through external guidance (be it religious doctrine, an authoritarian state or the rigid adherence to the "invisible hand" of the free market) that society is guarded from chaos. This myth also contributes to the frame that it is OK to be selfish and greedy until the law dictates it is not. In this way a society is created in which we – as frogs in a pot – turn up the heat by consuming as much as we can afford. And whereas we can blame the limited intelligence of the frogs mind for staying in the cooking pot, as humans we are very capable of realising that we have no alternative for planet earth. I will expand on this issue in Chapter 9 on the human response to the environmental crisis.

7 I take a more object relational approach than Freud though.

8 This could explain why we are attracted to beauty, but at the same time might shy away from it.

9 This association is only valid for interactions wherein one feels capable of taking charge and has an implicit sense of control. But when one is confronted with a threat of overwhelming proportions against which there is no defence or offence, fear is the primary emotion to emerge. This is the case for natural disasters, disease or superior enemies for example. In response to this fear, one tends to seek help from another person who is deemed more powerful. When one has a history of "powerlessness in interactions" and has a feeble implicit sense of control, then the focus is chronically aimed at the other. It is the other who is supposed to be responsible for one's inner emotional experience. And it is the other who is often experienced as dominant and indifferent at the same time. This pattern fits with an occupied attachment style. Then anger is mainly focussed on the other in order to persuade him or her to take action in benefit of the self.

10 This seems to be an important aspect of the fascination for firearms. A firearm has the potential to change fear into force, through the movement of a finger. On top of that, it enhances the reach of self-initiated violence. Unfortunately, this lessens the interpersonal feedback through the facial expression of the emotional state of the other. When pathways for empathy are diminished, diplomacy stands less chance. It is hard to be cruel to someone you look in the eye. Aiming for profit, the gun industry is very much aware of this fact and advertisement campaigns categorically dehumanise "bad guys".

11 See, for a discussion of the use of this distinction, Siegel, A. (2005). *The neurobiology of aggression and rage*. Boca Raton, FL: CRC Press.

12 See, for a critique on this standpoint, Carver, C.S. & Harmon-Jones, E. (2009). Anger is an approach-related affect: Evidence and implications. *Psychological Bulletin*, 135, 183–204. Interestingly, in the same article the distinction between positive and negative affect is brought up for discussion. The authors call for an alternative dimensional model in which affects of positive valence are not solely related to approach and affects of negative valence are not solely related to avoidance. Of course I agree.

13 This distinction might be of clinical importance in understanding the pleasurable aspect of resistance in psychotherapy and the hidden joy in making the therapist powerless (though this is an ambivalent phenomenon nonetheless, often ridden with frustration and guilt). I believe this to be a much overlooked facet of the *negative therapeutic reaction*. In some cases resistance can be thought of as an exertion of dominance on a devalued therapist in the absence of a firm inner sense of control and basic trust that makes the dependence on a helpful other bearable. See Freud, S. (1923). *The ego and the id*. Standard Edition, Vol. 19. London: Hogarth Press. 12–59.

14 One could argue that the aim of *freezing* is not to be found by the object associated with displeasure, and the aim of *grieving* is to be found by the object associated with pleasure.

15 A video of Dr. Tronick's Still Face experiment is uploaded by the University of Massachusetts, Boston and can be watched on YouTube.

16 Maybe some forms of mourning are so mentally draining because one has to repeatedly reconsolidate the notion of permanent loss and finite time alongside memory traces of oceanic feeling and unlimited gratification.

17 Mentalisation means the ability to think about emotions as experiences derived from subjective motives, which shape not only personal perspective but the perspectives of others as well. See Fonagy, P., Gergely, G., Jurist, E. & Target, M. (2002). *Affect regulation, mentalization, and the development of the self*. New York: Other Press.

18 The fact that humans are able to treat ideas and concepts in an emotional way as well – sometimes drawing paradoxical conclusions – doesn't take anything away from this basic function of emotions. To me, the growing amount of scientific evidence that other animals than humans are also capable of experiencing emotions is completely convincing. When we think about the evolutionary origins of mental faculties, we are bound to find differences in degree instead of in kind (like we do when physical properties are studied). The human species seems to be the undisputed front-runner though in the ability to experience internal conflict and to filter out information that isn't compatible with subjective assumptions. See, for instance, Bekoff, M. (2000). *The smile of a dolphin: Remarkable accounts of animal emotions*. New York: Discovery Books.

19 See, for a clinical and theoretical illuminative article, Freed, P.J. & Mann, J.J. (2007). Sadness and loss: Toward a neurobiopsychosocial model. *American Journal of Psychiatry*, 164, 28–34.

20 See, for a theoretically illuminative and clinically fertile way of dealing with extreme levels of arousal, Ogden, P., Minton, K. & Pain, C. (2006). *Trauma and the body: A sensorimotor approach to psychotherapy*. New York: Norton. I have had the great pleasure of hearing Pat Ogden speak in a workshop, experiencing vividly what the *window of tolerance* means.

21 This is the slow train of thought of Kahneman's System 2. See Kahneman, D. (2012). *Thinking, fast and slow*. London: Penguin Books Ltd.
22 In my personal opinion, there is no moral hierarchy in these two kinds of logic. When there is a confusion of tongues between matters of the heart and matters of the mind, moral intentions run the risk of being corrupted.
23 Bion, W.R. (1977). *Emotional turbulence in borderline personality disorders*. New York: International University Press.
24 In Freud, S. (1930). *Civilization and its discontents*. Standard Edition, Vol. 21. London: Hogarth Press. 64–145.

Chapter 3

Cartography for psychotherapy

***

It was not his choice to visit a military psychologist for his out of control emotions. Because that was what he was trying to do: to command his emotions back in line instead of regulating them within interactions. When I invited him to talk about moments that had made a disruptive impression, he immediately set aside our joint reflection in an outburst of rage against his "unprofessional colleagues". He completely ignored his own loss of military posture in the room, possibly because he couldn't face his loss of an internal sense of control. The first account of his deployment invoked an acute sense of powerlessness within me. But that is something that we couldn't talk about (yet).

I ask him why he wanted to become a soldier in the first place. He can't stand to watch and bear injustice "and never could", he says. He tries to adhere to strict principles. For him, a man is only worth as much as his word. "A soldier does what he says and says what he does." He developed himself in his professional career as a man who can be relied on. He is able to mix this straightforward attitude with a sort of humour that is not for the fainthearted, but unmistakably has a certain charm. I get the impression that most of the time he is perfectly able to defuse conflicts with a joke or a pun. He has little patience for "blistering stories", by which he means that he can't stand people who make excuses and ask for compassion. Possibly because his "lack of filter" fits quite well into military culture, he doesn't have a history of fights or arguments. He is a highly respected colleague who is valued by his commanding officer. Therefore, I have a strong suspicion that his heightened irritability has got something to do with his deployment. I tell him that and suggest that it is of professional importance to talk about his experiences. I still wonder whether he consented or obeyed.

I agree with his plea for good communications with the base. Especially on missions with a high level of threat, it is of the utmost importance that all of the colleagues keep this in mind, I firmly reply. It seems to relax him a little bit. He tells me that the Ministry of Defence has become too generous and soft on entry requirements. He himself stems from a military family. Both his grandfather and his father had been soldiers. They have told him stories from the old days, when military discipline "was taken seriously". "Back then, they didn't shrink from no form of violence to make sure that everyone was on the same page, both inside and outside barracks". I keep my reservations about his idealisation of aggression to myself and keep on listening. He tells me about the deficient mandate of peace missions, in which soldiers are placed in dangerous situations without permission to use force to take charge. When I suggest that it must have been difficult to be subjected to the arbitrary use of power at the road block while he was supposed to oversee peacekeeping efforts in the region, he emitted a deep sigh. "How is a soldier supposed to do his job in these kind of circumstances?" He tells me about the guard who kept grinning while playing with the safety of his gun. He described the clicking of the metal as an excruciating detail, knowing about the unimaginable enormity of the slaughter that had taken place there. He would have liked to teach the guard a lesson, but he refrained until his driver and he got permission to leave. He didn't say it in so many words, but our feelings and thoughts seem to coincide; it would have been in good family tradition to beat that sadistic grin off the guard's face. I tell him that it certainly was sensible to behave professionally, but that his heart told him otherwise. He gives me a short glance and a soft "yes". For him, it must have been intolerable to be subjected to humiliating cruelty without striking back. After this session, his irritability gradually diminishes. It seems as though he is more determined than ever to adopt military protocol, but somehow he got less rigid at the same time. Once again he is part of an army that takes action when human rights are violated, however limited. After a while he asks me with half of a smile whether we can stop now that he has lost his short fuse. That is fine with me, I reply spontaneously.

After the pieces have been put together, it is easier to recognise the roles for which I was casted in his interactional scenarios. Of course, I stood 1–0 behind from the start because he was sent by his CO. For him, I was the "pencil-licking" police officer who took notes on his transgressions; psychotherapy as a traffic fine. Possibly I also was an unprofessional colleague, one who doesn't know what really matters on a mission and who works in civilian clothes (in my own defence: only when not on a military base). He deigned me with his professional opinions while I probably was a primary example of the Ministry of Defence being too generous and soft on its entry requirements. Even though I was unaware of the precise contents of his interactional scenarios, intuitively I picked up that it was my only chance to take up my military role. With the authority of an officer, I suggested that we should talk about his short fuse. And it was from my own military experience that I could stress the importance of good communications and heightened alertness on a mission. It helped him to relax noticeably, possibly because he was able to see me as someone who has military professionalism in mind, someone more like his father. At the same time, it was important that I didn't bring up his military career for discussion, something that he did in the enclosure of his mind. Looking back on it now, I think that it helped him to disconnect me from the image of the sadistic guard and to lessen his feelings of powerlessness. He was seen as a soldier and not as a patient. The intensity of the experience at the road block was caused not only by the threat of violence but (probably even more) by the damage done to his military identity and devaluation of his self-esteem. He had withstood this psychological defeat with all his might – it had to be attacked or avoided – what had made him chronically agitated and irritable.

It was not until my psychoanalytic training that I realised how humiliating it is for a man to be labelled as "a short fuse". Within the army though this is a generally accepted term. It stresses that a faulty control over one's own aggression is a weakness that isn't compatible with military professionalism. A "true soldier" keeps a cool head and doesn't get carried away by emotions. From a professional perspective, this is completely reasonable. But with mental health in mind it is certainly not always beneficial to stow away overheated emotions in a private fridge.

***

Symptomatic phase and recovery: from contact and understanding towards trust and control

For psychotherapy to start off successfully, the therapist tries to make a connection – however small – on an emotional level in an early stage. This connection is the first step in building trust and hope for a successful therapeutic collaboration. Everyone has got his own set of expectations of change and how (not) to get there. That is why first impressions of the professional engagement of the therapist are so important. No one finds it easy to go into therapy, to invite someone else to look at parts of yourself that you struggle with and don't understand. And often people already have had a lot of negative experience in "the sharing department". These negative interactional experiences might also be integrated in a pattern of expectation that hinders an empathic attitude in others. Depending on the sensitivity of the therapist, repeated attention and appropriate timing is given to these defensive interactional manoeuvres. It takes courage to see a therapist about personal troubles, without knowing in advance what therapy might bring. This is often felt as the paradox of psychotherapy; in order to gain a better understanding of yourself and a more healthy relationship with yourself, it is temporarily necessary to lessen the usual ways of feeling in control and come into contact with more rudimentary and emotional layers of your personality. Some psychoanalysts call this "regression in service of the ego", which is thought to be a central element for opening up creativity (Knafo, 2002). In psychoanalysis, it is about the relinquishment of rational control and censorship in order to gain insight in internal and unconscious conflicts. This is captured in the analytic dictum of "free association". Besides that, I would stress the importance of the emotional sensitivity and availability of the therapist for the relinquishing of rational control. Before entering a state wherein intense and overwhelming emotions can be felt, it is important to know that you are not left to your own devices.

Emotions serve both the pleasure principle and the need for interpersonal contact. Emotions set humans in motion to fulfil vital needs through changing the interaction with others and set off in reaction to drives and needs. The distinction is somewhat artificial, but *drives* can be thought of as a stimulus from within through which an urge is felt to act in the outside world. This is where the pleasure principle reigns. A *need* reflects a shortage in the inner world – be it physical or mental – for which an active participation of the outside world is required. The principle governing needs are of the same order of magnitude as the pleasure principle and could be called the *need for contact*. We can see it unfold in all sorts of attachments behaviours, like a baby searching for safety through its parents. But the need for contact also plays a key role in the attempt to verbalise and understand the intricacies of the inner world (also with help from caretakers). The pleasure principle dictates that fulfilment is sought and frustration is avoided. The need for contact dictates that relations are sought and loneliness is avoided. In my opinion, these are the two basic principles that dynamically give rise to a range of personal characteristics, working with and against each other. No matter whether there is a surplus of inner arousal or a shortage that has to be filled up by the outside world, drives and needs energise us through emotions. That is why I believe that emotions and emotion regulation constitute an integrating framework for psychotherapy and psychoanalysis.[1]

We get acquainted with our drives and pleasures through contact with the other. And if we succeed in recognising and regulating emotional energy in a joint venture, both the internal sense of control and the feeling of connectedness are strengthened. This form of regulating emotions is of a higher level than controlling "unruly and unwanted" emotions mainly within the self. It also exceeds a long-lasting dependency on the other in order to keep the self in balance. Namely it enhances the capability to feel, think and act freely without forcing the self or losing contact with the other. Trust – in the self and in the other – is subsided understanding.

***

Talking to the non-commissioned officer, I learned that it was important not to make quick suggestions about his emotional turbulence. On top of that, it was crucial not to be content with a singular conception of his emotional life. The main experience at the road block wasn't one of fear and loneliness – that was my prime association – but one of humiliation and personal degradation. The effort it took him to keep his tension inside – and possibly his forbearance of violent action – felt like an admission of military failure. And that placed his identity in clear and present danger, his subjective worth as a soldier and as a human being. This key additional meaning only was raised because of my postponement of interpretation. I made an effort to keep my attention "open" and listen for all sorts of content that came to the fore within him or within me. It takes some clinical intuition and experience to recognise the right moment for making a comment, so insight is gained not only on a cognitive level but on an emotional level as well. And that is an indispensable step towards coping after a disruptive experience.

***

Symptomatic phase

Low sense of control and arousal tolerance. Overwhelming emotions and inability to integrate experience.

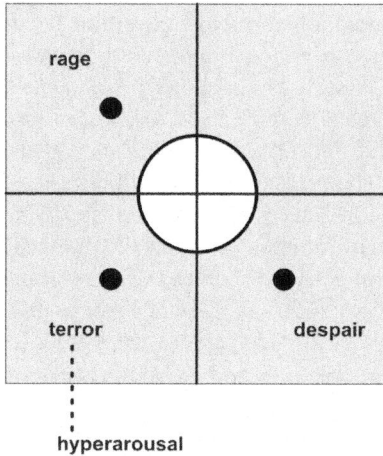

Recovery

Re-establishment of sense of control and arousal tolerance. Contact and reflection enable integration of experience.

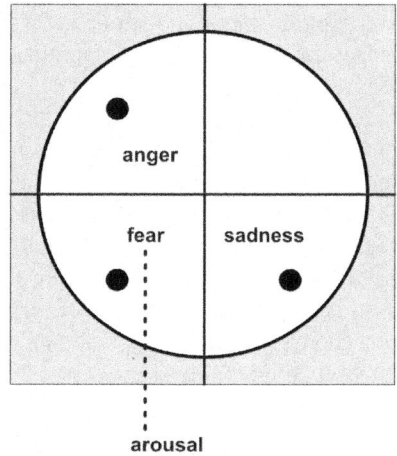

Figure 3.1 Symptomatic phase and recovery from an overwhelming emotional experience.

Within the Maelstrom model therapeutic change can be visualised as in Figure 3.1. It pictures two slices of the 3D Maelstrom model. The left slice displays emotional experience at the bottom of the vortex, wherein one feels overwhelmed and can't find words to reflect on actual experience. In the right slice, the way upwards has been found and emotions are contained and can be named. This makes it less difficult to access and talk about subjective experience. The emotional contact with the other loses its black-or-white quality and there is a building up of trust and confidence.

The return of the unmet need: symptoms and a chance to heal

The human psyche is very capable of keeping poorly understood and unruly parts of personal experience outside of consciousness. Probably this is for the better, for it generally enables us to function in a coherent way. Limited self-awareness definitely isn't an insurmountable handicap for healthy living. And when mysterious or disturbing parts rise to the surface in dreams or in art, for example, this doesn't need to put us off balance. It can also catch our attention and fuel our imagination.

Trouble starts when the return of raw, repressed or split-off emotional impulses leads to the emergence of symptoms, to a medical complaint that one just wants to get rid of. When psychotherapy is supposed to numb a particular part of subjective experience, what is really required is an even stronger censorship for consciousness. An emotional struggle that is deemed too painful runs the risk of being exiled out of awareness. When symptoms are so disturbing that daily activities are hampered, this wish is very understandable. The pathological part of this wish lets itself be felt as collateral damage. Overall intra- and interpersonal sensitivity is diminished. And when a symptom – for example an overwhelming emotion – is banned out of consciousness, one loses sight of the underlying motives that gave rise to the internal conflict in the first place. These are the sort of motives that search for a personal answer to questions like "who am I?", "who are you to me?", "where do I belong?", "what do I value?", "whom do I love?" and "what do I hate?". When one thinks to have all the answers to these big questions – and it's no coincidence that children are very preoccupied with these – the chance is that symptoms reappear in old or new form when suffering from another setback.

A symptom is not solely a sign of psychological crisis, but it also represents a chance to heal. When overwhelming emotional intensity has caused an internal split in the subjective experience of the relational world, the affective spectrum bleaches into a stark contrast of black or white. The other (or the self) is all good or all bad, friend or foe, big or small, strong or weak. In this two-dimensional world it is imperative to choose a side, because ambivalence is perceived as psychological disintegration. Then the return of the split-off is taken up as a threat, a weakness or a betrayal. The psychoanalytical viewpoint on this matter is not to mistake the symptom for the disease, but to focus on the rigidity of the splitting. For it is the implicit gap in the way we relate to others and in what we are aware of (and what not), that stirs up all sort of problems between the self and the other. Effective psychotherapy reduces splitting and enhances integration of fragmented subjective experience. A symptom depicts a disjointed and isolated part of the emotional inner world, in which the self is felt to be aching and alone. So it is a minimum requirement for psychotherapy to "listen to the symptom", even when the patient's only objective is "to get better". But when a symptom is reflected upon as a part that was out of sight until now, then a psychological crisis could become the starting point for personal growth. When suffering doesn't completely wipe out attention and personal engagement, the inner world might be expanded. The psychoanalytical invitation of free association is an incentive for exploring the self freely and fully. And when things go well, the integration of split-off parts (that were undifferentiated, forgotten, repressed or distorted) contributes not only to healing but to flourishing as well.

Some intense emotional experiences serve as a catalyst for personal growth. Other overwhelming experiences serve as an impediment and can be labelled traumatic. *Trauma* is the Greek word for wound. Psychological trauma is the wounding of the psychic skin (or stimulus barrier), caused by something sharp and intrusive or coarse and damaging. It pierces the protective psychic layer, also known as the psychic envelope (Anzieu, 1989), or tears it apart. With the Maelstrom model in mind, psychological trauma can be described as an overwhelming *confrontation* with a life-threatening danger (a psychological *stab wound*) or as an overwhelming *separation* from a vitally important other (a psychological *scrape wound*). Both of these emotional wounds exceed the tolerance of arousal and lead up to a severe loss of internal control. This might result in an impulsive fight-or-flight response (when dealing with a stab wound) or a crave-or-leave response (when dealing with a scrape wound). Besides that, these traumatic experiences can be perceived as an acute threat to the healthy sense of psychic coherence and therefore are further banned from awareness. Coping then (that is integration and regulation) remains incomplete. The intensity of emotional upheaval might temporarily be disconnected from awareness, but the connection between the memory trace and mental disruption stays unaltered.

When memory is triggered and parts of the experience enter abruptly into awareness, the traumatic event is *relived* (instead of remembered). Emotions retain their intensity because they are not regulated by higher mental processing. Motor activity is first choice for the unwinding of heightened arousal; the experience isn't remembered, but acted out. This might bring about abrupt episodes of reliving traumatic experiences but also a repetitive occurrence of trauma-related nightmares or the enactment of implicit relational patterns. The imprint of the traumatic event implicitly influences the whole of personality, but at the same time seems to be cut off as well. And when sensorial and relational memories pop up into consciousness, these can be extremely frightening and disruptive, against which one reacts with a fight-or-flight response on itself. Then memory becomes the enemy. Sometimes medication, illegal drugs or alcohol are used to obscure awareness defensively. Splitting, repression and denial then maintain their momentum, building up to a full-fledged syndrome like post-traumatic stress disorder.[2]

In Chapter 5, I will explore the topic of psychological trauma more fully, when a case of repetitive nightmares is discussed.

Psychotherapy and psychoanalysis

***

The non-commissioned officer came to see me sixteen times. At first his request for help mainly concerned the appeasement of his CO and the return to business as usual. Along the way, this was translated in how to handle his agitation and irritability. Once relieved from the sharp edges of his symptoms, he no longer had a need for psychotherapy. I suspect that he had accepted (or endured) more emotional closeness in our therapeutic contact than he was accustomed to in his adult life. And me being a man might have made it even more difficult.[3]

But what made the experience at the road block so disturbing for him? Why the road block, when he had went through numerous dangerous and tragic situations on his deployment? I suspect that there was something in the encounter at the road block that resonated with a dormant internal conflict. Something in this experience must have caused a real stir in the implicit undertow of his emotions and regulation, something that is related to sadistic humiliation and the unattainability of a safe haven.

***

The difference between psychotherapy and psychoanalysis might be formulated as follows, though it is somewhat reductive. Psychotherapy aims for symptom reduction and the restoration of functionality. Psychoanalysis aims for gaining insight in unconscious needs and wishes and the restoration of vitality.

His therapy most likely would have taken another course when his request for help was stated differently. For example something like: "Why do I get into trouble with authority, while I hold military duty in high esteem? What is the resentment within me for which people find me harsh and distant, while I don't want to avoid friendship at all?" Or even: "I don't want to alienate my wife from me, but I do so nonetheless. I want to change that." Ideally, psychanalytic therapy starts with a conflict that is experienced as internal. The psychological problem or struggle is acknowledged as something that resides within, instead of filing a complaint against the outside world. And to be completely clear: the capability to experience inner conflict and ambivalence doesn't take anything away from denouncing injustice in the world. It just asks for an additional sensitivity or interest in the workings of the inner world, especially when psychoanalysis is considered. Classic psychoanalysis – when someone lies down on the couch four or five times a week – still is arguably the most thorough method in terms of time and effort to get acquainted with one's inner world within the Western mental health system. The psychoanalytic motto of free association – to withhold oneself from censoring thoughts or feelings, however odd or disturbing they may be – is as radical as it is impossible. When free association falters and an untold story seeps through the cracks of the main narrative, be it felt or thought or fantasised, then an entry might be found to new or hidden insight.

It is completely fictitious, but what would it have been like if the soldier had lain down on the analytic couch? I want to share my thoughts, because it illustrates how working with the Maelstrom model in mind is helpful in capturing the emotional undertow in the therapy room. It goes without saying that I make use of other pieces of psychoanalytic theory wherever I can.

***

Looking back on the therapy of the soldier, it strikes me that I don't say it out loud that he would have liked to beat that sadistic grin off the guard's face. Apparently, something withheld me from verbalising this aggressive impulse explicitly. I only hint at it indirectly, thereby placing the impulsive aggressive act outside of the realm of military professionalism. If he was in psychoanalysis instead of psychotherapy, I would have come back on my indirectness, wondering whether it might be reflective of something that is going on inside him. It is not farfetched to presume that in the mind of the non-commissioned officer the impulsive aggressive act makes him less of a professional. But I wonder whom he would have identified himself with if he had attacked the guard? I suspect that it is his admired father, who didn't shy away from crackdown for the sake of discipline. By refraining from violent action, he possibly doesn't live up to the example set by his father, as he holds it within the enclosure of his mind.

At the same time, it also dawned upon me that the image of the sadistic guard got intertwined with the image of his father. Someone who threatens to use violence – without words but hard to miss – against the antagonist of his will. How did the non-commissioned officer as a child react to the severe treatment of his father? What sort of emotions did it stir up? I can imagine all sorts of emotions going through the son of a father who is a figure of authority within and outside of the family and who doesn't stand contradiction. And maybe secretly his father enjoyed this dominant position. The son must have sought a solution on the inside, as outward resistance was futile. Possibly his father also made clear that "blistering stories" weren't appreciated. So the son chose to become a soldier himself, walking in the footsteps of his father, and to bury his normal ambivalence regarding aggression. To allow the full range of his emotions to surface into consciousness and to stand up to his father could have been too much to ask for the boy living inside the non-commissioned officer.

It is not aggression that is taboo in the military, it is impulsivity and disobedience to higher command. Reflecting on my own indirectness, I think I, as a military psychologist, coincided with this strict order of things. It may very well be that he also felt betrayed by military command, which "set him up to fail". He was trained to take charge (from a very early age) but was instructed and forced to refrain from taking action. The impulse to act (and get "the bad guy") collided with hierarchical constraint (and the limited mandate of a peace mission).[4] His presence had to prevent the warring parties from fighting again, but he had to endure the presence of men who were responsible for the most inhumane sort of injustice. His emotional turmoil at the road block could be a dazzling mix of separation (from the safe haven of his base, from his military identity that prescribed that he had to take charge), fear (for harm to his colleague and himself) and anger (towards the sadistic guard but perhaps also towards his commanding officer who put him in this situation). It really is no wonder that he wasn't able to fully cope with all the intricacies of his emotional inner world. The encounter at the road block is full of "confrontation and separation" on many – concrete and mental – levels. The urge to take charge broke through at the exit on the highway in the Netherlands. He had held it inside for a long time and now found a venue with the policeman who stopped him and gave him a ticket. His anger may very well be displaced and originally aimed at the sadistic guard, his CO or even his father (figures of authority), which he couldn't permit himself to express openly. It would not only mean a breach in his professional identity of a soldier but also a desperate uprising against (his representation of) his father.

He also didn't go into the relational problems he had with his wife all that much. When I asked him what his wife thought of his irritability, he replied at the end of therapy that she said that he had progressed. It was perfectly clear that I didn't get access to that personal realm. Probably his marriage would have come up more in long-term therapy, where he would have had the time to explore his anger with his wife. His anger could have turned out to be vicarious if she was the "safe choice" for venting his resentment. Maybe he feared that he would turn into "a blistering story" and that he would fall off a pedestal instead of being "the soldier in control". And when I think about his wife, I realise that I know very little about his mother. It might be no coincidence that the image of the father seems to play such an important role and that the image of the mother hardly comes into focus. He wouldn't be the first to realise that the anger with one of the parents serves to prevent a conflict with the other parent. His father is "the likely recipient of resentment" whereas his mother is kept out of the firing line. I wonder – and I stress again that this is a fictitious example – what she has done to protect her son against the severe treatment from his father? Is she deemed as helpless as he was, or did he feel rage because of the betrayal by the woman he loved most? On what grounds is she considered to be powerless in attending to his well-being? In a psychoanalysis this could have become clear when he would have transferred his feelings towards his mother onto me. For example, he could blame me for not attending to his well-being very well, stating that I am only interested in his military deployability instead of his mental health.

But maybe I had already taken up a role from "an implicit mother-scenario" earlier than I realised. There had been topics which I felt to be conflictual but I was hesitant to ask about. Intuitively I witnessed but said little. In the end I am glad that the words I was able to speak got through and we made a tentative connection. It is part of my analytical training to be able to "sit on my hands and not to force a breach in the defensive psychological wall". For trust and control to grow, it helped that the soldier was given the time to decide for himself when he would open up a window, however little or short.

In order to come to terms with intense emotions, it helps to see behaviour (from the self or the other) as a result from inner and outer motives that are rarely completely understood. I am ignorant of the emotional experiences and implicit relational patterns of the soldier, but I listen respectfully and use my own sensitivity to imagine and to connect. Although it really is a mistake to come to any definite conclusions about the inner worlds of his parents, some things can be said about his subjective relational experiences with them. In long-term psychoanalytical treatment, he possibly would have had new thoughts about his parents, who they were and where they came from. For many adults still automatically put their parents on the childish pedestal which makes them "the most loving and strong parents in the whole world". This doesn't need to be problematic and it bolsters the sense of basic safety, that is; to feel safe in an outer world that is a lot bigger than you are and an inner world that is more turbulent than you can control. It becomes problematic when people hold on to premature solutions for conflictual and overwhelming emotions, and they get stuck in a clear-cut view of the self, the other and the world. Then implicit relational patterns become restrictive, the subjective freedom to choose is diminished and people feel trapped. To emotionally share and question implicit convictions in a safe therapeutic environment can be liberating. It doesn't redeem someone from all internal struggle or conflict, but it enhances the ability to choose consciously and give direction to one's own life. It reinforces the sense of control and the ability to be loving and strong in your own right and hopefully find meaningful pleasure in the process.

People tend to back down from the unknown, from what is unfamiliar or what is deemed impossible. It is a common obstacle before entering psychoanalytic therapy. And psychotherapy can have real impact, maybe a little too much for the non-commissioned officer. But then again, with half of a smile at the end he has let me know that we have restored some trust and control. And that is a big deal.

***

Intermediate closure

To end is to welcome what is incomplete. Like every psychotherapy, the loose ends of this text seem to demand further elaboration. But in both cases it is an illusion to think that completeness can be achieved.[5] The idea of completeness and perfection is a form of psychological defence, as it solidifies vital and dynamic constituent parts of the personality. Psychotherapy can be seen as the striving for the ability to live with one's incomplete and vital essence, without denying, repressing, forgetting or distorting it consciously or unconsciously. Because it is this incomplete essence that connects self and other, that connects us to life itself. A successful psychotherapy or psychoanalysis is an invitation to take part in life, knowing that wholeheartedness is fragile. It is an invitation to stay curious and creative, to be engaged and involved.

Psychotherapy is full of paradoxes. Someone seeks therapy because he is done with his problems and wants to get over them. He wants to get a grip. But first the sense of control has to be loosened for the underlying emotional dynamics to become visible. And in order to get a renewed sense of personal control, it is really helpful to share emotional troubles and insecurities even though the other doesn't have all the answers either. It can feel like diving in the deep with a buddy you have never met. And success in psychotherapy also depends on the embodied acceptance of our limited powers to control the human condition. It is about the ability to find happiness in being imperfect, incomplete and unfinished.

Half a smile really is not such a bad result then.

Notes

1 This theoretical simplification might also shed a different light on Freud's concept of the "death drive". The death drive is supposed to fuel the urge to alleviate all inner tension through destruction instead of creation. Personally I think it could be thought of as the bankruptcy of the subjective attempt to align the pleasure principle with the need for contact, after which both principles are deserted. One is implicitly convinced of the idea that pleasure is irreconcilable with human contact, and one can better renounce them both. The next best thing is the sardonic pleasure of destruction. Then all tension and effort are annihilated, leading up in its bleakest form to loneliness and suicidal tendencies. "Uncalled for" violence in the outer world can be thought of as an impulsive attempt to communicate this inner state of affairs to anonymous others. See Freud, S. (1920). *Beyond the pleasure principle*. Standard Edition, Vol. 19. London: Hogarth Press. 7–64.

2 More and more I am convinced that the criteria for diagnosing post-traumatic stress disorder in the *Diagnostic and Statistical Manual of Mental Disorders* (DSM-5) overstress the intrusive confrontational side of traumatic experience at the expense of aspects of separation and despair. Based on clinical experience, I would state that it is the accumulated effect of both life-threatening confrontation and separation that leads up to psychological trauma. See also the relatively new and clinically highly relevant concept of *moral injury*. Litz, B.T., Stein, N., Delaney, E., Lebowitz, L., Nash, W.P., Silva, C. & Maguen, S. (2014). Moral injury and moral repair in war veterans: A preliminary model and intervention strategy. *Clinical Psychology Review*, 29, 695–706. Also in 2014 David Wood published a gripping series of articles on moral injury in *The Huffington Post* (freely available online).

3 When words are mistakenly equated with action, then emotional openness might also be confused with sexual intimacy. Especially in the armed forces, a taboo rests on psychotherapy because of this alleged homosexual connotation.

4 This state of affairs might also reflect what it's like to be human, that is: not to be able to fully grasp who you are but still be responsible beyond your mandate. Total control of the unruly needs and wishes of our inner world is an illusion. At best we recognise this state of affairs within ourselves and within others and strive to do the right thing nonetheless.

5 In the words of the French poet Paul Valéry: "A poem is never finished, only abandoned."

Chapter 4

To turn a blind eye

The four basic emotions featuring in the Maelstrom model directly drive and orchestrate the interaction between self and other. But as mentioned in Chapter 2, there is a different type of emotion that contains the acute awareness of the separateness of the self and the other. Self-referential emotions, like shame and pride, have something to do with the way that we feel about the self. In this chapter, I will zoom in on shame because of its notorious complications in psychotherapy.

In essence, I will argue that the main implicit motive of shame is to blind the reflective eye, the merciless eye that is felt to judge and condemn. Shame is not a basic emotion but a self-referential one, that represents *the self as an object associated with displeasure*. This judging eye is often perceived as belonging to the other, in the outer world, but in reality is an inner representation of the eye of the other. By trying to blind the reflective eye, the implicit trust that one's inner world is acceptable and shareable is also under attack. For shame attacks the eye that is welcoming and understanding as well. This makes shame so hard to talk about, and it is arguably the most complicated emotion to get a hold of in psychotherapy. Also in this chapter, I put forward the hypothesis that shame has preverbal roots and gains its full strength in a period wherein psychological developmental lines are out of sync.[1]

Views of shame

Looking at the expression of shame, when someone shrinks and hides his face within his hands, trying to sink through the floor and to flee from every bit of daylight, one gets the impression that shame is an emotion that is intensely intertwined with eye contact. Shame is about seeing and being seen. Shame wants to get rid of all that, because it carries within itself a terrifying conviction; when you see me, you will be disgusted. Then I will lose you and ultimately perish. But how does this complete self-condemnation come about? What is it that makes shame such a powerful emotion, such a blitzkrieg on our sense of self? What is it that shame is fleeing from, that sets of shame in the first place? What are the painful roots of shame?

Shame is an emotion that brands the self as unacceptable. The classical psychoanalytical view on shame is that it corresponds with the gap between the actual self and the image of the self how it wants to be seen: the ideal self (Freud, 1914). It is an emotional reaction when one fails to live up to (other's or one's own) standards. These standards are extremely subjective and often unconscious, as they are mingled with unspoken or hidden fantasies (traditionally of grandiosity and punishment). "I show no one how mediocre I am, but when I grow up, I will dwarf Christiano Ronaldo with my football skills." Shame, then, is able to protect the self against painful exposure to a disappointing reality and stimulates self-improvement. These fantasies of an ideal self are a normal and healthy part of the developing human psyche. They hold great promise but also entail considerable risk. They make it harder to truly acknowledge vulnerability or powerlessness, to aspire to achievable goals or to seek consolation and share experiences that have been humiliating.

Schalkwijk (2015) describes shame as a self-conscious emotion, one that not only devalues the self in the present moment but puts the complete psychological identity under attack, without any control or defence. Intense shame makes you feel stupid beyond words, too ugly for love or too childish to be taken seriously. As is the case with all emotions, shame can both precede and follow conscious verbal thought. This is the reason that I prefer the term self-referential emotion instead of self-conscious emotion. Sometimes a disturbing thought makes your whole face clench like an inward fist, but at other times self-condemning thoughts just come along in the slipstream of the blood that rushes into your cheeks. No matter the path it took, the onset of shame is immediate and has severe consequences for feelings of self-worth and belonging. But even when it feels self-defeating and horrible, it doesn't mean that shame is a negative emotion in itself, so writes Schalkwijk. Shame is not necessarily the bad guy, as some people who act shamelessly show. If we wouldn't emotionally react to the opinion of the other, or of society as a whole, we would become ghost drivers in social traffic. Shame comes up when we are moving too fast in a self-serving direction, when we should hit the brakes because we are bound to fly off the handle in relation to the other. Self-referential emotions such as shame, guilt and pride play a key role in moral development. Together with love and empathy, these self-referential emotions fuel the inner motives for keeping an eye on the inner world of others and for "doing the right thing". It helps though when they are recognised for what they are: emotions instead of the final verdict of an inner Supreme Court. If we can regulate the discomfort of shame enough, we can see it for what it is: an inborn emotion that is part of the human condition and that unites us in humanity. Ideally, the presence of shame is a good moment to wonder: "what precisely is going on here and with whom?". But as mentioned earlier, shame tends to shy away from reflection.

The preverbal roots of shame

In order to shed light on the reasons that shame has such a profound effect on our mental state, we need to look at the role of eye contact in the early affective development of infants. From day one, babies learn about themselves and the world through the contact with the (m)other. Well before ideas can be put into words, infants gather sensory, emotional and social knowledge of their own bodies, the body of the other and the space in between. Within this constitutive dyadic relationship between the immature self and the (m)other, eye contact and mutual adaptation to the emotional expression of the other play a vital role that cannot be overstressed. Stern (2002) compared the nonverbal and mutual emotional interplay between mother and child with a dance. The mother takes part in the dance by attuning to the emotional expressions of the baby, with the baby's needs and window of tolerance in mind (Ogden, Minton & Pain, 2006). She mirrors the emotional expression vividly but also adds something to it that makes clear that she is displaying the baby's emotion instead of her own. This is called marked affect mirroring and it is a crucial ingredient for the development of the self (Fonagy, Gergely, Jurist & Target, 2002). The mother also adjusts proximity, the tone of her voice and pace of the interaction to her baby. All of these things, but maybe foremost eye contact and affect-mirroring, provide information on the inner world of the dancing partners. In this way, the infant learns that his own emotional expressions evoke a reaction within the mother, which informs him about his own inner state. It is not through cognitive reflection but through emotional dancing that the baby gets acquainted with his psychological inner world. He learns to recognise his own joy, by seeing his mother experience joy in reaction to his own. Through mother's eyes the door to his inner world is unlocked. And together with an entry to his inner world, the contrast with the outer world becomes more clear. Now the child can start to differentiate between the self (inner reality) and the other (outer reality). Stern calls this the development of the core-self-with-the-other. I reckon that this is the fundament of the sense of belonging in this world or, more precisely, that the inner world has its place in the outer world. And it starts to take shape well before the infant is capable of forming words and uttering sentences. It is the blueprint for self-evaluation and self-esteem later in life, when one is able to objectify oneself through verbal logic.

The human infant is completely dependent on the care of the other. For his physical and psychological survival, he needs the other to regulate his bodily and emotional processes. Mother's presence and attunement are necessary for calming overwhelming feelings of distress, panic, frustration or anger. When this nurturing relationship suffers severe disturbance, for example, in some cases of vital depression of the mother, the child is left to the unregulated intensity of his raw emotional inner world. This can have both acute and long-lasting effects on the development of the inner representations of the relationship between self and other(s). Immediate and without rational understanding, babies are alarmed when the eyes of the other stop to dance. The need to be seen is dramatically illustrated in the Still Face experiment (Tronick, 1989; a gripping video of the Still Face experiment has been uploaded on YouTube by the University of Massachusetts, Boston). In this experiment, a mother is instructed to freeze her facial expression for a couple of minutes after playing with her baby. The consequences are dramatic and heart-wrenching. At first the baby seems to experience the still face as part of the ongoing interplay. He tries to capture his mother's gaze to make it lively again. When this fails, the baby starts to protest and gets more and more distressed. He makes a screechy sound. And when the mother stays nonresponsive even now, the baby desperately tries to evade the eyes that reflect nothing. Some babies become lethargic within a couple of minutes and seem to drown within themselves. The psychological fabric of the baby seems to fall apart when reconnection fails. There is no reflection, no sign of recognition to be seen in the eyes of the mother and the baby might experience an intense mix of despair, abandonment and betrayal. In severe cases the baby might abandon the contact with his own inner world permanently.

Grown-ups are not dependent infants, but embedded in the implicit layers of our personalities lies an acute sensitivity to the absence of nonverbal signs of connectedness. Lack of lively eye contact has an ominous effect, both in reality (for instance, the empty look of a vital depressive person or the "1000 yard stare" in case of war trauma) and in fiction (for instance, zombies or black-eyed aliens). Freud (1919) wrote in *Das Unheimliche* about frequent occurring fears of children, including the loss of eyesight (though he only mentions losing one's own eyesight and not the eye contact with the other) and the soulless independent activity of the body (parts). Though he emphasises that the uncanny effect comes about because of the repression of something that was once familiar and threatens to become conscious again, another fundamental aspect of nightmare scenarios seeps through. That is when the other seems to be present, but mutual emotional contact is missing. Echoes of primitive and catastrophic fears become vivid again, such as the fear of annihilation or disintegration, putting the entire psyche on high alert. It is the infantile approach on survival that lets itself be felt.

Looking at yourself over your own shoulder

So eye contact involves dealing with the image how we want to be seen and our need to be seen at all. But there is more to eye contact than that. The attentive gaze of the other can also be restrictive and suffocating. We have an inborn need to be seen, but also a deeply ingrained fear of fusing completely with the other and of being devoured. Freud emphasised the importance of the father as the third person in the life of the infant, the one who opens up the mother–child dyad. According to classical analytic theory, this is met with intense emotionality, especially concerning the discovery that the mother has a relationship with the father as well and has to be shared. The psychological working through of this predicament is called the Oedipus complex. With the regulation of emotions in mind, we nowadays emphasise the importance of the third-person perspective (which is not necessarily bound to the figure of the father, though he also has a role as such). Not all emotional needs have to be met within a dyadic dance, but they can be viewed from some distance as well. It is the position of the third, of the observing outsider, that is incorporated and that makes it possible to shift in perspective.[2] Healthy psychological development entails both emotional dancing lessons and knowledge of the fact that one is moved by highly subjective motives, just as everybody else is. The ability to observe your inner world as populated with subjective emotional motives – just as other people – is called mentalisation (Fonagy, Gergely, Jurist & Target, 2002). When all goes well, children start to develop this ability around three or four years of age (Verheugt-Pleijter, 2009). The development of mentalisation enables the child to experience the world as more complex but also with more nuance. A single act can stem from a variety of motives.

The discovery of the third perspective allows the child to put some distance between basic emotional states and cognitive thoughts. An inner outsider has emerged whose position you can take. It adds an extra dimension to the inner world and constitutes a further layering of consciousness.[3] It also breaks through the illusory perfection of the dyadic relationship. It is a safe haven for feelings of frustration and disappointment about shortcomings in the idealised dyadic relationship. And in this safe haven we don't want to be visible all the time; we want to be able to free ourselves from the eye of the other. It is also an asylum for our imagination, where we can live out our most uncensored urges in fantasy and assign special meaning to our own place in the world. Yet again, for healthy psychological development to emerge, these perspectives have to be recognised and have to become basically shareable.

Some time ago I got sudden angry glances from our six-year-old son. He was playing on the floor and was surrounded by Playmobil toys. Epic battles were fought until he suddenly stopped and looked at me. At first I was surprised by his nonverbal blame, and I had no clue what I had done wrong. Then it dawned upon me that I messed up his game by looking at him. He answered me with a heartfelt "Yes!" when I asked him whether he found it annoying to be looked at like that. My eyes, full of fatherly love and pride, had had a horrible effect on the creation of his own playful universe. Smart as he is, he now sometimes asks me directly. He tells me that he wants to play and asks me not to look. Of course I fully cooperate. Fortunately I am "allowed to sit in the room", because he enjoys being together.

Shame is the emotional foreclosure of true self-reflection

Now we encounter a big paradox of shame. The shameful self-evaluation has a crushing effect on our complete sense of being, but at the same time we are often oblivious to the argumentation leading up to the self-condemnation and to the reasons that the verdict is so harsh. Who is the self that implicitly does the crude evaluation of the self? I put forward the hypothesis that it is the infantile self that reacts in a primary emotional way, dividing the world in objects that are *all good or all bad* (Klein, 2002, originally published in 1952), and just developed the ability to look at the self as if it is an outer object. The immature self is emotionally deemed *all bad*, fuelled by anger and fear towards the self. The ability to mentally represent the self (somewhere between eighteen and twenty-four months) precedes the ability to regulate intense emotions through mentalisation (starting from three or four years). These developmental lines just keep a different pace (Thyson & Thyson, 1990). And it is precisely between these developmental milestones that shame comes into play.[4]

So when we discover the self (that is, when we are able to represent the self in our minds for the first time), we treat it in the only way we can: we react with our raw and basic emotionality. Through implicit mental association a connection is made between the unempathetic eye of the other and the worthlessness of the self. Above all, it is through the eye that is capable of reflection but fails to be empathic that the proof of the self's inferiority is seen.[5] And the loss of the emotional dancing partner is experienced as catastrophic. So we slash and burn the "unrelatable" self in anger or we back down in fear, in a blind attempt to restore emotional contact with the other and to fulfil the need for attachment. The hope for a loving connection with the other is preserved at the expense of an *all bad* image of the self. This is the nonverbal birthplace of shame.[6]

Thinking it through, what shame does is to blind the eye that reflects the self and through which we feel ignored, objectified, powerless or worthless.[7] It is the condemnation of the dismaying self that shame is trying to undo, by doing it self before it is done to by the other. The self's worthlessness is made top secret, in order to guard the self from relational breakdown. But it is a psychological catastrophe to fully coincide with intense shame, because it implicitly acknowledges the verdict that the self is worthless. That is why shame also defends the self against shame, for it is shameful to be ashamed. Shame takes up arms against itself. Shame expresses itself not only on the outside (we make ourselves small, hide our face, don't speak and avoid attention) but also on the inside. We stop to think freely about ourselves and to reflect more fully on the whole of our personal situation in the outside world. We fruitlessly try to avoid the hammering refrain of self-condemnation (stupid, stupid, stupid . . .). We can be full of the emotion of shame while at the same time we desperately try to avoid having any conscious thought on the matter.

So we act without thinking as if we have to protect ourselves against judging eyes on the outside and make them blind. But really it is the inner sight on the self, the mental representation, that is ferociously opposed. "Shame means defeat and deserves no mercy", says the one who is full of shame, before poking out his own eyes.[8] And the punishment is solitary confinement in a vulnerable emotional inner world.

Now we get to the bottom of the painful essence of shame. It is a merciless devaluation of the self and a massive attack on self-reflection. It tries to blind all eyes, in both the outer and inner world. And by doing so, all hope is abandoned that one can meet eyes that can provide consolation and understanding. Eyes that – no matter the bad – can see the good in you. Eyes that see what is going on inside you, even before you know yourself. And eyes that can tell you that it is going to be all right. In a rushed attempt to evade judging eyes, compassionate eyes are overlooked, the eyes that dance to your emotional inner world. To put it differently: in an emotional attempt to regulate the self-referential emotion of shame, the co-regulation of basic emotions is sacrificed. To overcome shame, the basic emotions of anger, fear, sadness and joy are left alone without guidance. And in the case of severe humiliation or bullying, the ability to use fantasy as a healthy playing field is corroded. It breeds a bitter sort of realism, wherein there is little tolerance of the needs of the inner emotional world.

Maybe this perspective also sheds some light on the reasons that shameful experiences can leave such extremely vivid impressions in our minds, while at the same time the shameful narrative can be hard to integrate within our life's history. Shame aches like a splinter under the surface of memory. It is sharp and painful like an alien fragment, which resists incorporation in a coherent narrative. But it is also felt to contain some dark truth about the self and it forms a black hole in the inner universe, from where no contact seems possible.

Verbal foliage of shame

In a shameful state of mind, fleeting thoughts easily attach themselves to the theme of self-condemnation. Every outer sign of imperfection, of shortcomings towards an idealised image, can be taken up as further justification of self-devaluation. Too small, too big, too weak, too blunt, too flat, too round, too bald, too hairy, too black, too white, too normal, too strange . . . all these bodily characteristics and more can quickly associate with shame. When a bodily characteristic is seen as a betrayal of an ideal image, then the thoughtful admission of shame means a demeaning surrender to a humiliating reality. A realistic self-image then cannot be accepted, because "I shall never be confused with the ugly, needy and pathetic people in this world!" Shame is sometimes masked with a thin veil of pride. "I share my unruly hair with Einstein, you know." Emotional expressions of shame (blushing, for example) and disappointment, are ignored, fought or denied. The only focus is on the ideal, as a shield against the reality of one's own humanity.

But even more than by our naked bodies, we tend to be ashamed by our inner vulnerabilities: our lifelong dependency on others, our need for other humans to be human, the selfish aspect of our emotional impulses and the limited control we have on ourselves and our relationships. Those vulnerabilities are not seldom masked with fantasies of grandiosity and dreams of fame. As mentioned earlier, these fantasies have an important reassuring function when real empathy is hard to find. When a life's history is too full of unfavourable circumstances, then this reassurance can become so pressing that one is forced to forget that it is mere fantasy. In this manner, narcissistic defences can merge into personality pathology. Exposure to a mutual view on reality then becomes a source of shame that debunks the idealised narrative.

Another common narrative in which shame plays a key role is not about the idealised self but about the idealised other. The other is then implicitly experienced as almighty but uncaring or mean. The full responsibility of one's own feeling is then ascribed to the (lack of) action of the other. "You should be ashamed! You make me feel this bad, so you should fix it! I won't let you get away with this!" The experience of the demeaned self is then not fought in the self, but fought in the interaction with the other. Pointing to the possibility that it is shame that rears its head and that everybody has personal responsibility for coping with inner turmoil is often put aside as a shrewd attack on a righteous complaint.

Certainly it is not easy to admit being ashamed and recognise it as a personal emotional reaction. It becomes even more difficult when one is brought up with strict and punishing norms and values. Especially when particular inner experiences are labelled as sinful, as is the case in some religious doctrines, it becomes hard to psychologically own aggressive or sexual feelings yourself. These then aren't signs of your humanity "in the face of the greatness of God", but become proof of personal inferiority for which one needs to seek forgiveness within the religious community. It can seriously hamper the inner freedom to get to know one's mental world, when acceptance of subjective experiences is seen as disloyal or even a betrayal of a shared holy ideal.[9]

Shame hides behind basic emotions

So when the ability to represent the self mentally is added to the mix of basic emotions, a new category of emotions sees the light. Self-referential emotions such as shame and pride are essential building blocks of further moral development (among others).[10] Then, thinking in terms of the Maelstrom model, is there a way to conceptualise shame as a basic self-referential emotion? I suggest so, particularly because it is the eye through which the self is represented that does the harsh evaluation. The reflective eye[11] becomes a source of rejection and distress, because it sees the self as unrelatable. In short: *shame looks at the self as an object associated with displeasure.* It is the imagined visibility of the disgusting self that is reacted upon in a primary emotional way. When self-reflection raises intense levels of fear and anger, it is reacted upon with unadulterated fight or flight.[12] The reflection of the self in the eyes of the other (even though it is only imagined by the self) is experienced as *all bad.* This experience is filled with pain and despair, which is hardly tolerable without a moderating third-person perspective. And the malicious twist is that *the implicit motive of shame is to blind the reflective eye.* Consolation is ruled out in advance.

Displayed within the Maelstrom model, intense shame looks something like Figure 4.1.

Now we can differentiate various basic emotional expressions of shame. Once the self is represented as unrelatable and unlovable, then there are four ways in which shame deals with the imminent visibility of this presumed fact.

- First, the loss of the possibility of being relatable can spur the self into a saddening isolation. The self gives up to seek consolation or reconciliation. In the outer world contact with other people is avoided, as it would only amount to nothing. In the inner world faith and hope are shattered, and there is no refuge or rescue.

- Second, the threatening possibility that the unrelatable self becomes visible can become a pressing reason to anxiously avoid any sign of attention. The main theme here is not to draw any attention to the self, for that would spell danger. In the outer world this will contribute to being overly impressed by others and general underachievement. In the inner world this results in a general loss of self-worth, interest and confidence.
- Third, an overpowering confrontation is felt with the visibility of the unrelatable self that has to be fought off. Others are actively chased away, under the pretence of aggressive bitterness or even (paradoxically) with an exaggerated show of one's own unattractiveness. Inner self-reflection is hyperactively evaded, sometimes through the use of drugs or through the manic emergence in a virtual world.
- Fourth, the visibility of the unrelatable and unlovable self is actively attacked. The alleged demeaning opinion of the self is taken up as an act of intrusive aggression. Others are forced "to show respect" as a meagre substitute for relatability.[13] When this aggression is turned upon the self in the inner world, a harsh and self-destructive attitude ensues that might lead to emotional armouring[14] and in severe cases to suicidal tendencies.

So when we talk to someone who is secretly ashamed, we not seldom encounter intense feelings of sadness, fear or anger. These basic emotions can take their

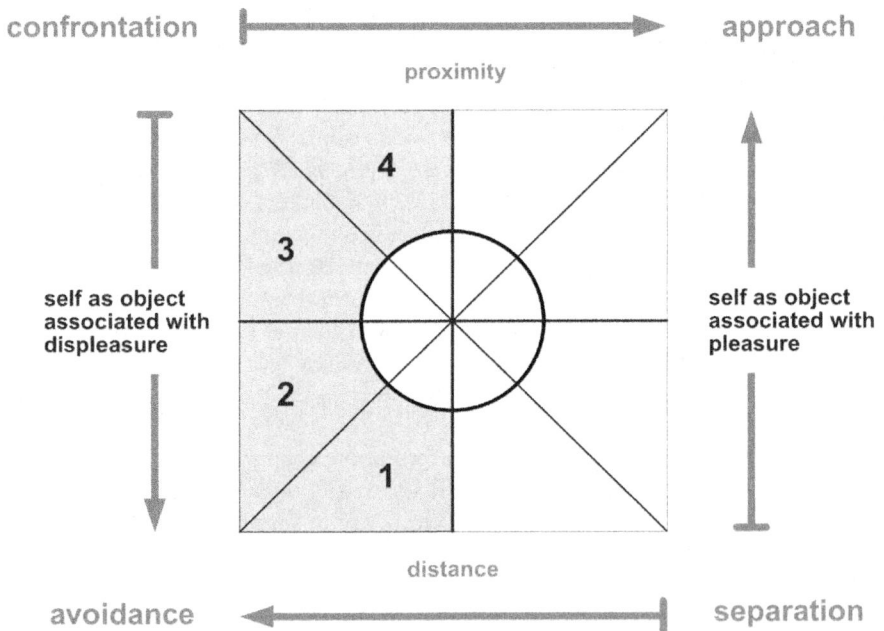

Figure 4.1 Four faces of shame.

toll on the dynamics of the relationship, especially when the hidden shame is not acknowledged. It is hard to listen carefully, to do good or to provide comfort, when one meets an unwavering sense of unrelatability. Psychoanalytically this might lead to all sorts of complicated transference-countertransference enactments. As a therapist, one might feel neglected or negligent, powerless or merciless, or downright under attack. It is a serious test for the mentalising capability of the therapist. But of course the one who is in need of help the most is the one who feels that his inner world is banned from daylight. So what can we do to help?

Open your eyes and tell me what you see

Telling someone who is in great distress that it is shame that is causing the emotional trouble seldom helps. For someone who doesn't have the ability to reflect on the experience of being distressed and recognise it as a specific emotional state, shame sounds like a verdict or an alienating label. Remember that it is in the nature of shame to dodge reflection. For someone who is able to connect his psychological predicament with a hidden sense of shame, hearing about shame can feel like being mercilessly exposed. It is the emotion that spurs the self into hiding that is dragged into broad daylight. And this highly vulnerable sense of self might easily wither in the sunlight of attention. So one has to proceed with caution.

Maybe the decisive factor is that there is no shortcut. Shame has to be faced and shared the same way as other emotions are processed. But by calling out shame too soon, it sets off an aversive reaction that feels like a breach of trust and a step back. Therefore, it might help to become more familiar with the different aspects of shame, in order to make tentative emotional connections without pinpointing shame with all its complicating associations. For instance, in psychotherapy, I might say something like: "I get the impression that it is hard for you to confide in me. Is there something on your mind, maybe something I said or did, that makes your efforts seem futile? Did I miss something or did I appear dismissive?" I welcome all sorts of reactions, certainly the ones that convey disappointment, anger or fear, because those are the ones that take the most courage to express openly.

With the various aspects of the Maelstrom model in mind, it is also possible to help to find words for experiences that are not yet verbally recognised as an emotion. For instance, with some clients I feel the need to measure out the amount of eye contact very carefully. When I take notice of that urge and when I assess that an interpersonal comment doesn't surpass the tolerance of arousal, I might convey my impression that eye contact is not self-evident or even burdensome. Also I might "think out loud" and wonder about the variety of things we can read in the eyes of the other. Or even that sometimes a look can feel like a poisonous sting that one has to monitor very cautiously. This kind of intervention gains strength when it is linked to a common experience or interaction, for example, when someone is upset because of the time in the waiting room, feeling exposed as someone who needs help because there is something wrong inside. Even more powerful is the association with a relational experience in the here-and-now of the therapeutic relationship. I saw a young woman once who changed her haircut between sessions, combing her hair half in front of her face. I couldn't suppress the thought that this change of style was more than a matter of fashion. Though at first I had made a spontaneous remark about the new look, I took the time to get a feel of her inner motives. It occurred after a session in which she had confided in me more than she used to. Though the thought crossed my mind that she had constructed a fashionable fence before her eyes, her proud presentation simultaneously made the impression that she shared something authentic. And because the confidentiality of the prior appointment didn't seem to have weakened, the change in personal appearance looked like a successful way in which she could implicitly express being sensitive for eye contact and shame, without the need to break off relations completely. After a while, in which she discussed some of the intricacies of her friendships, I made a tentative interpretation about her hair. I wondered whether her being so frank last week might have something to do with her new look, a haircut behind which she could take cover but also could look around to see what is going on. I asked what it is like for her to see the reactions she gets from other people and whether she is curious what I think of it. Boldly stating that she can withstand any opinion, she also admitted to be eager to hear my thoughts. Then I could express the impression that the change in her appearance was an authentic expression of how she deals with the intricacies of personal contact. And because she was an adolescent who needed more outspoken therapy, I added that in my opinion authenticity looks good.

I try to share the perspective of my client and give tentative words to inner experience (maybe with some humour of my own). I once heard myself say: "You certainly know better than to put your trust in someone who needed an education to listen properly." Of course when someone chuckles and approves, I stop and wonder at the reasons that this seems so self-evident. But even when some of the ice is broken, everyone needs time to make up for themselves whether they let themselves be seen and whether emotional connection is possible. So, as a therapist, it is also important to be patient and to have trust in nonverbal impressions of emotional connectedness, even when they can't be talked about yet or are very scarce. A quick glance, some lessening of muscle tension, the sudden use of the coat stand instead of sitting with a coat on the lap during the prior appointments; signs like these might be indicative of a growth of interpersonal trust. But no matter the circumstances, it takes a leap of faith to admit that one is ashamed and to talk about the wish for invisibility. The punch line is that we all know this wish for invisibility only too well. *Not seldom such a confession leads to an empathic reaction, to the relief of both persons involved.* Though it may be hard to accept that we aren't as perfect as we wish to be, it is a relief to be able to meet the other in our human and flawed state of being. Shame loses its blinding effect when we can see beyond the two-dimensional image and get a grasp of multiple inner layers, contradictions and possibilities. It is not unequivocal but it is the only firm foundation for a realistic sense of self.

Notes

1 Though the onset of shame is well before puberty, these periods resemble each other in the way that developmental lines don't keep the same pace. In puberty the maturation of the sexual body precedes the psychological adaptations that enable taking up personal and relational responsibility. This usually contributes to severe emotional turmoil in teenagers. In this chapter, I will ponder on the developmental lines that are involved in the onset of shame.

2 Certainly there are more factors that spur this development. I want to name one here, and that is the process of separation and individuation as described by Margareth Mahler.

3 See Chapter 8.

4 We see the self in black-or-white until the invention of the colour TV of mentalisation.

5 One could argue that shame is first experienced in full strength in the period that the parental "no" (when the child ventures too far) is associated with the self. The eyes of the other aren't negligent then, but are the eyes of authority. However, the empathic dance to the inner world is (temporarily) broken. The latter, when experienced intensely, might be taken up as "the evil eye".

6 Elucidating and clinically useful is the work of Donald Nathanson. See Nathanson, D.L. (1994). *Shame and Pride: Affect, sex, and the birth of the Self*. New York: W.W. Norton. In his "Compass of shame", he summarises four ways in which people react to shame. In short: people react with fight-or-flight when ashamed, and this reaction either targets the self or the other.

7 That is the reason that it is shameful to be treated as an object or to belong to a group that is known for its victimisation. "The realization that one belongs to a group that could be humiliated and mistreated with impunity, of course was shameful", the Dutch psychoanalyst Louis Tas wrote in a comment on the flight of German Jews to the Netherlands in 1938.

8 Like Oedipus did.

9 In my opinion, healthy psychological development helps a child to tolerate the ambivalence that springs from multiple and sometimes contradicting needs. I state that there is no single ultimate claim on the truth, but it is the capability of changing perspective that provides some security. It helps when a child is allowed to sometimes contradict itself, to come up with magical solutions and to have all sorts of feelings, even when the parents are not spared. To acknowledge that you can love someone but also that you are able to wish the other to be dead. The relief is in accepting that the wish is not the same as the act, and not all feelings and wishes are meant to become reality. In healthy psychological development, the ability to reflect on contradictory feelings has a moderating effect, instead of leading up to a polarisation of the inner debate.

10 Though this chapter focuses on shame, pride can be conceptualised as the opposite take on self-reflection. Instead of an impulsive ban, the reflection of the self in eyes of others is experienced as completely satisfying, as *all good*. In a proud state of mind, the eye of the other is implicitly associated with welcoming and fulfilling experiences.

11 The "reflective eye" is a representation that stems from the way that the self is seen by the other in the mind of the self.

12 I believe that this conceptualisation is completely in line with Nathanson's "compass of shame".

13 Going out in places where disinhibiting drugs like alcohol are used, sometimes a "wrong look" is all it takes to get involved in a fight.

14 See, for an elucidating psychoanalytical view on the possible reaction of a lack of maternal containment on the preverbal child, Bick, E. (1968). The experience of the skin in early object-relations. *International Journal of Psycho-Analysis*, 49, 484–486. Bick recognised the development of what she called "the second skin" as a primitive defensive reaction. Though I am not suggesting a self-destructive reaction in these infants, the physical fixation of arousal leading up to emotional atrophy is vividly described. I believe that this mechanism can also become active in the aftermath of intense shame.

Part II

Emotional turbulence

Chapter 5

The interpretation of repetitive nightmares

In the next three chapters, the previous theory is used to outline the emotional turbulence underneath some common forms of psychopathology. This chapter zooms in on the phenomenon of the repetitive nightmare.

Have you ever wondered whether your dreams mean anything? Maybe you find most of your dreams meaningless, if you remember them at all. But maybe you immediately remember one or two "big" dreams, dreams that you dreamt years ago and that have stayed with you, hinting at an important essence. Normal people are divided into those who think that dreams are a kind of meaningless neural noise and those who think that dreams have latent meaning. Psychologists are as divided as normal people. Freud – being in the latter camp – was most proud of his work on the interpretation of dreams, for it opened up vistas on the hidden mechanisms of the psyche. His main thesis was that the function of dreams is to preserve sleep by means of fulfilling potentially abject wishes within the realm of the dream. In this way the dreamer doesn't need to wake up and act, because pleasure is attained in the virtual midnight world.

But Freud struggled with the repetitiveness of nightmares, because it seemed to contradict his main thesis that dreams are wish-fulfilling. And worse even, people often wake up from nightmares, which is exactly what dreams should prevent. Freud first dealt with this by drawing the strange conclusion that nightmares are failed dreams. Twenty years later, in "Beyond the pleasure principle", Freud hypothesised that repetitive nightmares are anxiety-driven attempts at mastering a traumatic input, because he felt that it is the failure of mastering that renders the input as traumatic (Freud, 1920). He made an allusion to another function of the psychic apparatus that seemed to be more fundamental than the pleasure principle "without contradicting this principle". This function seeks to minimise the level of tension in the psychic apparatus to a lifeless zero. So the Freudian "death drive" was born.

The death drive as a theoretical concept never gained the face validity of its counterpart the libido (vital sexual energy). And with it, the psychoanalytic theory of dream interpretation has had a lot of critique of other psychologists. This even went so far that the whole idea of dreams carrying meaning was attacked.[1] But overall, most research nowadays points to the idea that dreams can carry meaning and serve various functions within psychic life, such as the processing and consolidation of salient information into long-term declarative and procedural memory. But not surprisingly, the discord found a new terrain and opposing arguments are formulated on the meaning of the term "meaning".

I suggest that the attribution of meaning to dreams is strongly influenced by the emotional reflectivity of the awoken dreamer. Meaning then isn't a solid or concrete thing; I view it as an (inter)subjective phenomenon closely connected to feelings of vital fulfilment in a distant place or time, in the inner or outer world, or from a transcendent perspective. The gratification of needs is therefore not meaningful per se. To be able to experience meaning, one needs to be able to empathically transport oneself to a distant or greater perspective, outside of the realm of immediate and nearby bodily pleasure. In other words: the ability to find meaning also depends on the ability to take a reflective stance towards your own emotions.

The thing about nightmares is that the emotional intensity is so gruelling that we can hardly bear to take the time and think about them. Caught in a raging Maelstrom, it is hard to discern the various emotional currents that created it. Which way do they flow and what course makes sense? Nightmares are full of terrors and despair, with a highly emotionally charged urgency to act or escape. There is a pressing need to act first and think later and even not to look at all.

Sometimes nightmares reflect actual experiences, as in some cases of posttraumatic stress disorder (PTSD). But I reckon that the level of emotional intensity is not the product of a single experience, but the result of cumulative feelings of terror and despair of associated memories, fantasies and implicit regulatory patterns. These emotionally charged memories, fantasies and patterns, from past and present, both explicit and implicit, are associated with recent shocking experiences. The overwhelming emotional intensity defies self-evident ways of dealing with the world that have become trusted and automatic. We use them without thought, until a shocking experience shows the limits of their usability. And especially when we aren't aware of associated images and patterns, we have a hard time to regain some sense of conscious control in the midst of the emotional intensity of the nightmarish experience.

In this chapter, I will look back on the therapy of a soldier suffering from PTSD.[2] More specifically, I focus on the question of what is it about nightmares that makes the worst one the most susceptible to become repetitive. I will argue that the worst one is so psychologically overwhelming and intricate that it is too hard to listen to the preverbal emotional narrative. It is about things we can't stand to think about or stem from the distant preverbal past of our personal history. It has the potential to break our hearts, to annihilate our sense of security and to shatter all that we believe in. But when something from within, something of vital subjective importance is not heard, it will continue to speak up until we find a meaningful way of dealing with it. It is another clinical case out of the early years of my career, and meanwhile I was learning the basics of eye movement desensitisation and reprocessing (Shapiro, 1995). This established technique is used to disconnect specific visual memories from overwhelming emotional intensity and make more adaptive thinking possible. Alongside this, I will reflect on the psychodynamics that are set in motion by psychological trauma.

Fearing friendly fire

***

On a Tuesday morning in a staff meeting of a mental health unit of the Royal Netherlands Army, we discussed the case of a soldier who patrolled his own garden at night and was found lying in the bushes by his alarmed neighbours. He is a man in his early thirties named Harry. He is assigned to me and a week later he passes my doorstep, somewhat uneasy but colloquial as well. His lack of formality is not without warmth but also makes a negligent impression to me. He has severe trouble sleeping, for more than a year now. He claims to be irritable, low on energy and forgetful. His work has deteriorated, he says. He seeks out isolated spots in the workplace, something he is able to do because of his highly specialised skills and function. He barely tolerates the presence of colleagues, "because they only create further distractions".

Harry lives alone in a small village, besides the village where his father lives, the only relative he is in contact with. His mother died after a short illness when he was two years old. He was raised by his father, who worked at an international firm. Together, they frequently moved within and outside of the country. To me it feels like that they haven't been able to grow roots anywhere. His father is retired now. My client worries a lot about his father, because he drinks too much and his health is deteriorating. He visits him whenever he can to cook for him and take care of household chores. Harry has had several intimate relationships with women, but never lasting more than a year or so. He claims that it is hard to combine his work with a relationship; he is frequently out on manoeuvres and has completed several tours abroad. He tells me: "That is just the way it is." He has been a soldier since he left school, but now fears for his career.

I ask him about his trouble sleeping and his nighttime activities in the garden. Since his last tour, he has had repetitive nightmares and sees strange shapes in the dark. He gets very tense when telling me this and he is covered in sweat. He is lost for words more than once and I try my best to help him collect his thoughts. At the same time, several options go through my mind: is he re-experiencing traumatic events, am I looking at a psychotic breakdown and is he using alcohol or drugs? I ask him bluntly whether he is using alcohol or anything else to relax. He used to drink, he admits, but he claims that he is completely off the booze now. He stopped cold turkey on his tour and hasn't touched a single beer since. He says that his life is complicated enough as it is and furthermore he sees what the alcohol is doing to his father. He doesn't want to go on the same road.

I invite him to talk about his tour and start asking factual questions. Again rivers of sweat. It doesn't catch me off guard and I am determined to hear about his experiences, then and now. It was his third tour, Harry tells me. Because of his sought-after skill set he is based on an international camp without any colleagues from the Netherlands. He found like-minded people in a foreign platoon who – contrary to himself – left the base frequently to go on patrol. When I ask him about events that stand out personally, he quickly sums up five episodes. Two of those still haunt him, he says. Then he tells me he got shot at. Thick clouds had made dusk fall early that night and he was on his weekly run along a path on the outskirts of the base. Suddenly gun shots were fired. He hit the deck and tried to see where the shots were coming from. Before there had been a lot of regional turmoil because of an important political event coming up, and he wouldn't be surprised if he got shot at to provoke further international intervention. He waited for the guards to react. Suddenly it dawned upon him that the colleagues he befriended had thrown a little private party on the base that night. What if they impulsively reacted by returning fire? No one knew that he was there, laying on the ground. The idea that he could get caught up in a crossfire invoked a disorientating panic within him. His dark silhouette in this peripheral area could surely be mistaken for that of an insurgent. Given the expert shooting skills of his colleagues, he feared friendly fire the most.

I don't choose to discuss the (un)likeliness of this graphic scenario with him, but simply acknowledge the terror he felt. He lives through this experience repeatedly in his nightmares, lying alone in a shot no man's land. He wakes up gasping for air and covered in cold sweat. Meanwhile his anxiety has flared up for falling asleep. Especially dusk has become troublesome: when there is just enough light to see possible intruders, but not enough to discern them. That is why he has made it a habit to ban every bit of light from his bedroom, by blocking the edges of the curtains and the door with towels and tape. "It's better when it's pitch black", Harry says. And he claims that it is the only way to ease his hypervigilance and to fall asleep.

It certainly has some logic to it: to diminish sensory stimulation in order to calm down his overstimulated mind. But he does so with military rigour, thereby exposing himself to sensory deprivation. And it is known that sensory deprivation might induce hallucinations. During the process of falling asleep, hypnagogic hallucinations can occur, revealing images of persons. The illusionary intruders were so frightening that he decided to go on patrol in his own backyard, in order to secure his home turf. This is what his neighbours saw, which they decided to report. I bring up the unintentional effects of his understimulation for discussion and invite him to explore other tactics that might help him to relax and orient in the here-and-now. He removes towels and tape and starts to play tranquil music instead. At first he listens to the same piece repeatedly all through the night. Later on he only uses the music to fall asleep. It is piano music that is both soothing and helps him to feel grounded. But the dusk holds more surprises for him than this.

There is a second event that still haunts him. The week after the shoot-ing incident the befriended platoon got hit by an IED (improvised explo-sive devise). A colleague he got along with very well was fatally wounded. He was brought back to base in a terrible state and died shortly after. The ceremony after which the colleague's body was repatriated, went by in a blur for my client. The lasting image is that of a coffin being carried into a colossal transport aircraft. After his own return home, Harry hardly mentioned his tour to his Dutch colleagues. There was a big reorganisa-tion going on in his unit and he thought that his colleagues had enough on their minds already.

We have agreed to meet once a week. The nightmare wherein he is lying alone in a shot no man's land keeps haunting him for the first two months. Fortunately for him and for me I receive training in EMDR and we try out this intervention together. During EMDR, Harry holds the image of getting shot in his mind and the physical arousal is soothed by the alternative thought "I am safe now". The reduction of arousal is successful, but he remarks – somewhat taken aback – that it is only logical to realise that he is no longer in danger. It is an anticlimactic sentiment that will return like a boomerang, but more about that later on.

The reduction of arousal opened up a reflective space wherein his night-mare could be seen from different angles. What looked like a stereotype initially, an accurate copy of a traumatic experience of vulnerability and powerlessness, turned out to have many layers. It pointed out to be no coinci-dence that it was exactly this experience that stirred up his emotional dream world. With his personal history in mind, meaningful narratives transpired echoing his traumatic ordeal.

***

An inner bog fire

Thinking about Harry's predicament, my attention was caught by the discrep-ancy between his single repetitive nightmare and the multiplicity of his unsettling experiences. I wondered whether early patterns of emotional regulation and other emotionally overwhelming experiences collided to create a perfect storm. Let's look at some pieces of theory on regulatory patterns, the stratification of fear and PTSD first.

Early childhood experiences, and especially basic ways of regulating emo-tions, can create a fault line between mental health and psychopathology, as they give rise to implicit models of relating to the inner and outer world.[3] These models are stored as non-declarative memory traces and therefore are hard to bring into verbal consciousness. We are poorly equipped to explain, let alone predict, who runs the risk of developing post-traumatic symptoms after a life-threatening situation and who doesn't. It dawned upon me that a crucial element in the equation might be found in the multiplicity of fear.

Does the threatening situation strike a nerve, a distressing scenario from the early years, wherein a traumatic exposure was felt to the unfiltered powerlessness of a child, who is utterly and desperately dependent on the parents? With Harry I thought of the death of his mother at his second year and of the ways he gave meaning to the image of her in his inner world. Is there an implicit safe haven in the inner world, or were the parents experienced as failing in the provision of emotional safety? How did the development of the sense of autonomy come about, given the intricacies of his attachment history? For children who experience traumatic events, the mentalising availability of the primary caregiver turns out to be an elementary factor for the development of psychopathology, like PTSD or behavioural difficulties.[4] The lack of an emotionally available reflective parent (like a mourning father) seems to be even more predictive for the development of psychopathology than objective aspects of traumatic events themselves. The felt experience that others are willing and able to empathise and process emotional undertones is a *sine qua non* for a secure feeling of being at home in your own inner world. It then becomes an inner place without a pressing burden of being alone and feeling helplessly overwhelmed. It is this mute blueprint that underlies the feeling of having a secure base in the world. It shapes the relationships in the constantly evolving here-and-now with our selves and with others we love and hate.

Besides explicit and implicit factors in regulating emotions, the multiple layers of fear also add to the complexity of psychopathology. I will give an example of this stratification with psychoanalytic literature[5] and the Maelstrom model in mind. It is not a hierarchical list of fears, nor does it strictly follow the timeline of human development. Also, the kind of danger that fear warns us of might come from the outside as well as the inside. Here is the list (without any pretence to be complete).

Fears concerning *physical and psychological integrity*

- Fear of annihilation
- Fear of disintegration or falling apart
- Fear of fusion or dissolving emotionally
- Fear of losing the sense of self
- Fear of losing the coherence of one's mind

Fears concerning *security in relatedness*

- Fear of separation or the loss of a loved one
- Fear of the loss of love of a loved one
- Fear of an attack by a hated one
- Fear of persecution by a hated one
- Fear of isolation
- Fear of moral judgement

Fears concerning *control*

- Fear of impairment and powerlessness
- Fear of vulnerability and helplessness
- Fear of unpredictability, including unruly emotions
- Fear of losing one's identity
- Fear of losing the sense of control in one's mind

In PTSD there is a mixture of failing explicit and implicit strategies for regulating emotions, as well as a terrifying experience that has multiple layers. Remember the comment I made on traumatisation in Chapter 3, on the traumatising overlapping of intrusive and separative interaction. With the stratification of fear in mind, a rule of thumb can be articulated for the origins of psychological trauma. Panic and fear might become overwhelming and a shocking experience might become traumatic, when:

- one feels utterly powerless and helpless in a situation that is life-threatening or that violates personal integrity; there is imminent danger in the outside world for the self or for a close other.
- there are aspects of both confrontation and separation involved.
- the experience raises emotional urgency on multiple levels; simultaneously flames are ignited in the inner world.
- there is a failure of explicit and implicit regulation of heated emotional experience; it sets of an all-devouring blaze in the inner world.[6]

Especially when our implicit assumptions of regulating emotions are affected, we become psychologically vulnerable. For a child to see his parents fight and harm each other violently, this might certainly destroy the sense of a secure base and of parental control. The idea that the parents can be trusted and relied upon might be seriously damaged. Another well-known and often implicit assumption is that "a lot of bad things happen to other people, but not to me", sometimes sustained by the related assumption that "bad things don't happen to me, because I am a good person". Besides the more explicit ones, we all have our share of implicit assumptions that don't stand up to logical scrutiny. It is the unconscious false bottom that provides us with a sense of safety and well-being, when real solid ground is lacking. In conclusion, a shocking experience becomes traumatic when we fall through both real and false bottoms. Layers of intense fear wash over us. Then we lose trust in the way that we understand the world we live in and the relationships between our self and our beloved and hated others. Then nothing makes sense anymore.

Within the Maelstrom model these various pieces of theory can be visualised in a single frame (see Figure 5.1). The dark dots depict the overwhelming emotional aspect of the intrusive nightmarish scenario, whereas the open dots

confrontation |———————————————▶ approach

proximity

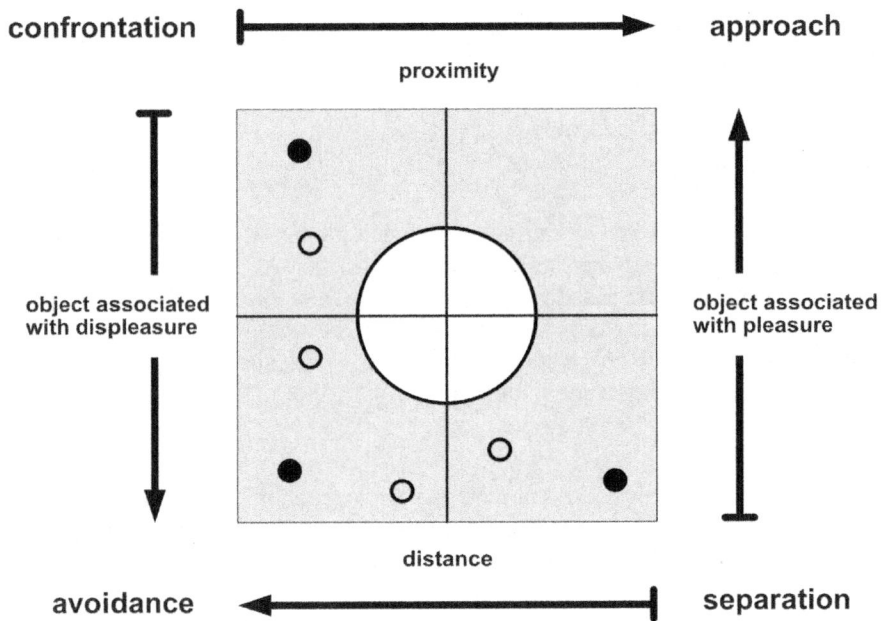

object associated
with displeasure

object associated
with pleasure

distance

avoidance ◀—————————————| separation

Figure 5.1 Dreams and nightmares don't have a single meaning, but multiple layers.

depict both conscious and unconscious representations that are strongly emotionally associated.

***

What made sense to Harry? Which fears beset him? Does he fear for his physical and psychological integrity, for his sense of security in relatedness or for losing control? Which beliefs and illusions has he got trouble holding on to? Is it the unpredictability of reality that gets the better of him, in spite of his personal level of skill and professionalism? Is it the impending loss of the reassuring presence of his father that renders him emotionally vulnerable? Is his trust in military comradery falling apart? I do not know, I can only guess. And what causes the stagnation of his unconscious creativity? Why do his dreams reach a deadlock? Why is the theme of "lying alone in a shot no man's land" repeated over and over again?

***

But before these questions can be addressed, let's reflect a little more on the things that can change fluid dreaming into a repetitive nightmare.

Nightmares are orphaned dreams of terror

I assume that dreaming reflects a basic mechanism through which raw emotional representations are associatively interwoven. The dreamed scenario is a condensation of an emotional tapestry that is moving in various primary and often preverbal ways, sometimes conveying a transcending meaning. The fear within us drives us to seek safety. Desperation and powerlessness make us wish for supernatural powers or an omnipotent saviour. In our dreams, we don't experience the fulfilment of all our wishes, but the emotional undertones can certainly let themselves be felt. The dream is the most liberated among our free associations, as it is relieved of rational and realistic scrutiny. But in order to consciously assign meaning to a dream, we need our emotions and dreams as well as our rationality and relational reality. We need someone to see and hear us, in order to get to know our self. And as adults, this important other is often our reflective self. Our emotions need someone to listen, accept and understand. It is the way in which our conscious mind learns to think and feel about our subjective mindful state.

And like we all need someone to see and hear us, our dreams need us to become meaningful. Like children need the sensitive reflection of their parents to learn to think about their feelings and to feel about their thoughts, our dreams need us to do the same. Especially dreams that are overloaded with feeling, with terror and panic, are in need of a sensitive and reflective inner space. In other words: nightmares especially need "parental compassion" and emotional containment. But what happens when the parents are too scared themselves? What effect has fear on reflection? Impulsively, they tend to look away and avoid contact, with dire consequences.

Let's pretend that a nightmare is a child who is overwhelmed by terror and panic and isn't able to tell what upsets him so much. And let's pretend that the dreamer of the nightmare is a parent who lacks the reflective space to empathise with the emotional urgency without being overwhelmed herself. I suggest that the fate of the nightmare resembles the behaviour of an overwhelmed child that is emotionally cut off from an empathic parent.

The Still Face experiment was mentioned in Chapter 4. In this experiment, the mother is instructed to freeze her face for two minutes amidst a playful time with her child. The effects on babies and toddlers are dramatic, as they desperately struggle to gain her attention and restart the emotional dance. Most children show various tactics, from screaming, fighting, crying, turning away, shutting their eyes to silent lamenting. Some children are inclined to cling more to their mothers (while others tend to fend off contact and turn inwards for consolation). If this pattern for seeking emotional attention grows pathological, it might result in an insecure attachment style. Even when empathic attention is found, the emotional upheaval isn't easily soothed. These children continue to place a great emotional appeal upon the parent, while it is not articulated what this appeal is exactly about. And for an exhausted parent the child's nagging behaviour is quickly labelled as the source of the problems. The trust is gone.

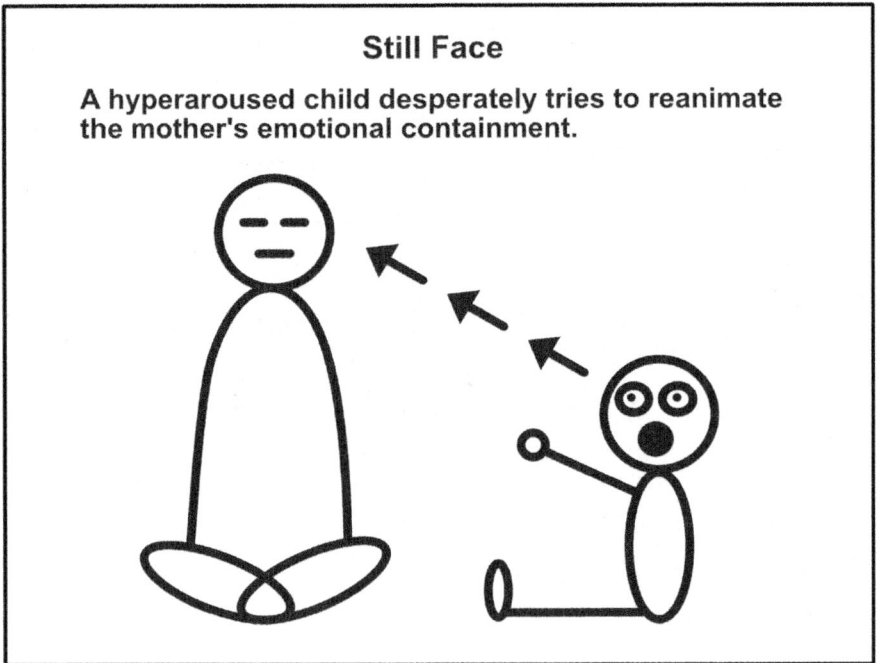

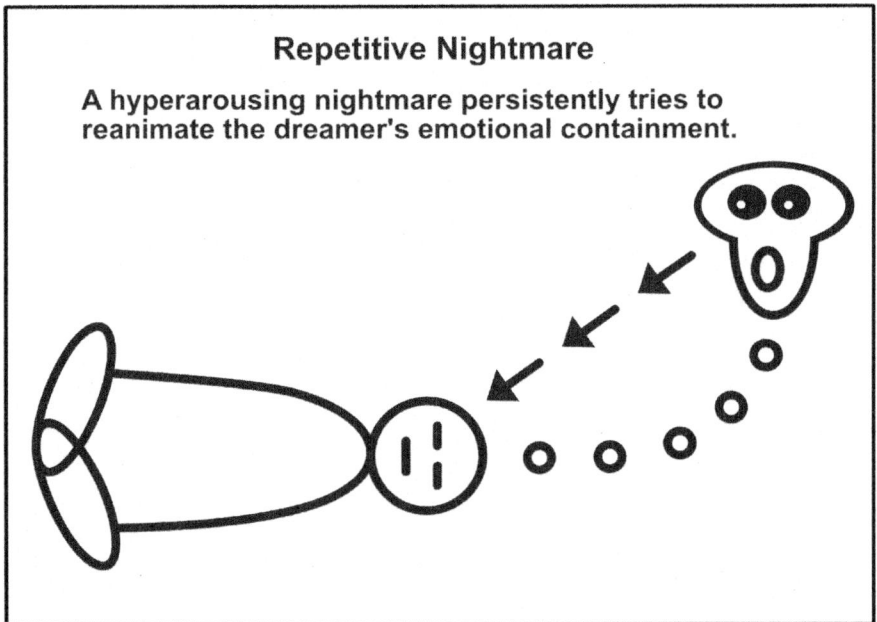

Figure 5.2 A repetitive nightmare is a dream of terror that meets a "still face".

So maybe nightmares repeat themselves like preoccupied attached children continue to make emotional appeals to their parents. The repetitive nightmare is the ongoing "temper tantrum" of the inner dream world, infused with explicit and implicit layers of fear. It is a misunderstood attempt at reanimating emotional containment and self-regulation. Figure 5.2 is a graphic representation of this state of affairs.

Dreams and nightmares are the result of an intertwining of raw emotional scenarios, based on actual and fantasised experiences riddled with rudimentary impressions. Past and present overlap and aspects of the therapeutic relationship can also become part of the presented dream. So when someone tells me about a dream or nightmare, I am aware of unforeseen intricacies. Not only might the dream reveal important pieces of an unchartered inner world, but also the trust between the other and myself is at stake. Can Harry trust me with his nightmare? Am I prepared to listen to him, even when I myself feel overwhelmed, powerless or downright nauseous? Do I trust myself with this task that I cannot oversee?

Reclaiming the frontline

***

Back to Harry. He did something that never happened to me in my career before or after. He gave me a pet name, at least that was my impression. My first name is Daniël, but he started to call me Danny. It was clear that he thought that Danny suited me better. I asked myself whether I found it belittling, but I didn't. Nor did I get the impression that there was a seductive homosexual undertone to it. My pet name sounded to me like the name a child gives to his teddy bear. A great variety of roles can be assigned to me as a psychotherapist, and I guess that this is one of them. One of the things that a teddy bear does is to help cope with all kinds of fear when mommy and daddy are not around. And a teddy bear is the safest bet if you seek someone who you can trust with your stories of vulnerability.

The teddy bear is related to the psychoanalytic concept of the transitional object, coined by Donald Winnicott. A transitional object derives its psychological value from its ability to mediate between the inner and outer world and often is associated with the representation of the mother. Years later, a clever student noticed that Danny sounds a lot like nanny, something I had never thought of.[7] Also, in the therapy with Harry, I don't recall to have asked him about nannies. That surely was an omission, for with his father working and travelling, young Harry undoubtedly had nannies. Probably Harry had experienced multiple separations when his father and he had to move repeatedly, following the job.

Both of us were focussed on his nightmares and on the use of EMDR, which proved to be a very effective tool. Like surgery it severed some of the problematic emotional associations from his nightmare, thereby lowering overall arousal to a manageable level. This helped to see more of the hidden layers that resonated with his experience of lying alone in a shot no man's land, even though at the same time it may have disconnected others.

The fear of being shot in the dark by his own colleagues, of being killed by friendly fire, is associated with a fundamental uncertainty about back support. The side that he needs to be trustworthy, the side for which he is blind and for which he needs others "to watch his back", that is the side where deadly fire can come from. Exactly the persons he depends on the most are the ones that can wound him fatally. If we have another look, the story of his life seems like variations on exactly this theme. In the present, his father is drinking himself into sickness, possibly death. His father is the person who Harry feels most close to and depends on, but unfortunately that person doesn't resist the urge to drink and shorten the time that they have together. Being an only child with one parent left, that most likely is very unsettling for Harry, who also doesn't have a long-lasting intimate relation of his own. And maybe this too had something to do with letting no one come close enough to hurt him.[8]

The themes of friendly fire and defensive isolation also comes up in his work. His expertise makes him eligible for solitary work, stationed on international bases with varying collegial setups. And when he did connect and made new friends, the friend that he cared most for got killed. The lasting image of this personal loss is that of a coffin carried into an aircraft. At home he doesn't talk much about his tour with his Dutch colleagues. He doesn't ask for support, possibly because it feels more safe not to put himself in such a vulnerable position again. He seriously feared that his repetitive nightmares disqualify him as a soldier. It is another reason not to confide in his colleagues. It makes him all alone all over, dodging contact, seeking refuge in darkness and silence, like in a coffin.

Of course I encouraged him to open up to people. After EMDR had broken through the cycle of pseudo-normal functioning and flaring up nightmares, he starts to make more contact. First he makes progress regaining collegial fun and professional fulfilment. Relieved of the burden of his nightmares, he again finds pride in his military capabilities. On top of that he tells me – with a blush that I haven't seen before – that he has started dating. Fortunately things are going in the right direction when I have to tell him after a year of therapy that I am designated for a six-month tour abroad. The frequency of our appointments was decreasing already, and he tells me that he doesn't need to continue with a colleague of mine. He tells me that he is confident and curious of the road ahead.

Nevertheless, I notice that I am sorry that we can't continue our talks. Who knows what a prolonged therapy on psychoanalytic tracks might have brought? It reminds me of the anticlimactic sentiment in his voice, commenting on the effectiveness of EMDR that it is only logical to establish that he isn't being shot at any more and that he is safe now. Harry also might intuitively have felt that there is more to the story of his repetitive nightmare than that.

***

In order to make sense of dreams, the only truthful approach is to follow the associations of the dreamer. So there is an inherent obstacle when a nightmare is so emotionally captivating that free associations are no longer possible. Then the transition from a nightmare into constructive fluid dreaming is threatened, and new meaningful arrangements of relational representations seem out of reach. I wish Harry and I could have had more time to reflect on his nightmares and dreams, for I believed the therapeutic bond to be firm and emotionally attuned enough to investigate his dreams together. Then I maybe could have helped him to make sense of his dreams, empathically tuning in when he is lost for words, in order to co-construct a meaningful narrative that is emotionally alive.[9] In particular, I notice that I associate easily regarding Harry lying in a shot no man's land and the familial circumstances in his earliest childhood. Taking the fantasised nature of these associations into account, I will share them here nonetheless.

***

Let's consider an association between the drinking colleagues and his drinking father. Maybe his father's drinking has made Harry acutely aware of an unpredictable streak in his father. Even if there never had been any physical violence, being an only child of a single unpredictable parent, this would have been an unnerving experience for the young Harry. What is a father capable of, in the inner life of a son? Thinking in the lines of a child trying to make sense of the incomprehensible death of his mother, maybe the man that is deemed almighty is held responsible. His father, being "the best shot", could be suspected (in the mind of a child) to somehow have caused the death of the mother. But with one parent left, psychologically the only child wouldn't have had the luxury to vent his anger or to turn away. The fundamental need for attachment would have made that very difficult. In a defensive reaction, the child might unconsciously decide that it is better to join the one that you cannot (afford to) beat.[10] A career in the army, with its institutionalised brotherhood and international operations, makes perfect sense then.

Another daydream I had was about a child lying alone, between two parties that have killed each other. I can imagine how Harry might have believed that his father never got over the death of his mother. And how the retirement of his father has robbed him of the professional distraction of this unbearable loss. Drinking himself into oblivion could have strong ties to the salient absence of his wife and mother of his son. But being the son, how can Harry psychologically adapt to a tragedy that is bigger than the life of his father? And at the same time the chronically suppressed fear of becoming an orphan turns into reality. Losing not one but the two most important persons could be a fate that is worse than getting shot yourself. Maybe it is farfetched, but seeking refuge in the darkness and silence of his hermetically sealed bedroom makes me think of a grave, possibly the dreamed grave of his mother where Harry found some illusionary comfort. At least psychotherapy has helped Harry to find comfort in the real world again.

And there was another surprising catch. Six months after the start of my own deployment, I was waiting for my flight home. Suddenly I hear a familiar voice shouting "How are you doing?" Surrounded by colleagues there is Harry, smiling. He tells me that it wasn't his time for another tour, but when his own company was assigned, he volunteered to join. It is the last piece of his recovery, he tells me. Not only did he want to get rid of his nightmares, in which he succeeded, but he wanted to be a soldier in real life again, "out there". Standing next to a colleague, he adds that this surely beats their deserted Dutch base. I sincerely wish him all the best.

The aim of Harry's therapy hasn't been to eradicate the possibility of becoming terrified ever again, but to deal with feelings of terror and despair in such a way that his life doesn't become restricted. For Harry it is not only about his physical safety, but also about being able to deal with danger and to stay connected. Perhaps it is even about the vicissitudes of love. Therapy helped him to be relieved of some of the most intense emotional upheaval, which enhanced his sense of control and freedom in his professional and relational undertakings. It was obvious that I didn't provide all the answers; I wasn't an EMDR expert or an authority on dream interpretation. But maybe, by being "Danny", I had been the right therapist for Harry. And maybe we shouldn't focus that much on the repetitiveness of certain nightmares, as if it is a characteristic of the nightmare itself. Maybe it is better to put more effort into listening, especially into listening to preverbal emotions.

***

Notes

1 See, for a recent example, the Hobson versus Solms debate.
2 I first presented this case on a Dutch Lemion congress on dream work in 2016.
3 Also known as Internal Working Models or as Implicit Relational Patterns. See, for an elaborated example, Ladan, A. (2014). *Dead certainties: On psychoanalysis, disillusion, and death*. London & New York: Routledge.
4 See, for example, Coates, S. & Schecter, D. (2006). Preschoolers' traumatic stress post-9/11: Relational and developmental perspectives. In: Wachs, C. & Jacobs, L. (eds.), *Parent-focused child therapy; attachment, identification and reflective functions*. Lanham, Boulder & New York: Rowman & Littlefield, 93–110.
5 For instance, Nicolaï, N. (2016). *Emotieregulatie als basis van het menselijk bestaan. De kunst van het evenwicht*. Leusden: Diagnosis Uitgevers.
6 The inner blaze is used here as a metaphor for emotional hyperarousal, through which one feels the urgent need to act, save or seek help while there is no opportunity to do so.
7 Harry is raised bilingual.
8 I don't think it is a coincidence that his father never got married again. I believe that Harry could have "got this message". And at the same time, in a certain sense, Harry seemed to have become the wife his father had lost.
9 In my experience, working with dreams isn't primarily about solving an analytic puzzle, but it is about creating a sphere of poetic receptivity. In my early professional years I made the unsettling discovery that several therapies (and work with dreams) went better when I was a little bit ill. Later on I understood this to be a sign of my intellectual hyperactivity, standing in the way of a more emotionally attuned way of understanding.
10 What is known in psychoanalytic theory as "identification with the aggressor".

Chapter 6

On obsessive compulsive behaviour

Losing control of the need to feel in control

***

Lauren has already been diagnosed with obsessive compulsive disorder (OCD) and uses medication when she decides to see me. The medication helps her to handle her obsession for the threat of accidentally poisoning others. Her balance still feels somewhat unstable though, and she wants to give "a talking cure" a chance, however hesitantly. Despite her well-spoken presentation, or maybe because of it, I notice that I become a little bit cautious and weigh my words with extra care. Control seems to be a delicate issue, leaving little room between feeling too much and feeling too little. In my head, I start to wonder about links between unspoken subjective experiences and the symptomatic surface. We decide to start therapy aimed at understanding her symptoms in a psychological way, to strengthen her sense of balance. I intend to use my understanding of the mechanisms found in emotion regulation and in dreaming, to help Lauren get a grip on her unfathomable symptoms.

***

Our dreaming minds use a perplexing variety of associations to link elements together and form dream scenarios. According to Freud, this puzzling variety serves to make sure that the fulfilment of hidden wishes doesn't reach hyperarousing levels that would cause the dreamer to wake up. For example, elements can be condensed, displaced or caught in an image that only makes sense when it is thought about in words. These transformative mechanisms operate in a layer of the psyche where the reign of emotions isn't as restricted by rationality as in conscious thought. It is in the same layer of the psyche where the preverbal flow of emotions can give rise to neurotic symptoms in waking life. These kinds of symptoms can be as bewildering as dreams, but can start to make sense once they are thought of in terms of condensed, displaced or concretised elements that can convey emotional meaning.

***

A couple of years ago, a polite young man named Luke came to see me with such a bewildering symptom. He reported that he started to sleepwalk six months ago. The sleepwalking didn't bother him that much though, but each time his girlfriend came over and spend the night with him, he would urinate on the floor of his room while sleepwalking. The general practitioner had found no medical cause and Luke was at a loss when he came to me. In his family history his older brother had a prominent role, because of his maladaptive behaviour and frequent fights with their parents. Also, when Luke had introduced his girlfriend into the family, there immediately had been a quarrel between her and his brother. In an attempt to subside heated emotions, the parents had decided to pay for a brand new apartment for their oldest son. Luke had then moved into the former room of his brother. I found it remarkable that in his account he never expressed any kind of anger towards his brother, his parents or his girlfriend. It was clear that he had developed a pattern of withholding his anger and had cultivated his role of "the good son", the one who doesn't trouble his parents. So, thinking out loud, I start to wonder whether he could be pissed off but didn't feel comfortable to express it. (In Dutch the word "pissig" also means angry.) It set off a train of associations, conveying a wide array of situations in which he reluctantly had withheld his anger. Also, it became clear that he was trying to make his former brother's room his own. Urinating on the floor impressed us as a possible sign of marking his territory. In the following weeks it helped him to re-establish himself, ultimately deciding to leave his room and look for a place of his own. It struck us both that the involuntary urinating ceased overnight.

Starting therapy with Lauren, Luke crossed my mind. I wondered what "being poisonous" meant in her inner world.

***

The terror of one's own rage

Obsessive compulsive symptoms, such as the chronically repeated act of washing hands, are notoriously difficult to treat with interventions aimed at a verbal understanding of underlying psychodynamics. An interpretation that links possible meaning to symptoms not seldom evoke lengthy argumentative discourses on the pros and cons of the interpretation. The washing of hands may point to getting rid of dangerous bacteria or other people's filth but might as well refer to getting rid of things from the inside such as guilt or forbidden lust. So an analytical search for emotional meaning of symptoms initially doesn't do much for someone who is suffering from OCD, as lengthy discussions often become a line of defence against an inner felt reality. There is something about obsessive compulsive symptoms that is inherently rewarding, in spite of great suffering at the same time (for instance, some people literally wash the skin of their hands). In this chapter, I will argue that obsessive compulsive symptoms may have multiple implicit emotion-regulatory functions and that the reward also can exist of the warding off of an inner felt reality that is even more devastating than losing your actual skin.

***

Lauren is an academic professional and a married mother of two girls. She is held in high regard for her intelligence and sensitivity by her colleagues. People tend to use her as a confidential mediator, a role which she often takes up. But lately she has developed some disabling symptoms that revolve around keeping an ultra-hygienic regime in and around her kitchen. Everything is meticulously disinfected and all thinkable is done to prevent food from becoming contaminated. This regime is getting out of control, as it forbids the children to play around the kitchen or to invite friends at home. Also her husband isn't permitted to move freely though the kitchen. The only thing Lauren is able to comment on the rigidity of her regime is how unbearable it would be if someone got poisoned from food coming out of her kitchen.

Lauren isn't a stranger to obsessive compulsive behaviour, but it never got in the way of her personal life as it does now. She finds the negative impact on her family very troublesome. Both her parents are alive and well, though her father is somewhat of a hoarder himself. Last year the father of her husband died from a disease that was largely denied. The all too real process of the progressive disease combined with the disavowed need to talk about it together had made her husband struggle with loss and mourning. According to her, this was the reason that he had started an affair in the aftermath of the death of his father. It seemed like a sexualised form of self-medication: an affair in order to feel alive. Though she didn't condone the affair and he had chosen to end it for the sake of their marriage and daughters, she felt burdened by the thought of robbing him of this defence. He hadn't had the opportunity to say goodbye to his father or to mourn with his mother and brother, and she didn't want to be the one who prevented him to "come alive again". His sullen despair weighted heavily on her.

Lauren speaks with great empathy about her husband's plight but also is able to reflect on the ambivalence she feels towards him. She vents her anger on his affair, but she remains remarkably composed doing so. Even when he still utters doubts about their marriage, she isn't overwhelmed by the thought of breaking up. Talking to her, there is an unmistakable impression that she is in control.[1] The one thing that she is not sure of is what is coming out of her kitchen when she doesn't pay attention.

Sometimes we think we know why we feel what we feel, only to discover later that our certainty has blinded us from hidden motives. Lauren never seems out of control of her emotions, except for the fear of poisoning others. Being understanding and nurturing to others, her husband, her daughters or anyone else for that matter, is such a big part of who she is, that an uncontrollable intensity of rage seems alien to her. (In Dutch the word "giftig" means both poisonous and extremely angry.) The sheer thought of losing their girls is so devastating that an unspoken Medea motive is out of the question.

***

An enacted mantra for an unspeakable threat

Life events, such as death, divorce or disease, have the potential to stir up basic emotions to uncontrollable and overwhelming intensities that are difficult to master. In those kind of circumstances, we might encounter parts of ourselves that we aren't acquainted with. We might be swept away by an emotional current, urging us to act impulsively, become paralyzed or have all sorts of reactions that are implicit or explicit attempts to regulate emotional intensity. That is why people often say that you don't know how you will react until you actually live through a stressful situation. I don't think that that is modesty speaking, but a realistic account of the limits of the human capability to consciously know and predict subjective experience and future behaviour. We humans really don't know precisely what is cooking in our inner kitchen. And preventive psychotherapy never has become popular; psychoanalytic psychotherapy helps people to get a grip by coming to terms with the emotional upheaval that has already been stirred up inside. And this surely can be a monumental task by itself, because of the Gordian knot of conscious and unconscious emotions, stemming from our own subjective experience or vicariously embodied, rooted in actual circumstances or in implicit relational patterns. To unravel such a knot might seem impossible, especially if one is feeling overwhelmed in the first place. Some might decide that concrete action is the way to go, giving up on the search for an emotional meaning of symptoms.

***

Maybe Lauren also had declared some parts of herself not only as unknown but also as unknowable in order to move on. But by doing so, these exiled parts remain to exert influence through continued but "senseless" emotional arousal. And because of associative processes like condensation and displacement known from the psychoanalysis of dreams, this arousal can easily become attached to new but somehow related objects. This arousal, stripped of its raging or despairing origins, can become a threat of its own. It may serve as a signal and raise anxiety for a devastating loss of control.[2] Instead of feeling deadly rage, for example, disconnected hyperarousal can become a terror about food becoming poisonous and venomous, threatening to kill the very people you love. And of course this horrible scenario has to be prevented at all costs. It seems plausible that Lauren's ultra-hygienic regime in her kitchen is an enacted mantra for a threat for which she has no relatable words.

***

Because the source of the emotional upheaval is not considered and regulated, it keeps on instigating the emotional urge to act. Obsessive compulsive behaviour, like a mute mantra, has to be exerted repeatedly in order to steer clear of danger. But safety and redemption always seem one harbour away. And the mindless repetition becomes a source of despair of its own.

Controlling the outcome instead of addressing the emotion

***

My working hypothesis at this point is that the emotional upheaval that set off Lauren's bout of obsessive compulsive behaviour is best characterised as anxiety for murderous rage.[3] Even when we don't know what exactly it was that fired up the rage, we can use the Maelstrom model to think about how it would lead to obsessive compulsive behaviour. Though obsessive compulsive behaviour can have multiple functions in itself, on which I shall reflect in a short while, a prime motive is considered to be the (re)gaining of a sense of control. Pathologic rumination and repeated behaviour are believed to be instrumental in avoiding a dreadful outcome that is unspeakable, but in this concretised way illusorily manageable.[4] The repeated behaviour serves to bolster the sense of control, thereby temporarily improving the tolerance of arousal and lowering emotional intensity. In other words: repeated behaviour is used to force unbearable emotions into submission. Fighting against fear of contamination in the kitchen is less overwhelming than battling a venomous rage in the caverns of her soul. Though Lauren probably never took this into conscious consideration, her implicit emotion regulation could well have taken over in lack of words that suit a subjective experience that doesn't appear to be personally relatable at all. Modelled visually, it looks like Figure 6.1.

***

Figure 6.1 illustrates how rage can become a source of terror of its own, from which it is hard to distance oneself because it comes from within and is intensely gripping. Unconsciously outsourcing the murderous threat leaves room to regulate the intensity of the emotion, because something can be done in the outer world to regain control. Terror is transformed into fear, at the cost of awareness of the source of the emotional upheaval and of long-term (co-)regulation.

So the occurrence of obsessive compulsive symptoms in the course of emotionally stirring circumstances might point to implicit regulatory mechanisms. OCD can have several defensive functions and can be a concurrence of implicit ways of regulating emotional experiences by fixating attention and repeating action.

- Obsessive compulsive behaviour provides a reassurance (however short-lived) that something can be done to avoid a dreaded outcome. By keeping the counter meticulously disinfected, Lauren experiences a gratifying (but fleeting) sense of control. It consequently lowers the subjective experience of the intensity of dreadful emotions.
- Simply acting on a basic emotional urge might be felt as a relief from a burden of ambivalent consideration or of feelings of alienation (until obsessive compulsive behaviour starts to feel alienating in itself).

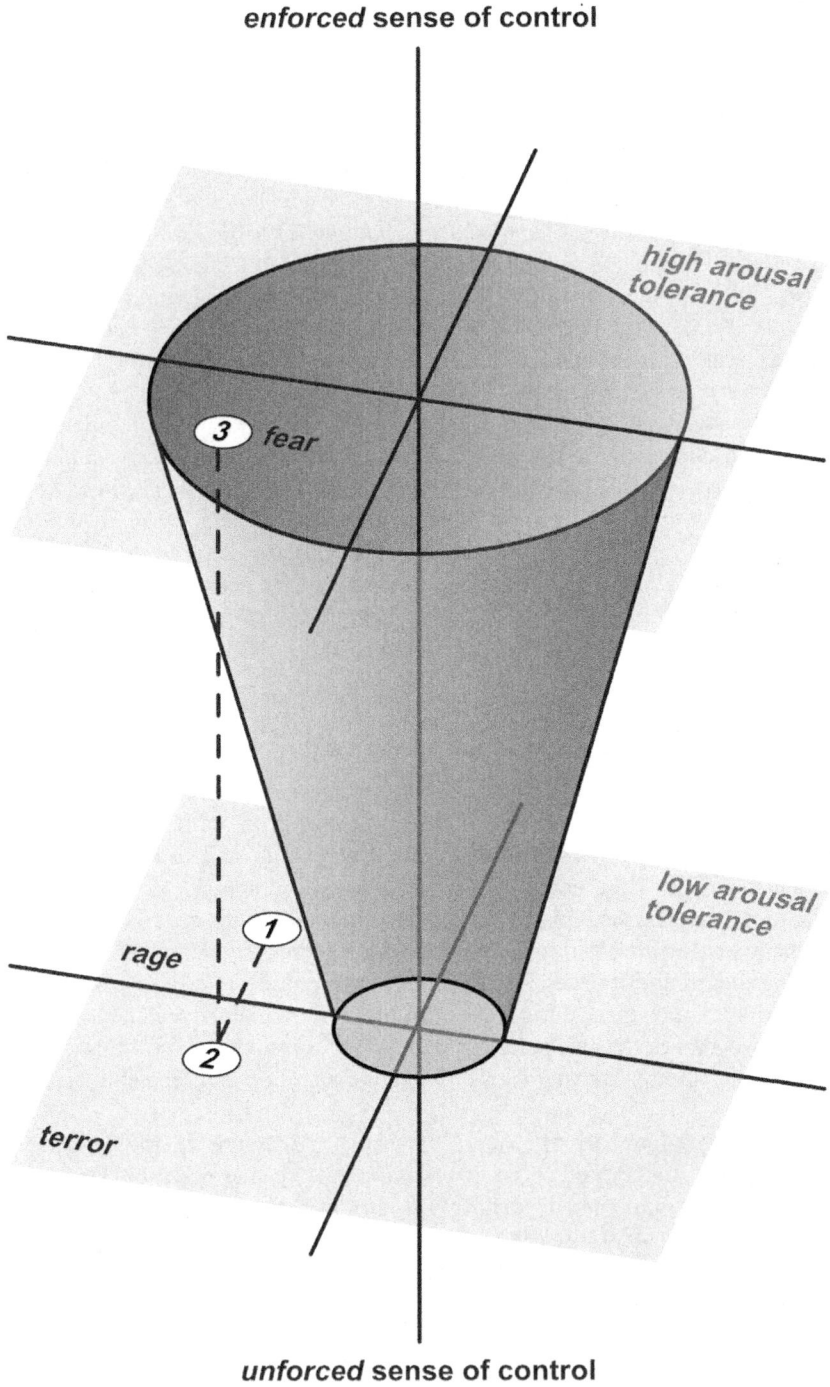

enforced sense of control

high arousal tolerance

3 fear

low arousal tolerance

rage   1

2

terror

unforced sense of control

Figure 6.1 Obsessive compulsive behaviour temporarily enforces a sense of control, thereby diminishing emotional intensity for a while. 1 = hyperaroused rage, 2 = terror of one's own rage, 3 = enforced and seemingly controllable fear.

- Perpetually focussing and acting on the outside world might serve as a means to avoid looking inside. It is hard to reflect on what is going on inside when your hands are very busy.
- It temporarily reaffirms the illusory conviction that one is capable of controlling one's own subjective experience. It defers the (re)consideration of the stunted boundaries among what is felt, thought and done.

But the cost of obsessive compulsive behaviour is twofold at least. First, and most often this is the reason that people seek psychotherapy for OCD, there is an accumulation of collateral damage. OCD tends to infiltrate all aspects of life, as it ultimately fails in providing the control and safety that it seeks. It might not only affect one's ability to consciously focus attention, but also have a detrimental impact on intimate relations, professional aspirations and having fun in general. In sum, it is bad for the ability to love, work and play. Second, and this is an unseen tragedy that makes it even worse, there is a basic part of the emotional subjective world that is abandoned and at a loss. Somewhere down the line a rupture has emerged that painfully separates intensely felt subjective experiences from soothing or fulfilling interaction with others. And because it is a part that is deemed unspeakable, it seems to speak for itself that the only one who can help you is you. Not seldom there is a pervasive sense of loneliness that is unquestionably accepted as a sad fact of life.

Emotions move us but don't define us

***

Even though Lauren suffered a great deal under the regime of her OCD, forcing her to use medication, it wasn't easy to consider the possibility that her symptoms could be evoked by an unidentified emotion like rage. The mere thought could bypass a comprehensive regulatory structure, what could cause her to feel defenceless and to become defensive towards me. First we needed to make sure that it is safe to make contact on an emotional level. Part of that was that she needed me to be clear about my thoughts and intentions. I had told her that she could make use of my experience as a therapist by picking my mind, and I would tell her openly what I think and feel. And if it is something that I am not sure about, such as a hypothesis on a puzzling subjective experience, I will say so. It is up to her to feel and think it through, deciding whether it is an insight that holds any truth or not. I also expressed my belief that it takes time to achieve this and that she is welcome to use it. Initially, this was enough to help us on our way.

She insisted on using a low dose of medication that helped her but didn't prevent her obsessive compulsions completely. As time went by, she got more frustrated about these recurring bouts of OCD, sporadic expressing irritation about the lack of effectiveness of her therapy and only hinting at my feeble effectiveness as a therapist. On one such occasion, I addressed the topic of anger. She was very quick to stop me in my tracks, turning on herself and explaining that she should be more patient instead of criticising me or her therapy. It was clear that this is dangerous territory that is unsafe for her to venture into. But her growing tolerance of arousal had already enabled her to openly consider the possibility of criticising me. I felt that it was important not to leave the topic of anger alone, for it would be left for her to deal with alone, which could result in anger turning towards herself. Lauren preferred to criticise herself instead of me.

So I reflected on what had just happened, on her turning on herself instead of criticising me. I felt the tension level rising and that it was on me to find a way out again. Lauren's eyes were fixated on mine and she wasn't able to speak. I said that I thought that anger is a very complicated emotion for her, as it is for a lot of people. And sometimes the thing about anger that is so complicating is how it makes you feel about yourself. If we urgently need to feel accepted, we dare not permit ourselves to feel anger. And if we don't look at emotions as the things they are, as temporary subjective states that motivate us to take certain action, but look at them as solidified objects that make us "good and relatable or bad and unrelatable" persons, it becomes hard to get to know your own heart. For all kinds of emotions live within us, sometimes teaming up and sometimes contradicting each other. And anger, as other emotions, has a voice, a meaning. I asked Lauren whether it is OK for us to listen to her anger together and find out what it is about. Implicitly I communicated that I was up for her anger: it wouldn't destroy me either. She nodded.

So we gave thought to anger and rage. According to the Maelstrom model, we should look for an intense confrontation with an object associated with displeasure. In her therapy with me she experienced displeasure through the frustrating attempts at regaining control. What was it that Lauren felt so confronted by outside the therapy room? The usual suspect was her cheating husband. It certainly had made her angry, but it didn't seem to overwhelm her. Maybe there was something else going on underneath the surface. It was something she said that caught my attention, something about her own childhood. While we were talking about her subjective experience of her obsessive compulsive behaviour, she claimed that it is partly genetic, as her father has been hoarding as long as she can remember. The thing is though that he calls it a hobby and the rest of her family thinks nothing of it. She added that besides hoarding, her father also has had several depressive episodes, something that she didn't mention before. Lauren describes him as a very gentile and caring man, who is sometimes impossible to reach. There have been several periods in her early childhood wherein her father fell completely silent and wasn't able to work. For weeks and months he had lain silently in his bed. It has taken a toll on the marriage with her mother and on her personally. Her mother had often turned to Lauren as a confidential mediator, a role that she had ultimately mastered.

I started to see a parentified child in Lauren, one who has trouble recognising her "childish" needs as an adult. Being asked to take up a role that is well beyond your years and is impossible to fulfil is being asked to give up a part of your youthful self. Just being a daughter hadn't been enough to reach her father, who was periodically silently unreachable or completely absorbed in his activities. And her mother had sometimes needed Lauren more to be a listening adult than a playing child. No wonder Lauren had used all her talents to become the one who is both caring and in control, at the expense of her own childish needs.

Then I started to think that maybe it wasn't her husband having an affair, but her husband having a depressive episode that had been so confronting and stirred up a powerless rage. The times that her husband had acted on routine, devoid of feelings of pleasure and meaning, first appealed to her caring and composed parts. She was the one on whom her husband and their daughters fell back, and meanwhile she also took it upon herself to become a liaison in her family-in-law. But despite of all her efforts, it didn't seem enough. She wasn't able to reach her husband or find reassurance that she was a lively part of his emotional world. It had seemed like he had given up, not only on the world, but on her. Her whole life threatened to fall apart. The resonance with her childhood experience is poignant. In relation to the two most important men in her life, all her efforts appeared to be ultimately futile. Lauren faced the dilemma of how to be angry at the man she loves while he is suffering. How can you be angry at someone who is giving up?[5]

Yet another layer came into sight when Lauren added casually that she had been a very happy and contented baby. Because of that, her mother had made it a habit to put Lauren in bed next to her depressed father, "who needed a bit of sunshine in his life". Lauren at first didn't give it another thought, but I couldn't scrub off the image of her as a baby, being put by her mother next to her depressed father. It overwhelmed me to feel and think about those moments, in stark contrast with the neutral tone in which she told me about them. What is it like for a baby to repeatedly lose the touch of a lively mother and find yourself next to a sullen father? I have told Lauren how this image keeps on popping up in my mind, raising questions about its meaning. It made her look more openly, lending my wonder to see herself as it were. She then said she pictured herself as a baby, puzzled and stiffening up near her father, who was kind but at times lethargic. She wanted to pick the baby up, soothe her unrest by holding her and let her play again. I nodded as we both felt the urge to care for those "childish" emotions that never had a chance to be expressed and recognised.

***

A premature loss of childhood

***

Denominating Lauren's anger didn't relieve her of her obsessive compulsive symptoms. Maybe anger was a part of her "inner poisonousness", but it wasn't clear what her anger was all about. Was there something else "cooking in her inner kitchen" that she so desperately tried to disinfect?

Something that she somehow associated with life-threatening visceral experiences, detrimental to vitality? It was after Lauren had sensitively pictured herself as a baby that she started to feel resistance to the burdensome weight of her parental responsibilities, as well as moments of numbing fatigue and loneliness. More precisely, she started to recognise them because she knew these feelings all too well, but never had been able to give words to them. She had always felt the need to put them aside as soon as they emerged. After growing up as a child who "brings a bit of sunshine in her father's life", she had become a woman who had trouble giving voice to both her light-heartedness and neediness. She had an enduring sense of all-encompassing responsibility for the well-being of others. And even more than for her father, she had always felt the need to be a mother for her mother. Her mother had lost her mother when she was only a child, and Lauren had been repeatedly praised by her mother for "being such a good listener whom she could tell anything". This had shaped their relationship, wherein her mother continued to call Lauren several times a week to vent. Lauren had grown up with ideas of how to be a parent through the eyes of a child, for she was only a child when she took up this adult task. And in the eyes of a child, a parent should be concerned, omnipotent and always available in times of need. So in order to live up to this overburdening ideal, she had to suppress her own childish "maladaptive" feelings and needs. In order to look after the child in her own mother, she had abandoned the child within herself.

Lauren had had an upsurge in her obsessive compulsive behaviour when her daughters were born. She then was obsessively concerned with not causing catastrophe, such as blowing up the house, and repeatedly checked whether she turned off the gas. Now she suddenly remembered when her obsessions turned towards cleaning her kitchen and meticulously preparing food. In 2011 there had been an outburst in Germany of E. coli bacteria, spreading towards neighbouring countries and causing severe illness and even death. The horrible scenario that had crept into her mind was that she unwittingly could infect her children, who would unwittingly infect all the children of their school. Because it takes several days for symptoms to develop, she couldn't be certain if this scenario wasn't already becoming reality or not. She felt that an imminent danger threatened the lives of all the children in the village and it was up to her to keep them safe. In the doom scenario the children would become ill and die, and an inquiry would demonstrate her guilt for giving them infected food.

When she told me this, I remembered the international media coverage of the horrible outbreak, but also I noticed the issue of disproportionate responsibility and guilt. It resembled the disproportionate sense of responsibility of a parentified child, who is used to carrying out a task that is only under imaginary control and who hadn't developed firm psychological boundaries between self and other. Also in her doom scenario only the children were infected. It then became clear how her own motherhood had felt like an impossible burden, not because she didn't love her daughters (on the contrary) but because she felt so powerless against all the threats in the world that could harm them. Becoming a mother once again made her feel that she was the designated bearer of responsibility, who should protect others from every harm. Her own "childish" feelings and needs had to be abandoned even more. The depressive episode of her husband and his "irresponsible" affair had left her feeling even more alone bearing this impossible weight of parental responsibility.

Now our efforts to understand her anger were getting somewhere. Though in her darkest imagination the lives of her children were at stake, it didn't seem to be motivated by a repressed vengeful motive of a modern-day Medea. Her rage seemed to be an emotional reaction to the powerlessness she felt in her overburdening notion of adult motherhood, a notion that stemmed from the time wherein she had felt that she could be a child no longer herself. Lauren was only a child when she felt the emotional appeal to parent her parents, so her anger also had a childish murderous intensity. In her mind she had good reasons to keep her anger locked up inside. And even today, her mother needed her more to listen to her than she was able to listen to Lauren.

So her anger seemed to be an emotional impulse to get rid of an overburdening sense of lonesome parental responsibility. The feared doom scenario would uncompromisingly lift this burden of her shoulders, be it in the most dramatic way possible, for she would be a mother no more. The thing that made this primitive emotional wish understandable was that she had become a mother (in a psychological sense) much too young, when she had needed to be a carefree child herself. The task of being a bit of sunshine in her parents' life had become so self-evident and all-consuming that is was hard for her to feel the burden of it. For Lauren, this was just the way it always had been. Being able to recognise her angry motive and to differentiate between feeling angry and being guilty of a murderous crime or of fatal negligence helped Lauren to identify what it was that she felt so confronted by. The nearly daily telephone calls from her mother, her loneliness in bearing the weight of parental responsibility, the way in which family and colleagues found it self-evident that Lauren was the one to go to when you had a problem. She needed to separate herself from the subjective necessity to take it all up onto herself. And yet, at the same time, she didn't want to lose it either. It is hard to give up on something that you do well. She needed space.

Connecting to her ambivalent anger opened up a new way for considering her own needs. It helped her to shift focus to the question what it was that she wanted and needed to feel heard, cared for and lively again. Not only did it lift a heavy veil from her tone within my consulting room, it helped her to establish healthy boundaries between her mother and her. Also she connected with her husband in a new way. In the meantime he had entered therapy himself. It helped them both to deal with their unspoken personal histories, communicating and finding new ways in which they could support and love each other. Of course this didn't go without ups and downs, and Lauren wasn't transformed into a different person. But from then on emerging oppressive urges to clean helped her to become aware of unmet needs that she had kept within for too long. It instigated her to find other ways to feel good about herself, besides being a sparkle in someone else's eye. It helped her to find her voice for feelings that were left unspoken before.

***

Getting to the bottom of a conflicted emotion doesn't make it magically go away or provide an univocal picture of what to do next. In my opinion, powerless rage is not a conclusion, but an emotional reaction filled with frustration and aimed at regaining a sense of control, even if control seems to be nothing more than destroying the status quo. And Lauren's lonesome plight had become her internalised way of coping without running the risk of asking for help and getting no for an answer. What emotional awareness does, is help to see emotion in context and to differentiate between confounding factors. It helps to get a clear picture of "what belongs to me and what belongs to the other", what belongs to "then" and what belongs to "now", however disillusioning this might be in itself. Also it helps to get a grip on implicit modes of regulation that might have started to live a life of their own and have turned into symptoms. Emotions are unruly but vital sources of living, enabling us to flourish when not treated as pathogenic germs.

Notes

1 Installing a "countertransferential" sense of powerlessness in me as a therapist. Lauren never seemed to appeal wholeheartedly for help, as she presented herself as the psychologically gifted person that she also is.
2 Whereas fear can be described as a reaction to a threat from the outside, anxiety might be thought of as a reaction to a threat stemming from the inside.
3 To quote Marion Solomon: "When strong emotions arise and are not regulated within the containment and safety of a secure attachment, it becomes difficult to distinguish between impulses of anger, the arousal of anxiety, and early-learned defences against frightening and painful affect." Solomon, M. (2009). Emotion in romantic partners: Intimacy found, intimacy lost, intimacy reclaimed. In: Fosha, D., Siegel, D.J. & Solomon, M. (eds.), *The healing power of emotion: Affective neuroscience, development, and clinical practice.* New York & London: W.W. Norton & Company, 232–256.
4 It is only when obsessive compulsive behaviour gets so out of control that it interferes with the sense of self, that it becomes a psychological burden on its own. For example, when someone is aware of his life falling apart because of the detrimental impact that OCD has on relations, work and joy, but cannot withstand the need to repeat, then OCD becomes the enemy.
5 And how could you not be?

Chapter 7

On depression

When the emotional Maelstrom grinds to a halt

***

Sebastian had taken pills to calm himself down, preparing himself for a final jump off a huge student apartment building. He was desperate and saw no other way out, but was very scared at the same time. Standing on the roof, his fearful doubts got the better of him and he decided that he could not kill himself. With a mix of disillusionment and self-blame, he slowly walked down every step for eighteen floors. Standing on solid ground, he felt utterly lost. He went home.

During a three-week admittance to a psychiatric hospital, personal talks and antidepressive pills helped to suppress his suicidal tendencies. Sebastian had frequent appointments with an empathic psychiatric nurse, who discussed his conflicted wish to kill himself as something that could be understood instead of acted upon. Being a bright adolescent, Sebastian quickly picked up on this. He was dismissed from the ward and referred to the Dutch Psychoanalytical Institute for therapy aimed at gaining personal insight. I met Sebastian there.

***

Within sight but out of reach: on adolescent breakdown

Suicidal tendencies are not necessarily a sign of depression per se.[1] The impulse to commit suicide can have multiple determinants, both internally and externally, and it usually does. Tragic conflicts and losses in someone's personal history, thwarted emotional needs and vanished perspectives of the future can get entangled with self-destructive forms of shame or guilt. Unspoken fantasies of getting back at the other,[2] getting back at one's despised physical body[3] or getting back at life itself, might scaffold the wish to end one's life. And at the same time, fantasies of reuniting with lost loved ones might replace the process of mourning and can exert a pull into death. In adolescence especially, when there is an urgent need to integrate one's inner experiences in order to make decisions about the course of one's life, the viability of these emotional dynamics is put to the test. The psychological drive for separateness in adolescence might lead up to an unbearable conflict with unfinished business, getting in the way of securely feeling connected. This might happen when an adolescent experiences a conflict of loyalty to opposing parents, when he is confronted with a reality that is much more complex than a previously held worldview can contain or when he is at a complete loss concerning one's inner motives. These kind of conflicts hamper the ability to think about one's feelings and to feel one's thoughts through, leading up to primitive ways of regulating emotion.[4] In my experience, suicidal tendencies in adolescents are more often caused by an unspoken and constricting conundrum of emotional needs than by the all-encompassing deadening flatness of a vital depression. When integration seems impossible and the sense of emotional direction is lost, life can be too hard to deal with.[5]

***

Sebastian really had a lot going for him. I saw a bright young man, verbally gifted, with an intense hunger for contact but very conscious, even cautious, in his efforts not to be ponderous. Polite, articulate and friendly, learning to become a teacher and in a relationship with a girl one year older than him. A bright future seemed to be within sight, but for him it felt out of reach. He had reached a dead end in his efforts to reconcile his various emotional needs.

Despite his first competent appearance, I noticed myself wondering about his hurt and vulnerability. Sebastian made good use of my invitation to take the time to explore what was on his mind and what was going on in his heart. As months went by, a picture became clear of how he got so entangled and stuck. Born as the fourth child in a religious family of seven, Sebastian had distinguished himself with his Christian oratory. Already at an early age, he had spoken on several religious meetings, where he stood out and was praised for his inspiring words. Hearing him speak, I could surely understand why people had high hopes for him. But around four years ago, he suffered a crisis in his faith, leaving the dogmatic way of practising his religion behind him.[6] This was frowned upon by his mother and siblings, who were very devout in their wish to see him fulfil his religious potential. Also he was the only one of the seven children who wished to see his father again, who had moved away after divorcing his mother and had entered a new relationship. Father was not to be talked about within the family, as the subject immediately touched an open emotional nerve. So Sebastian's decision to see his father anyway wasn't merely frowned upon but thought of as downright erroneous. Though Sebastian felt very close to his mother and siblings, he also felt an unbridgeable gap between them and himself.

Two years ago one of his closest and most admired friends had unexpectedly killed himself. Sebastian told me that this friend had been very intelligent and sensitive and seemingly had succeeded in leaving orthodoxy and finding a personal meaningful way to practice his religion, something to which Sebastian himself also aspired. He was left with a lot of unanswered questions concerning the death of his friend. His own religious uncertainties further deepened his sense of disconnectedness.

And on top of all that, confronted with his own doubts about asking his girlfriend to marry him, something he felt obliged to do, he experienced both agitated and depressed moods. He struggled with the idea that his mood swings were proof of his misguided ways, blaming himself for feeling miserable. In what way could this ever be part of God's plan? Where did he fit in, while he was feeling so screwed up? The future seemed within reach, but he felt so utterly out of touch.

***

Neither fulfilment nor solace

***

Sebastian was obviously severely struggling, and he had been for quite some time. I learned that two days before his attempt to jump off his apartment building, he had had a talk with a counsellor, giving him practical advice on his relational issues. Sebastian felt very misunderstood but wasn't able to communicate that. Instead he gave up hope and decided that counselling couldn't help him. Immediately I felt a subcutaneous pressure not to make the same mistake. I should refrain from giving him advice or telling him what to do. But underneath his eloquent story, the emotional conflict was felt with his intense hunger for both contact and guidance. It dawned upon me that it was not the practicality of the advice given to Sebastian by the counsellor that was so disappointing, but the implicit message that advice was all that Sebastian needed to go back into the world again. He needed me not to become the next man to give him fatherly advice and send him away. I shouldn't be misled by his competent appearance and better tune in on his craving for contact. He had suffered from too many losses of male figures, whom he could relate to and possibly identify with. It had left him with an idealised image of what it means to be a man, for he should become a better man than his father and tragic friend had been. Understandably he struggled to live up to this image.[7]

On a basic emotional level, I felt that a vital part of his plight concerned saddening losses and an unconsoled need for a developmental male relationship. After the divorce, Sebastian hadn't seen his father for five years before deciding to seek contact again. In the eyes of his mother and siblings, father not only had needlessly hurt them but also went against God's will by leaving his wife and children. Sebastian had grown up with the idea that his father's behaviour was inexcusable and that he was led astray by the temptations of the flesh. When entering puberty, Sebastian's religiosity became more intense and orthodox, perhaps as a way of distancing himself from his own sexually maturing body. He had acquired a taste for sublimity. It offered him guidance and a certain prestige, but later on he felt more and more constricted by this dogmatic way of believing. At the depth of his crisis, he felt that God had left him but felt guilty for believing that at the same time. Maybe God hadn't left him, but why wasn't he able to feel Him close again? He had surrounded himself by Christian friends, most of them years older than himself. With these friends, he could talk openly about matters of religion and his personal experience. Sadly the friend that he most admired and felt close to had ended his life without leaving a note. At the time of his own suicide attempt, Sebastian had lost contact with the most important men in his life, leaving him at a loss with the emotional intricacies of his own developing manhood.

Within a two-dimensional representation of the Maelstrom model, Sebastian's struggle can be pictured as revolving around matters of separation and disconnection, leading up to a stagnation in his developing sense of self. A straightforward strategy for reunion seems fraught and impossible. Reunion with his father is a very sensitive matter, because of both familial and personal issues. The suicide of his friend had shockingly severed their bond and abruptly ended their mutual involvement. And his own suicidal thoughts further created distance in his feelings of closeness to God, as he considered them sinful. But to turn to the opposite direction and follow the tendency to part himself, denouncing his faith and his need for contact, seems equally impossible and self-destructive. It would feel like cutting a part out of his own flesh, mutilating the sense of who he has been and of who he might become.

Also Sebastian showed little inclination to turn his highly aversive sense of disconnectedness into something that he could blame someone else for. It is not uncommon for people to turn their sadness into anger, forcefully breaking free or attacking the object of their unsatisfying longing.[8] But for Sebastian that wouldn't fulfil his basic emotional need either. He didn't expect any good to come out of that, as it conflicted too much with the longing he felt.

Another way to deal with an emotion that is fruitlessly pressing for fulfilment in interaction with the outside world is to regulate the felt intensity of the emotion itself. In the Maelstrom model this is depicted utilising the third "sense of control" axis. But the ability to regulate internally, is also based on how the personal history of emotional contact is internalised.[9] Abrupt ruptures and unrepaired emotional mismatches might leave scar tissue that stands in the way of emotionally opening up to other people and break through self-condemning solitude. Sebastian used to find solace in his relationship with God and his belonging to a close-knit Christian community. But going through a religious crisis, he had to face up to the reality of his broken home defencelessly. This was something that he couldn't talk about within his family, for it was an open emotional wound for his mother and siblings. And the relationship with his father was still too precarious for Sebastian to confide in him. The one he had turned to, his friend whom he shared a personal crisis of faith with, had abruptly left him in the most irreversible way. Following him in his footsteps was as luring as it was blasphemous. It left Sebastian with a bleak deprivation of emotional needs and failing strategies for regulating his emotional state. Within the Maelstrom model, the way up towards integrated emotions and a renewed sense of control felt blocked for Sebastian.

***

A depressed parting from vital needs and emotional arousal: feeling no point in reaching out or moving on

***

Fortunately Sebastian was able to make good use of the sort of therapy that was offered. Over time, a whole range of matters concerning his personal life were covered. We talked about the bleakness of his feeling of disconnectedness, the discrepancy between feeling low and having high ambitions, his conflicted craving for recognition, dealing with his own unwanted guardedness in intimate relations, his sexuality laden with inner taboos, standing his ground in familial arguments and re-establishing open communication, troubles with how and what to study, his love for art, and finding a new way to practise his religion and experience sexuality and intimacy. Of course in reality it wasn't as neat a sequence as I suggest here, but grosso modo it outlines the progressive developmental line that made the therapeutic effort worthwhile. Concerning all these matters, Sebastian had elaborated thoughts and feelings that he shared with me in an increasingly open and playful manner. It helped him to get to know and own his emotional inner world, besides lessening the pressure he felt to live up to dogmatic ideals. And the fact that both his parents supported Sebastian's therapy, even though they were still at odds with each other, definitely helped to turn around the developmental stagnation.

***

Neuropsychoanalysis has come up with a new hypothesis of the basic mechanism of the inner dynamics of depression.[10] Thought to be a core concept of depression is a form of social loss, exposing someone to experience separation distress.[11] This first reaction is also known as the "protest" phase, in which reunion with the loved object is sought. One could say that this is the phase wherein someone is truly crying for help. But if reunion fails to happen, a second mechanism is activated aimed at stopping the futile outcry and preserving energy. Subjectively this transition is felt as "giving up hope" and is also known as the "despair" phase. An enduring miserable and sad feeling hinders the acceptance of the separation fully, in the sense that it also diminishes the urge to seek out new companions. Solms (2018) states that the emotional experience of giving up hope is part of an adaptive reaction that is advantageous for survival, as energy levels are lowered and attracting possibly unwanted attention is averted. As such, an evolutionary meaning is found on the function of a depressive state in the deeper layers of emotional processing. Narratively I describe this state as "gloomily waiting to be found" while longing sadness and hope are inhibited. This seems to be a paradoxical core of vital depression: it is an overwhelming sense of disconnectedness without feeling the slightest urge to reach out or move on. In the 2D Maelstrom model, this position is located in the right corner of Figure 7.1.

Sebastian's initial predicament is probably best understood as belonging to the "protest" phase of separation. Despite his problems, he hadn't given up hope completely. One could say that this was the thing that stood between him and a state of vital depression. When someone does give up hope, not only for interactional fulfilment of emotional needs but also for (co-)regulation of the inner emotional state, the transition towards "despair" is made. I would suggest this as an object-relational addition to the mechanism put forward by Solms on the inner dynamics of depression. For the other can concretely fulfil a vital need – by feeding, warming and providing familiarity, for example – but also can play an elemental role in the co-regulation of emotions, through empathy and reflection. When this latter process comes to a halt, one falls prey to one's own unmoderated emotional tendencies, leaving someone numb and forlorn. In the 3D Maelstrom model, this position is located at the bottom of the vortex, in the right corner below. From there it seems futile to turn to someone, get away from someone or set yourself in motion to try to find the way back up again.

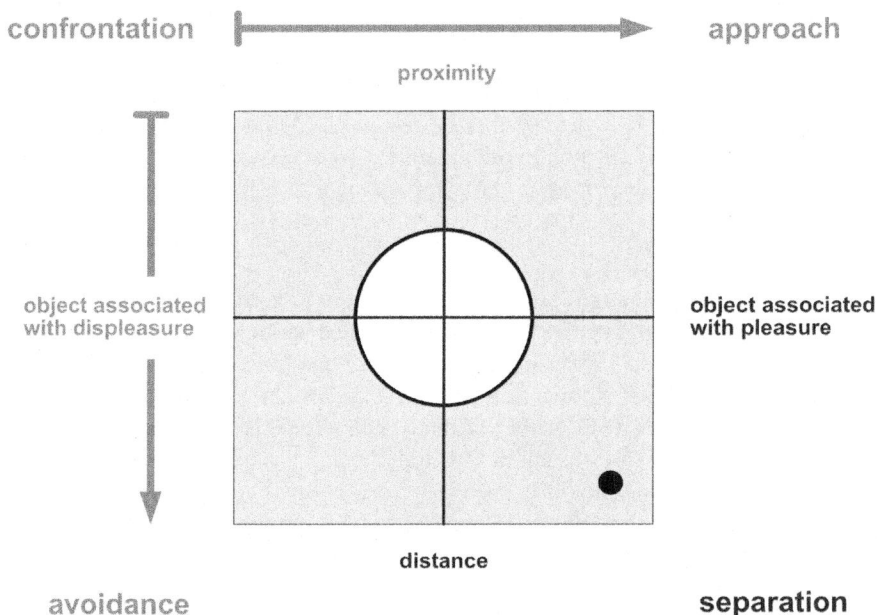

Figure 7.1 Feeling separated and stuck. When the action tendencies of craving (approach) and leaving (avoidance) appear pointless and when the emotional experience of separation can't be brought under the control of the self, living onwards might become a burden too big to bear.

And once this emotional state is relived repeatedly and internalised without reflection, it becomes a part of the implicit (lack of) expectations of social contact and of life itself. It forms the psychological basis for clinical depression, with its characteristic loss of motivation, energy and pleasure and a predisposition for toxic levels of shame and guilt. It feels like life is wasted on yourself. Awareness of vital needs is suppressed in order to sustain a biological state that is less energy-consuming and conspicuous. Emotional arousal drops as the psyche is set on "standby" instead of on "high alert". Metaphorically speaking, the emotional Maelstrom grinds to a halt, killing the emotional appetite for living life. Getting out of bed in the morning becomes pointless and every inclination to move only raises the question of "why bother?".

An addictive bypass

Because of its general clinical relevance, I will now try to link the topic of depression to addiction with a focus on basic emotional mechanisms, like a short intermezzo.

Another hypothesis stemming from neuropsychoanalysis states that drugs provide addicts with the feeling of fulfilment of basic emotional needs (Zellner, 2018). Drugs do so by acting on the subcortical emotional circuitry described by Panksepp and Biven in 2012. By engaging the SEEKING system and enhancing the effectiveness of dopamine, stimulant drugs can insert a core sense of enthusiasm in the world, provide energy (that is, optimise levels of arousal) to go out and have confidence that things can be done. Opioids on the other hand act on the PANIC/GRIEF system, temporarily relieving the addict of a sense of loneliness and insecurity. Together with the cognitive effects drugs have on learning mechanisms, these emotional aspects can broaden our understanding of the powerful grip that drugs have on the addicted mind.

These potent hypotheses can be translated to the theoretical framework of the Maelstrom model. So-called uppers like cocaine give the user a sense of vitality and invincibility, like being the winner of a contest, capable of overcoming every obstacle. Uppers seem to mediate the state that links aroused anger to a defeated adversary, thereby chemically producing the subjective impression that the battle has already been won and one can do anything. In the 2D Maelstrom model, this emotional transition is displayed as the upper arrow, leading up to joy after "chemical" victory. The focussed action tendency of "establishing dominance" subsides and makes place for high spirits wherein one wants and can do anything.

"Downers" on the other hand diminish the emotionally aroused state of separation distress and trick the mind to believe that the underlying need for reunion is already fulfilled. Drugs like heroine soothe unrest (arousal) and despair that spurs the tendency to seek contact and closeness, abolishing the urge to find a beloved other in the real world. When high on opioids, nothing else has to be done anymore. The chemical emotional message is that it is already OK, despite all rational considerations. The 2D Maelstrom model depicts this transition by the arrow on the right, pointing towards a blissful reunion.

Because modern drugs so potently can provide in enthusiastic energy and hope and are capable of relieving distressing feelings of loneliness, one can understand why people use drugs to self-medicate depressive feelings, especially when they can't put these feelings into words and think that their emotional state is incommunicable. Drugs chemically replace the subjective benefits of real achievements and loving relationships, virtually removing uncontrolled and unowned feelings of being worthless, stuck and abandoned. Of course, the effect is only temporary and the emotional neediness remains unmet in real emotional relationships.

When people chronically fall back on taking drugs to deal with mute and unmet emotional neediness, usually some feeling of shame emerges as drug use is considered to be an immature form of self-delusion. In essence it is make-believe. Most people have trouble acknowledging what they are doing when they do drugs. Addiction is often hidden and denied, for the self in the first place. Arguments like "I don't use that much" and "I could stop at any time" serve to disguise addiction as recreational use, keeping the emotional neediness out of awareness. This pseudo-neurotic defence doesn't hold up, as unsettling emotional lability breaks through after drugs run out. Then the need is felt to find and take new drugs, often in an impulsive and non-reflective state. Dependency on drugs is disavowed. The consideration of long-term goals takes second place and detrimental effects on relations, work and self-care can start to accumulate. When this "collateral damage" isn't recognised as the result of one's own inadequate coping, the unmet emotional neediness stays in the dark, continuing to exert its unsettling influence. As other people start to notice inappropriate drug use and emotional and behavioural dysregulation, the addicted person not seldom reaches a point wherein the hiding of drug use for others becomes more important than to get a grip on drug use personally. Critique on drug use can add to feelings of failure and abandonment that usually are part of the mute and unmet emotional mix that lures the addict into drug use in the first place. What might have started out as an attempt to keep unmet emotional neediness suppressed within the self can turn into a split between hidden drug-related behaviour and public non-drug-related behaviour, like two different conscious states "in parallel". The chemical bypass has become a relational taboo and keeps on undermining enduring positive feelings of connectedness and self-worth.[12]

Reconnect with life you can touch and that touches you

***

Sebastian didn't do drugs. Instead dormant fantasies of inspiring greatness served to bolster his affected sense of control and helped him to cope with intense and conflictual emotions. He needed these silent fantasies to regulate overwhelming emotional states. This invoked strong ambivalence towards these fantasies, as they were both comforting and surrounded by shame. On an intellectual level, they had spurred his development beyond his years. The praise from family, friends and teachers for his religious zeal and verbal brilliance had strengthened him, but later on they became troubling, as he began to find it hard to live up to these ideals in a personally satisfying way. His grades and academic performance were good, but the emotional need to excel put a heavy burden on him. It had worn him out and his self-confidence had sunk to a personal low, preventing him to upgrade his academic career.

On a personal level, these slumbering fantasies of venerable greatness prevented him to experience his subjective emotional self in full. Towards his inner world, he was always on the lookout, vigilantly registering every inner shift. He felt that he had to keep his inner motives in check in order to become the man who he felt he needed to be. This idealised self-image had guided him towards personal empowerment and social connectedness, but it had done so at the expense of his physical spontaneity and mental freedom. It had solidified his mistrust against uncensored emotions that linked his bodily needs to personal strivings. The continuing flow of emotional experiences always could produce feelings that were incompatible with this soothing idealised self-image. So repeatedly, when he looked into his own heart, the most disturbing thing he felt was that he wasn't good enough, a disappointment in disguise, a sinner of flesh and blood. This he had to fight continuously within himself, like a never-ending battle. Instead of experiencing his unruly emotions as an indispensable part of his inner dynamics, Sebastian tended to see them as deceptive urges that not only could led him astray but also could prove that he was a bad person. A good person shouldn't have intense carnal or competitive feelings, he thought. No wonder that it took a lot of his strength to continuously keep them in check. Lengthy periods of low energy were one of his most enduring and complicated symptoms.

What started out as an empowering and soothing personal ideal had become a draining and merciless self-image that left little room for spontaneous emotions. Therapy was about discovering the variety of his inner emotions, in order to strengthen a sense of self that is embedded in communicable bodily feelings and that is fuelled by vital energy. Gradually Sebastian let go of the overstretched parts of his idealised self-image. He reconnected to bodily feelings and related to them in a new way. He found new energy to take part in life. He acquainted himself with the various sources of his weariness, so that his weariness became a signal that emotionally something was stirring up. And instead of pursuing an ethereal ideal, Sebastian chose to change his academic study, bringing into practice what he most wanted to do. He grew to be a man of flesh and blood. With a taste for sublimity, of course.

***

Notes

1 See for example Jacobs Hendel, H. (2018). *It's not always depression: Working with the change triangle to listen to the body, discover core emotions, and connect to your authentic self.* New York: Spiegel & Grau.
2 Not seldom accompanied by secretive images of grieving others at one's own grave, filled with remorse and regret.
3 Like capital punishment inflicted on the hated body by the observing, reflective part of the self.

4 See Chapter 8 on "Developmental Issues in Normal Adolescence and Adolescent Breakdown" in: Fonagy, P., Gergely, G., Jurist, E. & Target, M. (2002). *Affect regulation, mentalization, and the development of the self.* New York: Other Press.

5 My dear colleague Lisette Daenen once told me that in adolescence the wish for death, as in suicide, often is an attempt to hide "not knowing how to live". In my personal experience, therapy with depressed adolescents not seldom feels existential, as in helping with figuring out "how to live".

6 He had developed an aversion to dogma, he explained.

7 As his therapist, I also got a feel of "all the high hopes" that surrounded and pervaded him. I should become the "hoped for" therapist, who didn't make the mistakes other professionals did. I felt that I should be perfectly able to understand the things he wasn't able to say in words. In an attempt to make this dynamic eligible for discussion, I told Sebastian in an early stage of therapy that it was not a question "if", but "when" I was going to get it wrong and disappoint him. For out therapeutic alliance to work, I needed him to pay attention to feelings of being misunderstood, as would I. Explicitly I invited him to talk about it when it happened, instead of dealing with it alone. There was something of bewilderment in his eyes, but he agreed. And he did.

8 In Kleinian terms one could say that the good object absent is the bad object present. See for instance O'Shaughnessy, E. (1964). The absent object. *Journal of Child Psychotherapy,* 1(2), 34–43. In other words: "You are no good when you are not here."

9 Think of Sidney Blatt's differentiation between anaclitic ("overly dependent") and introjective ("defensively separated") depression here, as two premature forms of boosting the sense of control. Blatt, S.J. (1974). Levels of object representation in anaclitic and introjective depression. *The Psychoanalytic Study of the Child,* 29, 107–157.

10 See for an accessible chapter: Solms, M. (2018). Depression in neuropsychoanalysis: Why does depression feel bad? In: Spagnolo, R. (ed.), *Building bridges: The impact of neuropsychoanalysis on psychoanalytic clinical sessions.* London & New York: Routledge, 39–54.

11 In the Maelstrom model, this is specified as an increase in physical or psychological distance that stands in the way of fulfilling interaction.

12 Heinz Kohut coined the terms "horizontal and vertical splitting". In horizontal splitting, the frustrated need to gratify infantile emotional impulses is partly repressed into the unconscious. This is the basis of a neurotic structure of the personality. In vertical splitting, this subjective need lives on in a parallel part of the personality that alternates with a part of the personality that adheres to the reality principle. It is the part that impulsively seeks to gratify infantile emotional needs and wishes without the restraint of reality that gives rise to overt pathological behaviour. See Kohut, H. (2001). *The analysis of the self: A systematic approach to the psychoanalytic treatment of narcissistic personality disorders.* Madison, CT: International Universities Press, Inc. (first published in 1971).

Part III

No emotion, no sense

Chapter 8

On emotions, the self and the mind

How personality is organised by integrating emotions

Looking at the Maelstrom model, one could get the impression that there is a fairly straightforward relation between emotional intensity and action (versus thinking). A feeble sense of internalised control is related to a low tolerance of arousal, leading up to high emotional intensity under stress and impulsive actions. But there is more to say about that, as every model is only a simplified representation of a part of reality. Emotional hyperarousal doesn't necessarily lead to emotional acting out, but can also trigger a broad range of defence mechanisms through which the psyche tries to uphold the sense of control and to realign internal and external flows of information. Defence mechanisms change the experience and perception of inner felt states and of outer reality in order to reduce the emotional upheaval to a manageable level. Defence mechanisms are therefore indispensable for everyday functioning, but they are also at odds with reality testing. Generally speaking, one can say that mature defence mechanisms distort inner and outer reality less than immature mechanisms.

Defence mechanisms come in all shapes and sizes (Freud, 1992, originally published in 1937). Personality is characterised by the inborn strength of the emotional drives and the predominant type of defence mechanisms that is used. This being said, it raises the question of whether we can specify the influence of personality organisation on basic emotional functioning. In this chapter, I will present a schematic overview of such an integration.

Underneath my line of reasoning lies the assumption that emotional experiences that are too intense to process can lead up to a wide variety of psychological defences and symptoms that are difficult to connect to their emotional origins. First I will propose three psychodynamic fault lines that can curb the coherent experience of an emotional state when the level of arousal is too high. These fault lines roughly coincide with the psychoanalytic differentiation between neurotic, borderline/narcissistic and psychotic defences. In distinctive ways, they can form a watershed in experiencing, expressing and integrating subjective emotions. As the full-blown subjective intensity of basic emotion is hampered, the evolutionary adaptive function of basic emotions withers. They no longer inform the self on the immediate state of the self in relation to the world, and further conscious reflection is stunned. Especially the adaptive functions of basic emotions (as conceptualised in the Maelstrom model) regarding how to deal with vital pleasure and displeasure, the handling of proximity and distance and the preservation of a sense of control are compromised. The three fault lines compromise these adaptive functions of basic emotions in specific ways. For example, a neurotic defence thwarts the handling of proximity and distance differently than a borderline/narcissistic defence does.

But first I will introduce this new concept of psychodynamic fault lines in more detail.

Three psychodynamic fault lines that can curb the integrated experience of emotions

The first fault line is the gateway between actual *emotional experience* and what can be incorporated into the *personal narrative*. It is the tension between basic emotional needs and wishes ("the id") and what can be acknowledged by the self and communicated to others ("the ego and superego"). It also alludes to the Freudian dynamics between conscious and unconscious material and the Cartesian schism between body and mind, given that the body is verbally mute[1] and the mind has representational language. As emotions operate in both spheres, the splitting of these spheres can serve defensively to minimise the full subjective experience of the emotional state. *"I am fine", says someone who would actually feel quite bad if he hadn't "forgotten" all about his dentist appointment.* In the case of repression, bodily felt emotional states are denied access to verbal consciousness because of their intense and conflictual qualities. This is considered to be the most important neurotic defence mechanism. Unwanted emotional tendencies are isolated in the experiential sphere, and attention is subsequently defensively diverted. In the short term it deflects overwhelming conflict from subjective experience, but in the long term it corrodes the coherence of the sense of self. Because no defence is full proof, some residual anxiety and shame remains that also refers to the act of defence itself.[2] The impact on reality testing consists primarily of distortions in the perception and recognition of the subjective inner world. Of course these inner blind spots have an inevitable effect on the perception of outer reality, as attention is restricted and biased in order not to re-experience the repressed emotional state. Motives for repression are in principle knowable from a reflective point of view.

The second fault line is the boundary between *self and other*. As basic emotions always refer to interrelating aspects of self and other, the subjective experience of the emotional state can defensively be split on this fault line.[3] When an emotion is overwhelming, both the personal and relational aspects of the emotion can be distorted in order to protect the self against a state of disintegration. *"I don't feel bad; it is you who is bad!", so a heated accusation states.* The self-informative aspect of emotion is silenced, as is the interactive appeal (that is presented as a factual statement instead). The boundary between self and other is the prime territory of borderline and narcissistic defences, which inextricably impacts the personal narrative of what is bodily felt as well. Prime examples are projection and introjection, whereby emotional states are mentally transferred from self to other or from other to self. Reality testing is especially weakened regarding the boundary between self and other, often resulting in confusion of what is part of the self and what is part of the other.

The third fault line demarcates *whether visceral state and sensory perception are merged into meaningful emotional experience or not.* This is fundamental for the bodily anchoring of subjective experience in the spatial and temporal characteristics of live interaction (that is, in the here-and-now). The developmental blueprint of this ability is formed by the moment-to-moment attuned interaction between mother and infant in the first year of life (Stern, 1985; Tronick, 1989).[4] This fundamental structuring process can be compromised when the psyche fails to integrate the ongoing flow of visceral experience and sensory perception, as is the case in dissociative fragmentation and psychotic decompensation (Gumley, Gillham, Taylor & Schwannauer, 2013). When emotions aren't integrated as intra- and interpersonal phenomena that are bound by interactional rhythms in space and time, they might operate as disembodied and alien agents that mentally can transcend space and time.[5] The coherence of meaning is accordingly shattered. Reality testing is severely distorted for the sake of preserving a minimal sense of self. When reality testing isn't based on "meaning making" emotions but hinges primarily on raw visceral state, then sensory perception gets distorted and *hallucinations* occur (to fit the visceral state). When reality testing hinges primarily on sensory awareness, then visceral sentience is distorted and *dissociation* occurs (to deal with sensory perception). In both cases, subjective experience is unglued from ongoing intersubjective processes.

When these "proto-emotional fragments" (or "id-entities") are projected onto the outer world, this gives rise to hallucinations and delusions. *"Evil is after me and watches me all the time", a psychotic defence states.* Imagery impresses as reality and television screens can contain secret messages. A cosmic plot enfolds wherein *"I have to fulfil a special role".* One becomes a lone actor on the alienating stage of one's own making.[6]

When these "unintegrated proto-emotional stances" are introjected back into the inner world, dissociative states of identification might ensue. *"Beatrice is not here, you are with me now", points to a dramatic switch in dissociative identity states.* Though they originate in rudimentary emotional subjectivity, these unintegrated states operate as separate reified agents. Dissociative identity disorder is claimed to be caused not by a multiplication of personalities, but by a lack of integration of various subjective states (Nicolai, 1997; Spiegel, 2008). The self is fragmented into a cast of actors, who consecutively try to cope with an ongoing reality that can't be dealt with by a single one of them alone.

The third fault line, which is akin to the psychoanalytic notion of psychotic defences, is compromised when inner fragmentation and delusional projection occur. It has an inevitable impact on the capacity to verbally reflect on the whole of subjective experience (the first fault line), while also the boundaries between self and other are blurred (the second fault line, which differentiates between me and not-me). However, there is an intrinsic difference that seems to be caused by the absence of meaningful emotional interaction altogether. Emotional motives are not only split intra- or interpersonally, neither are they split horizontally or vertically (Kohut, 2001, originally published in 1971), but they seem to be cut out "circularly". When emotions are unhinged from space and time, it seems as if they are surgically removed and without subjective ownership. "Psychotic/dissociative" interactions don't have a "neurotic or borderline/narcissistic feel" to them, as the ongoing relational dynamics inform communication only incoherently. Inimitable turns in intrapersonal experience and interpersonal contact often impress as devoid of meaning and bizarre, as they frighten and alienate the self and others.

In sum, we unknowingly defend ourselves against overwhelming emotional experience in three ways. The unbearable content can be *hidden within us* (the neurotic defence), it can be *projected onto other persons* (the borderline/narcissistic defence) or it can be *fragmented and dispersed* all over the place, inside and outside (the dissociative/psychotic defence).

These three fault lines are developmental hurdles to be taken before a mature, emotionally reflective perspective can arise. Especially in affective interactions in the first years of life, the foundations are laid for the merging of visceral state and sensory perception into communicable and meaningful emotions. Within live and attuned interaction the temporal and spatial aspects of emotion become firmly anchored.[7] In its wake the ability to differentiate between self and other grows, as does the ability to "mind the body" and reflect on one's inner experiences. When shocking events stir up overwhelming amounts of emotional arousal, psychological defences operate along these three fault lines to minimise subjective turmoil. By doing so, the need-fulfilling tendencies of the basic emotions are reduced. The pleasure principle – that is the innate tendency to focus and react to objects that are associated with pleasure and displeasure for the benefit of self-preservation and reproduction – is compromised. When the coordinated interaction tendencies of the basic emotions are disrupted, some typical symptomatic patterns of dysregulation emerge along the three axes of the Maelstrom model. People can have a hard time dealing with vital pleasure and displeasure, handling proximity and distance and preserving a sound sense of control. Struggling with these matters, people have a hard time figuring out who they are and discerning what they really feel and need.

Now a window opens itself through which we can see the interconnection among psychodynamic development, basic emotional functioning and a wide range of psychopathology. A three-by-three matrix can be contrived that relates these developmental fault lines with the three essential functions of basic emotions according to the Maelstrom model. In the resulting nine sections, some typical symptomatic clusters will be described. By doing so, tentative relations are formulated between a variety of symptoms and unintegrated emotional experiences. Hopefully, the clinical logic of these examples further illustrate the primacy of the

Table 8.1 Nine symptomatic clusters: patterns of emotional (dis)integration that are indicative of personality organisation

Basic emotional functions > Psychodynamic fault lines V	Dealing with vital pleasure and displeasure	Handling proximity and distance	Preserving the sense of control
Gateway between emotional experience and personal reflection	*Inner conflict about pleasure and displeasure*	*Inner conflict about proximity and distance*	*Inner conflict about control*
• Neurotic • Intrapsychic • Repression • Cluster C	Anger and fear inhibited: **Naively romantic** Joy and sadness inhibited: **Intimacy problems**	Joy and anger inhibited: **Conflict avoidant and overly worried** Sadness and fear inhibited: **Too up-front and overly active**	Lack of control and emotional underregulation: **Overly sensitive and nervous** Forced control and emotional overregulation: **Perfectionism and rigid composure**
Boundary between self and other	*Relational issues with pleasure and displeasure*	*Relational issues with proximity and distance*	*Relational issues with control*
• Borderline/narcissistic • Interpersonal • Projection and introjection • Cluster B	Joy and sadness towards self ("with") Anger and fear towards other ("against") **Self "all good" and other "all bad"** Anger and fear towards self ("against") Joy and sadness towards other ("with") **Other "all good" and self "all bad"**	Emotional approach of self and emotional avoidance of other **Push and segregate** Emotional avoidance of self and emotional approach of other **Pull and fuse**	Self is in control ("above") Other lacks control ("under") **Dominance** Self lacks control ("under") Other is in control ("above") **Submission**
Merger of visceral state and sensory perception into emotion	*Disintegration of pleasure and displeasure*	*Disintegration of proximity and distance*	*Disintegration of control*
• Dissociative/psychotic • Impersonal • Fragmentation and dispersal • Cluster A	Distortions in visceral experience (being overwhelmed or neglected) Severe mismatch of pleasure and pain (in self) and good and bad experience (with other) **Depersonalisation and compartmentalisation of inner states of consciousness**	Distortions in sensory perception (being overstimulated or deprived) Subjective experience unhinged from space and time and confusion of mental imagery with perceived reality **Derealisation and hallucination and delusion**	**Dissociative identification** with powerful "big" parts and vulnerable "small" parts **Delusion of grandeur** (self as omnipotent) and **delusion of control** (feelings, thoughts and actions are not deemed as one's own) **Disintegration of the sense of being an embodied subject**

processing of basic emotions for understanding psychopathology, as it links various psychological problems to (combinations of) unintegrated emotions.

The gateway between emotional experience and personal reflection

This is the first of the three psychodynamic fault lines and the classic psychoanalytic realm where most people think of when they think of psychoanalysis. It is about the tension felt when one takes the time to freely reflect on what is going on inside, while trying to suspend critical censorship. It is about what drives you, about needs and wishes, fantasy and impulses, regardless of social acceptance. Here the Freudian slip (of the tongue) might give a disturbing peek into an affective core that is mainly concerned with vital pleasure. It is about processes that we call "basic emotional".

The interplay of the four basic emotions in the Maelstrom model serves to coordinate dyadic interaction when vital needs are at stake. Differentiated interaction with others who are associated with either pleasurable fulfilment versus unpleasurable infringement comes about through the orchestrated workings of joy, sadness, fear and anger. When the psychological integration of these emotions is impaired, difficulties arise when dealing with matters of pleasure versus displeasure, handling proximity versus distance and preserving a sense of control.

When it comes to dealing with pleasure, full experiential and narrative ownership of joy and sadness are imperative. (See Figure 2.2 to recapture this aspect of the Maelstrom model.) Without the safety and freedom to feel bodily rooted yearning and satisfaction (that is without toxic levels of shame, guilt or disgust), the subjective experience of pleasure is impoverished. When joy (for example in the form of lust or play) is prohibited, spontaneous excitement is quarantined within the body and accordingly suppressed. Whether this inner conflict gives rise to overt symptoms (such as postural rigidity) or not, the mind has become restricted in navigating through matters of pleasure. The self is denied an emotional compass point that could lead to personal fulfilment in the outer world. It spells trouble for finding and keeping a fulfilling sexual relationship as well as lively and fun friendships. In Table 8.1, this is coined as *intimacy problems.*

Inhibited anger and fear form another example that can cause problems, particularly in dealing with displeasure. Think of someone who was raised in a family wherein expression of anger ("opposition") or fear ("weakness") was not welcomed because it was "not needed", while joy and sadness ("loyalty") were reinforced. It paints a deceptive picture of an idyllic upbringing that can imbue someone with an enduring inner conflict about the subjective experience of anger and fear. If the identification with these parental ideals is strong, the expression of subjective displeasure gets conflicted. A *naively romantic*, idealising and pleasing interpersonal attitude can become part of the personality organisation.

The ability to handle interpersonal proximity and distance also depends on the free access to basic emotions. Joy and anger are indispensable emotions when dealing with close and immediate interaction. In them, the psychoanalytic emphasis on sexuality and aggression resounds. When for example a child grows up with traumatised parents, who inadvertently distance themselves when the child expresses intense dyadic joy or anger, the integration of these emotions runs the risk of being blocked. When the child doesn't understand the parental withdrawal and unreflectively links it with his needs for physical and emotional intimacy and for self-assertiveness, relational proactivity will be depleted. Inner conflicts involving shame and guilt turn up when intimacy or confrontation come near. The proactive stance that ensues from joy and anger is repressed. When vital bodily experience is stunned, the mind will seek refuge in ideation instead of in relational experiencing. The mind is experienced as near, while the experiencing body is distanced. And accordingly, the mind will wander into *worry and conflict avoidance*, instead of the body coming into action.

While the expression of joy and anger might impress as proactive, sadness and fear seem to imply a reactive stance.[8] Interpersonal distancing by a young child (despite its own attachment needs) is not seldom a reaction to mismatches in emotional responsiveness and lack of reparations by the caregiver. Of course, children also want to venture into the world by themselves, but then the attention is on the world, not solely on the dyadic relationship. When the unfamiliar is too unruly to control, fear emerges and with it comes the cry for the protective and comforting caregiver.[9] Such emotional refuelling is elemental, and it is seriously jeopardised when fear and sadness aren't acknowledged. With the blockage of the physical experience of fear and sadness, the mind tends to develop the sense of autonomy on a fragile and feeble base. One tends to react regardless of personal well-being, becoming *too up-front and overly active*.

Also the sense of control itself might become compromised by the fault line between body and mind. The idea of the body "having a mind of its own" illustrates precisely that. Like the five-year-old child who was frightened to go onto the ice for the first time, said: "I really want to go, but my feet don't want to." One could metaphorically say that the child's body reacted *sensitively and nervously*. Fortunately this child was learning that his feet are also part of his "I". However obvious this might seem, a smooth interface between body and mind isn't easily established and maintained. Physical sensations aroused by unacknowledged emotions might bewilder the self, and the abiding regulatory attempts might contribute to the formation of physical symptoms. Somatisation is an example of not being in total control of the body, which is something to which the mind aspires that defends itself against overwhelming emotional experience by reducing it to the sphere of the body. In extremis, this leads to *emotional perfectionism*, aimed at controlling emotional arousal up to the level of *unwavering composure*.

The boundary between self and other

While neurotic repression renders conflicted emotions into the intrapsychic realm of the dynamic unconscious, basic emotions get lost in translation through the interpersonal borderline/narcissistic mechanisms of projection and introjection.

I call this the second psychodynamic fault line. When emotional regulation operates on this level of personality organisation, unregulated aspects of basic emotions are projected into others. The revolving interactions take shape along implicit relational patterns that implicitly serve emotion regulation (Ladan, 2014). In a classic analytic setting, these self-evident patterns can only be discerned through attentive mutual observation, instead of mere interpretation by the analyst. More modern techniques focus on recognising, regulating and owning one's own emotions, for example through mentalisation-based treatment (Allen & Fonagy, 2006) or dialectic behavior therapy (Linehan, 1993). Whatever the therapeutic approach, the aim is to improve the regulation of emotions and lessen both identity diffusion and the use of primitive defences (Kernberg, 1967).

So instead of internal conflicts, all sorts of relational issues arise. The dyadic relation between self and other is now prime territory for the owning and disowning of emotional states of mind. The two basic emotions that associate an object with pleasure are joy and sadness. When these emotions are confined to the self, while anger and fear are felt towards the other, a characteristic split ensues. Then the self becomes represented as "*all good*" while the other is represented as "*all bad*". This is the fundamental relational split that Melanie Klein first wrote about in 1929. It instigates black-or-white thinking and an attitude of "when you are not with me, you are against me". Ambivalence can't be tolerated. It can also be the other way around, when one confines all angry and fearful feelings to the self. Then a representation ensues of the self as "all bad" and the other as "all good". As both positions are severely biased attitudes towards the other, they often alternate to compensate for the untenable framing of the other. "*I am so sorry for yelling at you. You're not to blame: it is all me!*" Because this framing also is untenable, a vicious relational cycle of blame and self-blame might ensue. When reality is simplified and distorted, reality has a way of bringing complexity back again.

The way that proximity and distance are handled shows another characteristic clinical feature of the borderline/narcissistic personality organisation. This is particularly so when emotions leading to approach are irreconcilable with emotions that are leading to avoidance. When the self is taken over by fear, defensive anger or parting sadness, people tend to *push and segregate*,[10] as relating to the other is deemed as damaging to the self. The other is associated with something that is unbearable for the self. Vice versa, when the self is seized with joy, offensive anger or craving sadness, people tend to *pull and fuse* in order to internalise (projected) strength and consolation. Then the other is associated with something that is of vital importance to the self. And like the "all good/all bad" polarity, this polarity can also turn into an alternating pattern of push and pull, of segregation and fusion.

When issues of control are split along the boundary between self and other, another typical dichotomy unfolds. Control located in the self is equated with a lack of control in the other (and vice versa). Relationships become power struggles, characterised by *dominance or submission*. To be "above or under" the other becomes an enduring feature of interpersonal dynamics.[11]

Notice that two of the dimensions identified as emotional polarities along the boundary between self and other form the famous rose of Leary, also known as the interpersonal circumplex (Leary, 1957). He placed the dominance–submission dimension on the vertical axis, while the against–with dimension is placed horizontally. These axes are now also known as agency and communion (Horowitz, 2004).

I wish to add a small note on defining *idealisation and devaluation*. I reckon it is important to differentiate between the "all good/all bad" split versus the phenomena of idealisation and devaluation. In clinical situations, idealisation and devaluation are usually related to more complex processes. Idealisation can be thought of in emotional terms as the focus on joy towards the other, with whom the interaction might actually have threatening features. Devaluation can be thought of as the focus on anger, to defend against unacknowledged feelings of sadness caused by unmet attachment needs. As such, idealisation and devaluation can be understood as an attempt to bolster the sense of control, through the relational delineation of goodness versus badness and control versus lack of control. This conceptualisation also bears resemblance to the notions of positive and negative transference.

The merger of visceral state and sensory perception into emotion

The third psychodynamic fault line contains an essential premise of the Maelstrom model, namely that this kind of basic emotions operates at the juncture of the internal state and peripheral environment.[12] It is through the process of developing an emotion that our attention is focussed on matters of vital importance and imbue them with valence (as a precursor of meaning). Solms and Panksepp (2015) further make a convincing case for affect as the fundamental source of consciousness, on which I shall elaborate later on. It shouldn't come as a surprise then that in this realm of the psychotic personality organisation, at this merger of visceral state and sensory perception, we come across symptoms that seem to lack emotional meaning, that impress as impersonal, that distort consciousness, that lack orientation in space and time, that confuse inner imagery with outer reality and that ultimately disintegrate the sense of being one's body. See, for an elucidating object-relational formulation of this psychological state (Ogden, 1989).

The attentive reader might have noticed that in Table 8.1 two "psychotic" defence mechanisms are mentioned that I have labelled *fragmentation and dispersal*. Since Bion (1957), fragmentation is widely regarded as a defining element of psychotic defences. Personally I believe his following "excessive projection of these fragments of personality into external objects" to be a one-sided perspective that was instigated by Bion's wish to link it to Melanie Klein's concept of projective identification. It exclusively focusses on the movement outwards, as do other concepts like "primitive evacuation". But what is fragmented is not merely the inside scattering outwards; it is the surface between the inside and outside that is *dispersed* both outwards and inwards. Elements that are pre-symbolically integrated by the development of emotion are now left without further binding and without anchoring in the inner and outer realm. Regarding the subjective experience of the internal world, this means prolonged distortions in visceral experience, disintegration of the subcortical registration of vital pleasure and displeasure, and in the ongoing flow of consciousness. This inward lack of binding results in compartmentalisation, while the outward lack of binding results in (hallucinatory) evacuation. I propose the term *dispersal* because it doesn't prioritise an inward or outward movement: it refers to both. Also it refers to an absence of mind, though an absence of emotions "that make sense" would be more correct. Other primitive defences, such as disavowal and withdrawal from reality, as well as more comprehensive delusions, can be understood as resulting from fragmentation and dispersal.[13]

Problems with the experience of visceral states lead to problems dealing with vital pleasure and displeasure. This might occur in cases where people are severely and extensively emotionally overwhelmed or neglected. Especially when there is a severe mismatch between experiences of pleasure and pain, and both good and bad experiences with the other (for example, in case of sexual abuse by a family member), a shutting down of visceral experience in the form of *depersonalisation* might ensue. Further psychological processing of these kind of experiences might lead to *compartmentalisation of inner states of consciousness*. Pleasure and pain then are experienced in separate experiential spheres. Unintegrated and objectified experiences of pain can give rise to the idea of reified evil forces (for instance the devil or demons) inhabiting the inside or luring from the outside.

Severe distortions in sensory perception as a result of overstimulation or deprivation disintegrate spatial and temporal orientation and the handling of proximity and distance. Subjectively this is first experienced as an alienating sense of *derealisation*. It is important to note that overstimulation and deprivation are not inherent features of (a lack of) outer stimulation, but always have to be connected to (a lack of) constitutional stimulus filtering and the need for stimulation. Schizophrenia is known to run in families. In Panksepp's terminology, it is related to hyperactivation of the dopamine-dependent SEEKING system. This being said, we all know examples of severe overstimulation and deprivation that have led to loss of orientation in space and time and to confusion of mental imagery with perceived reality. Post-traumatic stress disorder is infamous for its repetitive reliving of the traumatic past, which is subjectively experienced as "near and now". These trauma related re-experiences are phenomenologically related to hallucinations (Hardy et al., 2005) and are associated with peritraumatic dissociation (Lensvelt-Mulder et al., 2008). Even though a trauma-related re-experience differs from psychotic experience in its dependence on memory traces, their underlying processes seem to have a lot in common. Psychotic experiences that are more elaborate and are built in the organisation of the personality can give rise to *hallucinations and delusions* that have a bizarre coherence of their own.

Disintegration of the sense of control has the most profound and disturbing impact on the ongoing flow of being. These symptoms are the most eligible to be equated with plain madness for most people. Within the inner subjective realm, successive identification with compartmentalised states of consciousness results in *dissociative identification*, both with powerful "big" parts and vulnerable "small" parts. These various "parts of the personality" lack integration, which is the ultimate goal in the treatment of these patients. In the outer realm, people resort to delusions in order to preserve a sense of control, however idiographic. During a *delusion of grandeur*, the self is experienced as omnipotent. The sky is the limit for what is felt to be under personal control. The reverse side probably would be the *delusion of control*. Then someone is convinced that his feelings, thoughts and action are not his own and that there is an external person (or force) who inserts them. This type of delusion is closely linked to persecutory delusions.

The tangible interface between the inner and outer realms is where the body ends and the world begins. Disintegration can also involve this intermediate realm, which results in the *disintegration of the sense of being an embodied subject*.[14] Fragility of the sense of being an embodied subject is associated with a wide variety of pathology, ranging from dissociative, psychotic and body-related, such as conversion, anosognosia, automutilation and anorexia.

Three interrelated sections of consciousness: emotion, self and mind

So now we have a wide-angle view on emotion, integration, regulation and psychopathology, based on a synthesis between personality organisation and emotion theory. Notions of consciousness and unconsciousness are interwoven and are notoriously hard to disentangle. Freud himself used both his topographical model (delineating levels of consciousness) and his structural model (delineating levels of processing drive energy) to get to a more accurate account of what was going on in the psychic life of his patients. His "iceberg" and his "egg" are attempts to reconcile these two fundamental aspects of the psyche. Recent neuroscientific findings on preverbal consciousness of affective states and suggestions for a psychoanalytic reformulation of drive theory seem to turn the iceberg upside-down.[15] One can imagine that revising such basic parts of psychoanalytic theory generates a lot of turmoil under professionals.

The outlines of Table 8.1 and especially the reformulation of defence mechanisms into psychodynamic fault lines offer the possibility to recapture some of the intricacies of consciousness. Figure 8.1 could be read as an additional fourth column in Table 8.1, but a separate display allows for a more precise elaboration of bottom-up and top-down processing. The figure shows how I envision three interrelated sections of consciousness.

I start with the notion that the psychodynamic fault lines can function defensively when under stress but that they are also the birth grounds of these psychic structures we call emotion, self and mind. Especially the differentiation between affective and cognitive consciousness seems to fit into this picture, as well as the concept of nested brain-mind hierarchies (Panksepp & Biven, 2012).

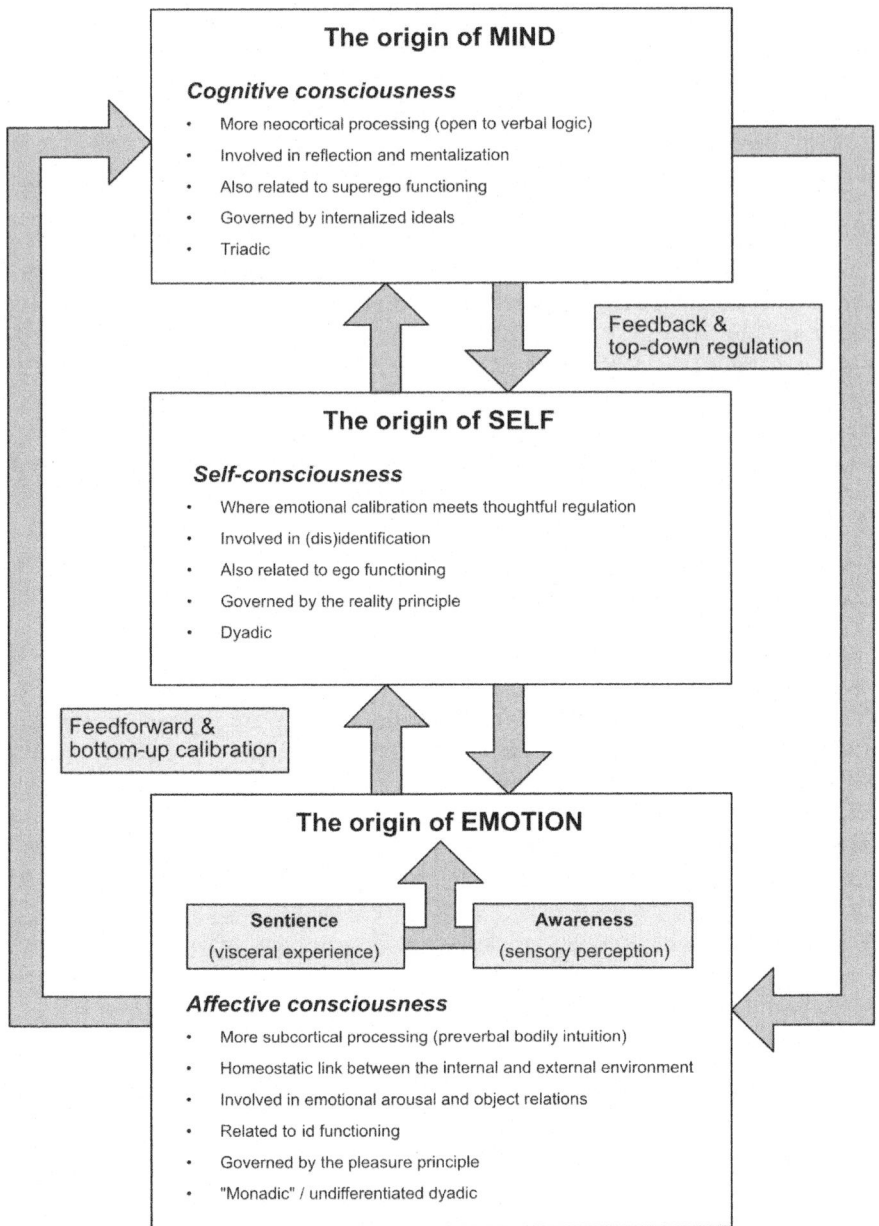

Figure 8.1 Three interrelated sections of consciousness: emotion, self and mind.

Only I reckoned that the concept of self-consciousness has not been given sufficient attention, the development of which is such an integral part of psychoanalysis and that has so many intra- and interpersonal vicissitudes.[16] Based on both psychoanalytic and neuroscientific insights into personality organisation, the origin of the self is positioned between the origin of emotion and the development of mind.[17]

A main psychoanalytic premise in this book is that affect precedes (cognitive) ideation. So we consider the base of consciousness to be the development of emotion out of physical and social needs that urge us to maintain internal homeostasis within an unpredictable outer world.[18] This is *affective consciousness* as is conceived of by Panksepp and which he meticulously linked to subcortical networks. (For practical usability, I propose to use the word *sentience* for the immediate consciousness of visceral experience, while *awareness* is indicative of consciousness as a result of sensory perception.) Affective consciousness lets you know that you *feel* something, through the use of body language. It also includes the immediate focus of attention on internal and external processes that are vital for your survival and reproduction. It is affective consciousness through which we recognise salience and that helps us distinguish what is important from what can be left unattended. In Freud's structural model, we are now in the sphere of the id, which is governed by the pleasure principle. Object relations are characterised by a "monadic" stance, by which I mean that the lack of discrimination between self and other results in an undifferentiated dyadic scenario.[19] Embedded in this "one-ness" (that consists of the vital first relation), the baby survives and thrives. Without this relational "one-ness", the infantile psyche disintegrates and infants might actually perish.[20] No one-ness can actually become none-ness.

With the discovery of the object as a separate entity, the notion of a separate self comes into existence. Here the foundations of the boundary between self and other are laid. This is the sphere of *self-consciousness*. Object relations can now be characterised as dyadic as the mother is understood as "not me", as an actual other. Through the bonds of attachment, the child continues to approach her as the guardian of vital needs of the self. Self-consciousness lets you know that *you* feel something. The thoughtful regulation of emotional needs by the mother serves rudimentary identification purposes. The empathic care of the mother lets the child know that he is a person in his own right whose needs can be attended. In healthy development, beneficial identifications are based on a variety of fulfilling interactions with caregivers. In this way, the child can learn to recognise his own needs and to attend to them. Therefore, it is also related to ego functioning, in its function of attending to the demands of the id in the face of the restrictions of reality.

Most Western people are accustomed to thinking of *cognitive consciousness* as the whole of consciousness. Here it is conceptualised as an evolutionary younger section of it. In this section of consciousness, objects are mentally represented and imaginarily manipulated through the process of thinking. Now we can start to apply verbal logic and think through various scenarios.

Cognitive consciousness is considerably dependent on neocortical activation and enables you to *think* about the way you feel. Also the sphere of the Freudian superego is opening up, which is governed by internalised ideals.[21] These ideals can exist of verbalised commands and restrictions but also of implicit nonverbal patterns, for instance, when shame is involved. Cognitive consciousness is triadic in the sense that it is now possible to become aware of being a subject amidst other objects that are subjects by themselves. Not only does it become possible to realise that other people have relationships that don't involve you (raising feelings of exclusion, jealousy and rivalry and so forth), but also a third-person perspective can be taken towards the self. It is a triadic ability to envision the self as the other in the eyes of the other who is a self in his own right. By now the ability to mentalise comes into full force.

Among these three sections of consciousness – and among emotion, self and mind – various forms of feedforward and feedback are simultaneously active. This can give rise to intricate loops that might complicate the primary sequence of affect before ideation.

The first evaluation of the subject's state and status is quick and emotional. It energises and informs the organism of the need for a (re)action in order to survive or reproduce. The self is the recipient of this emotional information and is potentially capable to act accordingly or choose differently. A crucial element in this equation is whether the self is capable of recognising the emotional information as belonging to the self. If so, the mind can function as the organ by which various scenarios can be considered. Then the scenario can be chosen that is the best combined fit for the biological, social and psychological needs of the self.[22] In this feedforward process the system is *calibrated from bottom-up*, mobilising evolutionary younger levels of consciousness in order to find the most adaptive reaction. The conscious mind appears in response to unmet emotional needs and this process is fuelled by emotional arousal.[23] The subjective experience of "too much calibration" is the experience of being emotionally overwhelmed. Then the emotional self can't be observed from a mindful standpoint anymore.[24]

The feedback process on the other hand involves *top-down regulation*, in order to dynamically counterbalance emotional arousal. Besides providing mental flexibility in considering various appropriate reactions, consciousness is concerned with preserving the sense of control.[25] That is why we can think about our feelings, as if we are monitoring them in a control room. We can wonder whether they say something about the self or the other and decide to come into action or not. Also it is through feedback that we are able to feel our thoughts. This is where we can fantasise all sorts of scenarios and consider our feelings in order to examine "how it would be like". Top-down regulation is also about considering the emotional impact of imagined scenarios, to guide us in our actions or to guard us from actually coming into action. Paradoxically, this is not always experienced as driven by a need to regulate arousal and to come up with viable solutions. We are driven to meet our vital needs in order to stay alive, but we also need to feel our emotional neediness in order to feel alive.[26]

If it wasn't for the ongoing integration of emotion, self and mind, people would not acquire mature defence mechanisms instead of primitive ones. Becoming familiar with the workings of your inner world doesn't make them much more predictable, but at least less scary. Then sublimation or humour can be used, instead of an irreflective use of dissociation or projection, for example.

Adapting the therapeutic stance in order to gain access to different sections of unconsciousness

In real life, people can be oblivious to various sections of their consciousness. You might hear people say "I don't know what I am feeling" or "I don't know what to think of my feelings". Also people might wonder whether a feeling is theirs or not.

The conceptualisation of consciousness in three sections (involving emotion, self and mind) paves the way for delineating different forms of unconsciousness. The "mind-level" of cognitive unconsciousness can be associated with Freud's dynamic unconscious (Berlin, 2011). The dynamic unconscious consists of anxiety-provoking feelings, thoughts, fantasies and impulses, which once were cognitively conscious (maybe barely) but have been repressed because of their emotionally conflicting qualities. These conflicted origins are in principle accessible for an interpretative mind (be it of the therapist or of the self). Therefore, analytic interpretation can be used successfully, especially when there is no insurmountable interference of implicit relational patterns. In her brilliant work with children, Anne Alvarez (2012) calls this the explanatory level: it is about figuring out *why you feel the way you do*. Therapeutic interventions from other schools, such as changing cognitive behavioural patterns or extending the experiential sphere, are also known to be successful.

On the level of self-consciousness, we enter the realm of implicit relational patterns that are associated with borderline/narcissistic personality organisation. In this realm, we encounter parts of the unconscious that aren't repressed but that could be considered idiographic blind spots for parts of reality. These blind spots have come into being because of the iteration of relational patterns that have made them implicit. The relational patterns stem from the subjective experience of reality, providing them with an intangible mix of objectivity and subjectivity. In psychoanalytic theory, these patterns are considered to be interwoven in the structure of the ego. They are experienced as inherent to the personality and unquestionably shape the subjective experience of new realities. Alternative takes on reality can be discussed but can't be felt by the patient as containing "visceral truth". Pathology doesn't involve inner conflict that much, as it mainly consists of relational issues with people who don't share the idiographic experience of reality. In order to therapeutically access this realm, the therapist has to be sensitive for surprising aspects within the dyadic couple. The therapist has to pay attention to the transference and countertransference, in order to become a catalysing part of the exploration of these implicit relational patterns. Also a mutual focus on trust and safety, as well as a clearly delineated working alliance, are essential for therapeutic progress. Only then, the subjective emotional experiences that stem from the problematic implicit relational scenario can be explored and reconsidered. It resembles Anne Alvarez's descriptive level, that sensitively clarifies *what is felt*. It involves developmental work on both recognising and regulating basic emotions.[27]

On the level of affective consciousness, we encounter a wide array of seemingly unintelligible symptoms that stem from the unrepressed unconscious and that have varying therapeutic implications. Underlying disintegration are overwhelming feelings of anxiety, despair and terror, so the first concern of therapy is to strengthen outer structure and stabilise disabling symptoms. The involvement of social networks and/or clinical admittance can be considered, as well as the use of medication. The presence of the therapist is the most vital aspect of the therapeutic alliance that promotes both security and integration. Especially it is the mind of the therapist that is both structuring and receptive and that ultimately enables the raw (proto-)emotional turbulence to calm down. This is not the place for astute interpretation, but for the welcoming of meaning through the sensitive exploration of experiences. In patients who are severely withdrawn, who are chronically dissociated or who are in autistic states, this might be done using what Anne Alvarez calls the intensified vitalising level of analytic work.[28] Interventions are made on a fundamental level of emotional functioning, even before the specific emotions are named and "assigned" to the patient. It is about gaining access to emotion itself: it is about *welcoming, gathering and structuring the fragmented parts of emotion itself*. Because only when emotion comes to the fore, things start to make sense and become meaningful.[29]

This chapter ends on the note that it is only human to struggle sometimes with the balancing of your emotions, self and mind. The next chapter, which is the final one of this book, will zoom in on the present-day crisis that is unsettling for all of us. Humanity as a whole is struggling to feel, own and think the environmental crisis through.

Notes

1 One could say that body language is wordless but ultimately emotional. Emotions are ancestral memories of basic evolutionary adaptive (inter)action tendencies that are embedded in our genetic code. See Panksepp, J. & Biven, L. (2012). *The archaeology of mind: Neuroevolutionary origins of human emotions*. New York: W.W. Norton & Company.

2 Then secondary anxiety and shame are added, anticipating the confrontational return of what is repressed. See, for a liberating form of therapy, Fosha, D. (2000). *The transforming power of affect: A model for accelerated change*. New York: Basic Books.

3 It could be argued though that a neurotic defence is a top-down inhibitory process that is fuelled by symbolic motives. Psychotic "defences" on the other hand seem to inhibit the full processing of emotional states from bottom-up, because the integrative capacity of the psyche falls short (for example, when it is flooded by raw and intense sensory and visceral input). The term psychotic "disturbance" seems to fit the bottom-up dysregulation better than does the term psychotic "defence". In my clinical experience,

borderline/narcissistic defences have both top-down and bottom-up inhibitory and dys-regulating qualities.

4 See, for a more recent operationalisation, Shai, D. & Belsky, J. (2011). When words just won't do: Introducing parental embodied mentalizing. *Child Development Perspectives*, 5(3), 173–180.

5 See also Bion's conception of "beta-elements", which consist of raw sense-data and inchoate emotional elements. Bion, W.R. (1962). *Learning from experience*. London: Heinemann. I suggest the term "id-entities" to describe these disembodied and unowned rudimentary sensory impressions and visceral-emotional states. These partial "unbound" qualia and the emanating motivational stance can remain in this dissociated state. In succession they can mistakenly be attached to inner and outer, organic or inorganic objects. In my mind the term "id-entities" captures these features of fragmentation, alienation and aberrant inner-/outer-adhesion quite well.

6 One finds the world to be filled with objects that are bizarre, as Bion lucidly explained. See Bion, W. (1957). Differentiation of the psychotic from the non-psychotic. *International Journal of Psychoanalysis*, 38, 206–275.

7 See, for a lucid review, Fotopoulou, A. & Tsakiris, M. (2017). Mentalizing homeostasis: The social origins of interoceptive inference. *Neuropsychoanalysis*, 19(1), 3–28.

8 This differentiation is often misused in gender stereotyping. For boys, it would be more OK to display joy and anger, while the expression of sadness and fear is taboo. For girls, it would be the other way around.

9 Margaret Mahler delineated this process in her definition of "rapprochement".

10 I use the word "segregate" here instead of the more common "separate" to accentuate the purposeful division of something that in fact is whole.

11 In a (sexually) violent context this dichotomy is also known as offender versus victim.

12 In line with Solms, M. & Turnbull, O. (2002). *The brain and the inner world: An introduction to the neuroscience of subjective experience*. New York: Other Press.

13 I believe it to be in line with a proposal to reconceptualise the psychotic disorders (such as schizophrenia) and rename them as "salience dysregulation syndrome". Three subcategories are identified: with affective expression, with developmental expression and not otherwise specified. Van Os, J. (2009). A salience dysregulation syndrome. *The British Journal of Psychiatry: The Journal of Mental Science*, 194(2), 101–103.

14 See, for a neuropsychoanalytic take on the matter, Fotopoulou, A. (2015). The virtual bodily self: Mentalisation of the body as revealed in anosognosia for hemiplegia. *Consciousness and Cognition*, 33, 500–510. See, for an analytic classic, Bick, E. (1968). The experience of the skin in early object-relations. *The International Journal of Psychoanalysis*, 49(2–3), 484–486.

15 Keynote lecture of Mark Solms on the 2019 congress of the International Neuropsychoanalysis Society in Brussels, entitled: "Proposed revisions to Freudian drive theory".

16 To give only three essential references: Mahler, M.S., Pine, F. & Bergman, A. (1975). *The psychological birth of the human infant: Symbiosis and individuation*. New York: Basic Books; Fonagy, P., Gergely, G., Jurist, E. & Target, M. (2002). *Affect regulation, mentalization, and the development of the self*. New York: Other Press; and Damasio, A. (2010). *Self comes to mind: Constructing the conscious brain*. New York, NY, US: Pantheon & Random House.

17 See, for instance, Dunn, B.D., Galton, H.C., Morgan, R., Evans, D., Oliver, C., Meyer, M., Cusack, R., Lawrence, A.D. & Dalgleish, T. (2010). Listening to your heart: How interoception shapes emotion experience and intuitive decision making. *Psychological Science*, 21, 1835–1844; Herbert, B.M. & Pollatos, O. (2012). The body in the mind: On the relationship between interoception and embodiment. *Topics in Cognitive Science*, 4(4), 692–704; and Tsakiris, M. (2017). The multisensory basis of the self: From body to identity to others. *The Quarterly Journal of Experimental Psychology*, 70(4), 597–609.

18 See, for an illuminating theory of how a lack (or falsification) of mental prediction leads to unbound free energy that is in need of top-down regulation, Friston, K. (2010). The free-energy principle: A unified brain theory? *Nature Reviews Neuroscience*, 11, 127–138. In this theory, the system has an inherent tendency to minimise free energy by optimising its predictions, which binds free energy. See also Solms, M. & Friston, K. (2018). How and why consciousness arises: Some considerations from physics and physiology. *Journal of Consciousness Studies*, 25(5–6), 202–238.

19 Like Winnicott's famous phrase: "There is no such thing as a baby." It means that there is no baby without a relationship with the mother, even if the mother is absent.

20 Consider the tragic fate of the children in the Romanian orphanage that were studied by René Spitz.

21 These ideals consist of symbolic predictions, that are accompanied by a sense of should and a sense of shouldn't. See Theriault, J.E., Young, L. & Barrett, L.F. (2019). The sense of should: A biologically-based model of social pressure. 9 January. https://doi.org/10.31234/osf.io/x5rbs.

22 A fourth dimension that is existential or spiritual could be considered here.

23 That is, the need to minimise prediction error, felt as unbound free energy. See Friston, K. (2010). The free-energy principle: A unified brain theory? *Nature Reviews Neuroscience*, 11, 127–138.

24 It disrupts mentalisation.

25 In other words, the set of interconnected predictions that underpin the implicit sense of control can only be reconsidered at the expense of vast amounts of energy-consuming attention.

26 This paradox might shed some light on the intricacies of sexuality versus erotica. Sexuality as a biological drive seeks fulfilment and tension relief, while erotica is about savouring and tension build-up. See for a hands-on, heartfelt and open-minded book: Lousada, M. & Mazanti, L. (2017). *Real sex: Why everything you learned about sex is wrong*. London: Hayhouse.

27 Other examples of therapies are transference-focused psychotherapy, mentalisation-based treatment, dialectic behavior therapy and schema therapy. Also the combination of individual and group therapy can be of great value.

28 Read for an excellent clinical account: Alvarez, A. (2010). Levels of analytic work and levels of pathology: The work of calibration. *International Journal of Psychoanalysis*, 91(4), 859–878.

29 Another example of a treatment tailored for severe dissociative disorders is the phase-oriented treatment of structural dissociation. See Steele, K., Van der Hart, O. & Nijenhuis, E. (2005). Phase-oriented treatment of structural dissociation in complex traumatization: overcoming trauma-related phobias. *Journal of Trauma & Dissociation*, 6(3), 11–53. An example of a treatment aimed at better regulation of psychotic symptoms (instead of symptom reduction per se) is acceptance and commitment therapy. See: Hayes, S.C., Strosahl, K.D. & Wilson, K.G. (2012). *Acceptance and commitment therapy: The process and practice of mindful change*. 2nd Edition. New York, NY: Guilford Press.

Chapter 9

Why it is so hard to talk about what matters most

Soaring temperatures, drought, severe storms, floods, melting ice caps, sea level rise, deforestation, desertification, pollution, habitat loss, biodiversity loss, faltering ecosystems, societal disruption, mass migration, mass extinction. Climate change is a euphemism, two words trying to contain panic.

In our life and times, and in all future ones, this is what matters most.

The science of it all, which is our most rigorously verified knowledge of what is going on, is undisputable. Multiple reports from the Intergovernmental Panel on Climate Change (IPCC) and the Intergovernmental Science-Policy Platform on Biodiversity and Ecosystem Services (IPBES) speak of irreversible tipping points and an unprecedented decline of nature. On top of that, there is scientific consensus that humanity's finger- and footprints are all over these alarming global changes. It has led geologists to propose "the Anthropocene" as the new name for the epoch we live in (Crutzen & Stoermer, 2000). The consequences of these ongoing processes are so extensive and so detrimental to our way of life and to life as a whole, that we psychologically struggle to digest this chunk of reality. The truth is not only inconvenient, it is overwhelming. And as psychologists know: when the human mind can't handle the truth emotionally, reality-testing withers. Also personal reflection is diminished and basic emotional impulses are left to be regulated by less mature forms of psychological defence.

Greta Thunberg's plea for urgent and realistic action at the United Nations Climate Summit in 2019 was both emotional and reflective.[1] Here are some of her words:

> You say you hear us and that you understand the urgency, but no matter how sad and angry I am, I do not want to believe that. Because if you really understood the situation and still kept on failing to act then you would be evil and that I refuse to believe.

Even though I believe that evil has many faces, she is right in stating that there is a lack of understanding of the situation. Still a considerable part of the world population is, or chooses to be, ignorant of the extent of the crisis. But ignorance isn't lifted by science; it is lifted by the will to learn. And we can only learn what we can fathom emotionally and what we can bear to accept as reality. Learning about this unprecedented existential threat of our own making makes us stare into the bottomless depth of who we are as a species. Few have the stomach to face that.

Most political leaders know this. That is why most of them fail to step up their action. Vigorous action would imply an urgent cause, which would alarm their constituency. I don't think it is a coincidence that we see a rise of political strong men, supported by people who need (illusory) reassurance more than honesty and moral leadership. It is a societal-political constellation that leaves a lot of room for the lobby of non-governmental businesses and industries, whose existence depends on the unsustainable status quo and whose guiding principle is profit. Politics becomes business and business becomes politics.[2] The catchphrase is: "Don't worry and keep consuming. Let us take care of business and everything is going to be all right." And business usually doesn't refer to nature.

This chapter is about why it is so hard to talk about the global environmental crisis and how to deal with our own emotional reactions and defences. First a bit of background information is given on climate change as a wicked problem and connected to the theory of emotion and regulation as proposed in this book. Elementary implicit attitudes towards nature are discussed, as well as shifts therein after learning about the environmental crisis. A user-friendly overview is presented covering common defence mechanisms and linked to some of the bewildering successes of fact-free politics and conspiracy theories. In conclusion, the point is made that there is no therapy like the truth. But in order to face the truth, we have to mind how we emotionally relate to our selves, each other and all of nature.

The environmental crisis is such a wicked problem because the perception of reality is limited by our capacity to process emotions

For years, climate change has been known to be a wicked problem. As the predicted change is steadily turning into a crisis, it is now known as a super wicked problem (Levin, Cashore, Bernstein & Auld, 2012). Indeed, there are many interdependent factors complicating the matter. The fossil fuel industry for instance has become so big and influential that currently it seems indispensable for global financial markets and geopolitical stability. There is hardly a product you can buy that hasn't got components shipped or flown in from all over the world using fossil fuel. Also the growing technological advancement of our societies chiefly add to the carbon footprint of each individual. Many are brought up to think that the wheels of progress, on societal and individual levels, are oiled by oil. Energy is power; who could argue with that?

Our collective and individual lives are so dependent on the consumption of natural resources that refraining from it seems detrimental to social success.[3] And that is exactly what we should be doing if we want to handle the environmental crisis.[4] It is like nature is saying to us: "Stop being so successful in what you do, because I can't keep up with you. Find new ways to thrive." Unfortunately it is hard to give up something that we do so well.

As taking up responsibility for the human impact on the environment seems to be at odds with economic growth within a capitalist system (Klein, 2014), information regarding climate change initially was associated with vital displeasure. Apart from the displeasure of environmental degradation, this kind of information was handled as a hostile confrontation with an economic threat. The alarming ecological predictions obviously haven't been integrated into corporate and governmental planning, as other issues were prioritised (Mommers, 2017). Short-term financial statistics have been decisive over and over again (as the long-term cost is unmeasurable). I state that the willingness to believe this kind of framing is based on a basic emotional mindset in reaction to traumatising intrusion and loss. It is the overwhelming intensity of surging emotions that sets us up for denying the environmental facts in more primitive ways than the cognitive choice "not to think about it".[5] Without the full acknowledgement of how humans deal with emotions, we will fail to understand why public and private discussions on the environmental crisis are so heated and depressing at the same time.

Using the Maelstrom model as a theory of emotion and regulation, I will now try to shed some light on the emotional dynamics involved in (the lack of) climate action.

Our love–hate relationship with wild nature

The most basic emotional awareness of the natural environment adds contrast to things that are associated with pleasure and things that are associated with displeasure.[6] What catches our attention are the things that marvel and delight us versus the ones that frighten and oppose us. It is emotional arousal that provides us with energy and focus to (re)act adaptively. Moreover, it is highly advantageous to be able to handle pleasurable and unpleasurable interactions flexibly. The capability to discriminate between them and fine-tune one's own (re)actions has additional evolutionary value. Only this capability is something that is not purely inherited. It is something that should be developed in real-life interactions. And frankly, it is a lifelong task to develop and sustain it.

When we struggle to handle our preverbal tendency to classify interactions as pleasurable or unpleasurable flexibly, we get stuck in a polarised view of the world. Not being able to take in your own emotional state and reflect on it dismantles the moderating effect of psychodynamic tension. It is part of being human that completion of this developmental task is unfeasible, though it is maturational to strive for it. Dependent on (early) experiences and the (implicit) messages they are brought up with, people tend to be divided between the ones who associate nature with pleasure and those who associate nature with displeasure. It is the caricature of people who would only feel joy and compassion for nature ("the lovers") versus the people who would only feel fear and opposition ("the haters"). Nature accordingly is treated as friend or foe.

Joy and sadness (the "love-pleasure-side") prompt us to seek proximity and to relish the interaction with nature.[7] It inspires us to investigate and study it, play in it, to immerse oneself into it and to care for it. Being in a natural environment, that is an environment that isn't created by humans, can install a nurturing sense of belonging to something bigger. It helps to put personal preoccupations into perspective. Being able to feel joy and sadness combined with the notion of belonging to something bigger than yourself endows us with feelings of connectedness, reverence and gratitude.

Fear and anger (the "hate-displeasure-side") prompt us to distance ourselves from the unmoderated influence that nature has on us.[8] It inspires us to be attentive, cautious, on the lookout for threats to ourselves and to the ones we love. The natural environment as a hostile place fills us with the sense of being vulnerable and reminds us of the fragility of our physical bodies. These emotions are as essential to our survival as joy and sadness. They help us to get to know our place in nature. Being able to feel fear and anger combined with the notion of being a small part of bigger nature helps us to focus on preservation and self-assertion amidst awe-inspiring nature.

As is evident from the description earlier, these quasi-antagonistic attitudes towards nature are two sides of the same coin. They are mentioned here because these different attitudes also lay down the groundwork for different reactions to climate change. But what is common in both attitudes is that both presuppose a vital interaction between humans and nature. The reality that our emotions make us aware of is that our dependency on nature is of vital importance. Without (acknowledging) the rest of living nature, humanity ceases to exist.[9]

We tend to treat this fundamental dependency on nature differently when we are limited to one of the two emotional mindsets. The pitfall for "the lovers" of nature is to become naïve and blind to the indifference and violence that are intrinsic parts of nature. Dependency is associated with pleasure and is sought after. The pitfall for "the haters" is to become paranoid and to abstain from a mutual nurturing relationship with nature. Dependency is associated with displeasure and has to be overcome.[10] From this viewpoint, humans stand above the rest of nature and may treat it as they wish. The all-too-common misconception is that this standpoint is not brazenly emotional and not in need of regulation.

When we take the emotional nature of our being fully into account, there is no denying our fundamental dependency on outer nature. Two aspects of outer nature, however, make it especially hard to fully acknowledge humanity's intrinsic dependency. First of all is the fact that nature is beyond human control. It is the essence of wild nature that it ultimately defies human regulation. We can allow it to flourish and we can destroy it, but we cannot design it as we would like it to be. The second point is that nature not only is independent of humans but is fundamentally indifferent about human existence. From a psychological point of view, these two facts are hard to swallow. Accepting vital dependency on an indifferent natural world leaves us psychologically defenceless. Most of all it conflicts with our developmental drive towards emotional self-reliance and mature object relations. It conflicts with our need to feel in control.

How is it possible then to face this psychological ordeal? First of all, it is important to realise that our love–hate relationship with nature stems from a basic emotional *dyadic* take on relationships. Such a dyadic perspective assumes that all relational processes are limited to the self and the other: no third perspective or alternative view is present. When we take our emotional nature into account but also mind our inner conflict with our dependency on nature, I believe that *respect* is what comes up. A core feature of respect is that it acknowledges one's dependency on the other irrespective of (the lack of) dependency of the other on you. Respect, as opposed to submission, surpasses the dyadic perspective. It is based on a deeper understanding and as such it is part of a mature, *triadic* and responsible relationship with nature.

Relating to nature's crisis: on craving, grieving and leaving versus fighting, freezing and fleeing

In addition to basic emotional attitudes towards nature, people have basic emotional attitudes towards nature's crisis.[11] An elementary differentiation in people's reactions to learning about the environmental crisis can be made on the basis of the "love-or-hate-nature" dichotomy. As few people are outright lovers or haters of nature, I will from now on refer to the various parts in most of us that either love or hate the interaction with outer nature. This formulation also does more justice to the ambivalence most of us experience.

For the parts in us that are driven by joy and sadness and associate the interaction with nature with pleasure, the sight of environmental degradation is experienced as a vital loss. The confrontation with it is experienced as an interactional distancing from a loved and needed one. It is like seeing your beloved grandmother fade away because of illness. As distance and intensity increase, an emotional point is reached that triggers a crave, grieve or leave response.[12] *Craving* urges people to seek proximity and restore close interaction with nature. It is the emotional foundation of the "back to nature" movement that brings the beneficial effects that nature has on us into focus. The emotional action tendency drives people to seek out natural environments. The point of *grieving* is reached when people find it impossible to either go back or move on. Our personal lives can become so full of technology and dependent on industry and our alienation of wild nature can become so complete that we are at a loss regarding how to integrate our way of life with nature's needs. Back to nature then is a no go, but turning our backs on nature is evenly impossible. I believe this to be the paralyzing foundation of the emotional experience that Renee Lertzman (2015) so appropriately describes as environmental melancholia. Especially when the gap between what people feel what should be done versus what they actually do is addressed, the concept of environmental melancholia is illuminating. It stops us in our tracks, as neither approach nor avoidance seems to alleviate our distress. The third type of basic emotional reaction to loss motivates us to *leave* the situation and give up on an unattainable reunion. The degrading environment is then considered to be a lost cause that is best to be avoided. It makes people turn to human-made environments (e.g. cities and virtual worlds) while downplaying the intrinsic value of natural environments. Caring for the natural world is left to others (e.g. environmentalists), whose despairing plight is bound to be forgotten.

Other parts in us (driven by fear and anger) oppose the wildness of nature as something to be fled from, tamed or beaten. Within such an emotional mindset, environmental degradation is picked up as further evidence that nature can't be trusted. It is experienced as a highly unpleasurable, even hostile confrontation. Nature's crisis only makes it more unpredictable and amplifies the tendency to fight, freeze or flee. *Fleeing* is the inborn action tendency to get out of harm's way. It urges us to seek shelter from the impact of environmental degradation. It makes us think like preppers, trying to stockpile supplies in case of natural meltdown. Within this state of mind it makes sense to invest money into a residency that is deemed safe, however illusory (O'Connell, 2018). Avid belief in the power of technology makes a flight from the surface of the earth seem a logical part of humanity's destiny, in search of other inhabitable planets.[13] *Freezing* is the basic emotional tendency underlying psychological shock, which interferes with an orchestrated reaction to approach or avoid danger. It is the shock and awe we experience while being confronted by (images of) natural disasters, like devastating floods or unparalleled storms. These are felt to be adversaries that are too powerful to fight against and too absolute to flee from. It induces in us a utter state of powerlessness and helplessness. The implicit logic of freezing is to let danger pass you by, not noticing you. Unfortunately one cannot sit out the environmental crisis. *Fighting* the environmental crisis is the third basic emotional reaction. It makes us want to take up arms and eliminate this threatening thing, regardless of the fact that we continue to exacerbate the threat ourselves. From this basic emotional standpoint, it makes sense to geoengineer our way out of trouble, despite the unforeseeable consequences of technological interventions on a global scale. Though fighting the climate crisis can also be done using natural methods like planting trees, the fighting state that associates the natural environment with displeasure has a tendency to use technological solutions for natural problems. Probably it aims to bolster the illusory sense of human control even more.

The climate has changed so much already that both mitigation and adaptation are necessary. Only a synergistic response to the environmental crisis has a chance of succeeding in preventing the further collapse of natural systems, including human societies. The whole gamut of human emotional reactions is needed to drive us to take all sorts of vital action. Even though all measures should be considered and multiple actions have to be taken, we have to take into account our inborn tendencies to buttress our sense of control and oppose vulnerable dependency. These tendencies tempt us into prioritising technological solutions that destroy (the inherently dependent relationship with) nature along the way. An even more cynical and ruinous policy would be to invest in the ongoing course of climate change as a way to shift the international power balance. Unfortunately, increasing military activity around the Arctic to back up national claims of thaw-ing natural resources does exactly that.[14]

Uncontrollable by nature: the environmental crisis is the ultimate reality test

The environmental crisis exposes how fragile the illusion of control over nature really is. But we can only face up to reality in a state of receptivity to its emotional ramifications. The intellectual understanding of reality is not the hardest part: it is whether we can handle the truth emotionally. Therefore, the hardest kind of reality to take in is an unnerving reality that is of our own making. It not only confronts us with basic emotions of overwhelming intensity but also forces us to deal with self-referential emotions like shame and guilt, as well as to reconsider our explicit and implicit ways in which we regulate our emotional states. The environmental crisis is causing a mental crisis in which external and internal threats get mixed up.

As mentioned earlier, the environmental crisis installs in us all sorts of impulsive (inter)action tendencies, from craving and fighting to leaving and fleeing. These tendencies stem from basic emotional states that also calibrate the way in which we perceive reality. This is the first obstacle for perceiving reality accurately: through basic emotions, attention is focussed on partial information that is intuitively deemed as vital. The emotional action tendencies can spur us into action without further inspection and reflection. Simply acting on an emotion bolsters our sense of control when we are successful in changing our relational environment. Dealing reflectively with an emotion on the other hand bolsters our sense of control when it leads to a deeper understanding of our connectedness to the world. The latter is a more mature and psychologically stable sense of control. However, the thing with emotional hyperarousal is that it corrodes the sense of reflective control in the long term. Given the psychological need for a sense of control, we dislike feelings that are too hot to handle. We are overcome by something from within that steers us instead of us steering us. "*I don't know what's got into me.*" And we find it hard to integrate motivating forces into our identities that seem to have a life of their own.

Facing up to the emotional reality of the environmental crisis puts pressure on the psychodynamic balance between our emotions and our sense of control. It is unsettling to note that our control is limited not only over outer reality but also over our inner reality.[15] But in contrast to our limited control, human impact on the natural environment is ever expanding. And as we fancy our control to be bigger, we wish our negative impact to be smaller. The environmental crisis confronts us with the detrimental impact of human activity on the natural world and on future generations. It begs the question: "What have we done?", and it is a question that the environment is answering with increasing force. The immense adversity of what is going on inevitably leads up to self-referential feelings like shame and guilt. And as every psychotherapist knows, shame and guilt are formidable obstacles to facing reality with an open mind. They hinder reality testing because they make you feel like you can't look reality in the eye.

The third obstacle to facing reality is that it undermines all sorts of implicit assumptions that we have about the world and our place in it. Semi-conscious fantastic beliefs like "*Mother Earth is infinitely good*" or "*Humans are the pinnacle of evolution*" are disparagingly over date.[16] Reality is hard to take in when your whole idea of your place in it crumbles and has to be revised. And though these fantasies seem somewhat childish to the rational mind, we all have them. Most of them actually stem from childhood, when our understanding of the world was developing and our beliefs were mainly guided by their ability to make us feel better. Indeed they have become ingrained in our implicit understanding of the way the world works. But the environmental crisis forces us to face the facts that the love of Mother Nature isn't boundless and that we are not her favourite children. Despite of all the riches of the natural world and despite of all our technological capabilities, we can't go on pumping up fossil fuels thinking that nature will take care of herself. We can't go on driving numerous species into extinction believing that extinction will stop at our doorstep because of our greater verbal capabilities. We have to curb our technological efforts to get as much out of nature as we can, if we want to secure a vital base for the future of humanity. Therefore, we have to curb our greed and let go of the assumption that the world is our oyster. Planet earth is a blue marble in space, and we are just temporary inhabitants like many others.[17]

To summarise, reality testing can be hindered by emotion, the self and the mind. And here I have only focussed on our direct relationship with nature and our emotional reaction to the environmental crisis. The action needed to minimise further degradation sets a whole new array of emotional reactions in motion[18] (and is for now less profitable as a business model). Though it is beyond the scope of this book, suffice it to say that we are both in the best and the worst position to take climate action. We are in the best position because our scientific knowledge and technological capabilities are growing faster than ever before. We can implement change with unprecedented speed. But we are also in the worst possible position because geopolitical dynamics depend heavily on technological control and economic power, which is largely based on the appropriation of natural resources and of fossil fuels. Our resources- and energy-consuming lifestyle and dependency on technology are so ingrained in our societies that it will take a huge shift in our collective mindset before we can bear the burden of change. We have to discover how to look after our vital needs sustainably instead of focussing on what we have learned to desire (through culture and corporate advertisement).

The politics of widening fault lines: neurotic, borderline and psychotic defences as political strategies

As the environmental crisis is too big for any person, political party or nation to handle alone, it is a truth that seems too hard to bear. I can think of no meetings in the private or public domain that are capable of psychologically containing and practically addressing the breadth and depth of the problem, other than an international gathering like the United Nations.[19] It takes the best of our combined efforts to meet the challenges that the environmental crisis imposes upon us. Failing to do so condemns us to an international prisoner's dilemma with the natural environment as an unforgiving judge.

On a national level, the resistance can be felt against both threats and restrictions stemming from the globalised world. Not is only global warming often treated as a threat stemming from the outside, rational restrictions for unsustainable industries are likewise opposed. A growing class of politicians takes advantage of societal resentment by giving free rein to unmoderated emotions. This populistic approach claims to be speaking for "the people" (versus "the elite"), but often is a brazen attempt to free basic emotional impulses from burdensome reflection. The reality of the environmental crisis that urges us to take an honest and responsible look at humanity is aggressively called into question. As ignorance is bliss, it wins a lot of nationalistic electoral approval.

I will now present a user-friendly overview to categorise the diverse ways we use to get rid of unbearable truth.[20] This framework is based on the psychodynamic fault lines as presented in Chapter 8. It might serve as a search tool for understanding your own fluctuating and ambivalent attitudes towards the environmental crisis. Likewise, it helps to see through various political strategies and formulate more effective responses to political arguments that thwart reality. It is a framework for debunking personal and political framing.

The first line of defence against unbearable reality for a sane adult mind is repression. The astounding truth of the environmental crisis is pushed beyond the gateway that links emotional experience to personal reflection. In other words: *when we think about it, our feelings are inhibited. And when we get emotional, our reflective thoughts stop.* In the previous chapter, this gateway is described as the neurotic fault line. When it operates defensively, it hinders the integrated emotional and reflective experience of reality. It protects us from feeling overwhelmed when confronted with the desperate plight of the natural world we are part of.

On a personal level, the decline of nature is driven out of sight and out of mind. Though the hint of knowledge is there, full-fledged emotional awareness of what actually goes on is obscured. Table 8.1 summarises some characteristic patterns of how this act of repression is achieved. For instance one can maintain a *naively romantic* outlook on reality, focussing on the splendour of nature and on inherent abilities to bounce back. And if nature is in serious trouble, there is a reassuring belief that science will find a way to revive it. Another example is a *conflict-avoidant* attitude, which keeps natural degradation literally out of sight. People avoid media coverage of global environmental issues and focus on their backyards instead. The experience of nature is restricted to a space that isn't emotionally overwhelming. The third example given here is that of *perfectionism*. In the spirit of rigidity, one can obsessively try to avoid having any carbon footprint at all, meticulously scrutinising all daily activities. The sheer amount of time put into this effort might serve to take the mind off the disempowering awareness of the scale of the crisis.

These neurotic attitudes do distort the perception of reality, but not in the most severe way. Therefore, they are not the most powerful defences against unbearable reality and overburdening responsibility. Moderate political strategies aim to support these defences through institutionalisation and legislation. That is how voters vote in a democratic society: they vote in favour of the policy that supports their psychological needs the most, even (or especially) when those needs haven't been articulated yet.[21] The political pendant of the out-of-sight strategy is to hide violence (like animal slaughter) and decay (like garbage dumps) from view and to outsource society's negative impact on the environment as much as possible (like ship disposal in Bangladesh, when you are not living in Bangladesh). The attentional bias is fostered towards growth and progress, while the decline of nature and international inequality are neglected.[22] Another secretive kind of policy is greenwashing, whereby small measures are taken to defuse motivation for fundamental change. Thus, emotional turbulence is soothed without taking appropriate action.

The second line of defence cuts deeper into the fabric of subjective perception and distorts reality considerably more. The unbearable part of reality is pushed beyond the boundary between self and other. It is like declaring the degradation of nature to be "someone else's problem that has got nothing to do with me". In Table 8.1, this kind of defence is listed as borderline/narcissistic. On top of intrapsychic repression, there is now substantial interpersonal projection and introjection going on. It protects us from severe attacks on feelings of self-worth by enabling us to wash our hands in innocence and put the blame on someone else. This line of defence is fortified when actual others are identified as scapegoats (like environmentalists or migrants but also like the capitalist elite).[23]

In the personal sphere, this kind of scapegoating emerges out of a "*self all good and other all bad*" mindset. The tacit argumentation is that the environmental crisis – if it is true at all – has no relation with what I am doing. The motto is: "Others have messed up and they should pay the price." Here we meet the tendency to *push and segregate* from others who are identified as evil-doers, while trying to *pull and fuse* with like-minded "good people". We seek safety in a bubble of equals, who join us in this defensive strategy. It makes it hard to have a conversation with someone who has different ideas than us. In order to keep a firm grip on these relational dynamics, we emotionally strive for *domination* as we are convinced that not being dominant means being submissive. Getting the upper hand is now becoming more important than being right. It is not the truth of the environmental crisis that matters; it is about the domination of the debate.

As the environmental crisis deepens, and in its wake a whole range of crises, the "neurotic defence" of moderate politicians starts to fall short in containing the emotional turbulence of this unbearable reality. Therefore, we see a rise in politicians of more extreme ("borderline/narcissistic") parts of the spectrum, who use cherry-picking and divisive narratives to dismantle the truth. The "*self all good and other all bad*" mindset receives a warm welcome in identity politics and fierce nationalism. It becomes "us against them". This is especially appealing to voters who are already in a state of psychological alert because of losses already suffered or the threat of future losses. Here is where people on the low and high side of the socioeconomic ladder find each other. The emotional tension between them is diverted outwards, towards people of other nationalities, race, religion, etcetera. National geopolitical power is prioritised at the expense of international crisis management. Political unions based on cooperation suffer from segregating tendencies, as national unity is enforced at the same time. Nature again is on the losing end.

We have to look at the most severe "dissociative/psychotic" defences if we want to understand some of the bewildering successes of fact-free politics and conspiracy theories today. This is the third line of defence that comes into operation when the emotional experience of reality keeps on overwhelming us. I want to stress once more that this kind of defence is not reserved for people who experience full-blown alienation, hallucinations or delusions. It is a mechanism that is engrained into our common psychological constitution and can function as the ultimate brake when we crash into a traumatising reality.[24] As discussed in Chapter 8, the unbearable admission of reality can be stopped at the merger of visceral state and sensory perception into emotion. Emotional awareness of the environmental crisis doesn't emerge, because of distortions in visceral and sensorial functioning. And when there is no emotion, there are no inherent valuation and attentional focus to drive thinking. Feelings and thoughts about the crisis aren't banned from the mind: they are halted before their development is completed.

It is the devastating numbness that can be seen in disaster survivors. The thick mist of *depersonalisation* blocks emotional overwhelming amidst the ruins of familiar reality. Media coverage of the environmental crisis has the potential to invoke bouts of depersonalisation, especially when it is brought without a caring eye for the humanity of victims and viewers.[25] Emotional processing is blunted and the entirety of reality can't be taken in. The arrested development of reflective thought hampers the re-evaluation of the misleading distinction between natural and human-made disasters. It can be staggering to hear people deny any relation to rising sea levels within the remnants of their flooded homes. Concomitant *compartmentalisation of consciousness* raises inner barriers between various emotional reactions to personal circumstances. This, for instance, can prevent the connection of traumatic loss to feelings of guilt and human responsibility.

In contrast to the inner mist of depersonalisation, *derealisation* can serve as a thick veil through which the perception of outer reality is distorted. The disastrous decline of nature is perceived as a bad movie that is both alienating and unreal. The present-day crisis is felt to belong to a different space and time. Again the defensive function is to protect us from an overwhelming emotional experience of reality. Imagination can take the place of the perception of a reality that is stripped from meaning, which is a key feature in the formation of *hallucinations and delusions*. We stop to believe our eyes and hold our preconceptions to be true, unable to recognise any psychological motive for doing so. The environmental crisis then becomes a certified hoax.

As realistic control disintegrates, it is fragmented and dispersed both in the inner and outer world. Internally we can be split into *powerful "big" parts and vulnerable "small" parts* that alternately preside. A coherent "stage director" (which would be a struggling, though comprehensive sense of self) is lacking. Intermittently we become victim or victor. We might start to behave accordingly, sustained by *delusions of control* (when your feelings, thoughts and actions are believed to be "inserted by others" and not deemed as your own) or *delusions of grandeur* (when the self is believed to be omnipotent). With regard to the environmental crisis, we might dwell in apocalyptic or nihilistic fantasies or imagine us to be the masters of the universe that can't be touched by derailed nature. The entire range of unpremeditated fantasies can be accompanied by the *disintegration of the sense of being an embodied subject*. It lets us feel like we can truly transcend subjectivity, space and time. Now the plight of outer nature is light-years away.

Political strategies that capitalise on the reality distortion caused by these kinds of defence mechanisms are found at the outskirts of the political spectrum, and they are increasing. These strategies actively seek to unhinge public opinion and reality. Emotional blunting (or depersonalisation) is promoted by continually framing emotional reactions to the environmental crisis as hysterical and delusional. Contempt and ridicule are used tactically to steer away from substantive discussion. By excluding it from the political agenda, the emotional urgency of the crisis is disavowed. Social media and filter bubbles are manipulated to invoke a restricted single-mindedness that blocks environmental awareness. The political aim is to compartmentalise public opinion and frustrate democratic debate, as the dialogue with dissimilar voices is subverted.

Likewise, the reality of nature's decline is aggressively called into question. Public awareness is infused with derealisation by public statements that you cannot trust established institutions and the media ("fake news"). Scientific reporting is obstructed by cutting budgets and implicitly demanding politically approved data. The lack of absolute scientific certainty is exaggerated to discredit science as a whole or selectively discard unwelcome information.[26] Investigative journalism especially suffers from ferocious attacks, as individual journalists and whistleblowers are demonised and persecuted. Diminished reality testing and orchestrated alienation lay the foundations for the dispersal of illusory stories. Public statements that blatantly lack scientific consensus are spread to undermine the distinction between truth and doubt even more ("fossil fuels are clean"). These representations and convictions obtain hallucinatory and delusional qualities.

The political leader is portrayed as all-powerful, stripped of any sign of human vulnerability. The leader is the saviour whose motto is "to make us great again". Omnipotence is appropriated and political leaders are attributed with godlike qualities. Powerlessness on the other hand is perceived as an alien trait. Confronted by inevitable adversity (such as natural disasters), the irrational but narratively coherent explanation is that there is an evil power at work that is not to be underestimated.[27] This power is not specified, so it can readily be used to point the finger to any convenient opponent. Even if the opponent turns out to be innocent, the conviction remains that there is an evil power to blame. Once conspiracy thinking comes into existence, it appears to be immune to refutation. The paranoid attitude is highly resilient, because the psychological defences at work are installed before an integrated experience of an unbearable reality has formed. People become oblivious of their own blinding rage and the essence of conspiracy theory is the assumption that you cannot trust your senses. Meaning is only to be found in plots that are hidden from view. That is how a leader who is blind to the environmental crisis but claims to be omniscient at the same time can be appealing to voters. He "sees" something that they don't.

Advocating defenceless truth: minding our inner nature for the sake of outer nature and our children

When you are in the midst of a crisis, the hardest part is not to find your bearings but not to lose your mind. Various kinds of protective measures against the subjective experience of an unbearable reality are built into our psychological makeup. Our own emotional impulses and defences can make us blind for the situation that has arisen. That is why it is so hard now to *think* about what matters most.

Talking about what matters most can be even more slippery, especially when the diverse ways in which we thoughtlessly distort reality are ignored. Instead of an enlightening discussion, we get lost in misunderstanding and confusion. The worst-case scenario is that we cannot sympathise anymore and become actual enemies.

We have to remind ourselves of the all-too-human tendency to fight a convenient enemy over the humbling act of cutting losses. Picking a fight can serve as the next defence against admitting the limits of our control. And at the receiving end, it is hard not to become too hostile when you are being picked at. Losing yourself in vengeful action is losing sight of what is at stake.

We need a realistic human response to the environmental crisis. And we need an effective response to the bewildering successes of fact-free politics and conspiracy theories. Many moderate politicians struggle to formulate a compelling answer. Insight in the personal and political dynamics of the matter can help in figuring out why this is so.

A concise analysis would be that in the political debate "the unbearable" is *projected* into the other through strategies used by the far sides of the political spectrum. *"You messed up, not we!"* is repeated over and over again. Besides irritation, this refrain triggers an internal conflict in the political centre, because the *repression* of the unbearable is undermined. Partial responsibility for messing up can't be denied, as humanity on the whole is responsible for the environmental crisis. Self-reflective moderate politicians find themselves feeling ashamed and guilty, while others seek refuge in toothless rhetoric that is intended to reinstall repression. This dynamic might also explain the inherent pleasure it seems to give some politicians of extremist parties to make their opponents feel bad and stumble, even though a realistic strategy for facing the crisis is nowhere in sight. On a personal level, these anti-democratic tendencies can strengthen the agitator's sense of control and boost feelings of self-worth.

But what unites us all – no matter the place on the political spectrum or the opinion on the environmental crisis – is that *no one wants this to be true*. Some choose to ignore it and turn a blind eye. Others claim that it is a problem of someone else that they want nothing to do with. A third group denies the reality of the crisis altogether and claims that it doesn't emotionally disturb them at all. But despite of our tendency to soften reality when we can't cope emotionally, we have to overcome the sulking oppositional teenagers within us. The mature thing to do is to face reality and take up responsibility, despite of the enormity and intricacy of the problem. And we really need each other if we want to have a fighting chance.

Therefore, I am in favour of a diplomatic attitude in the personal domain, while firmly advocating defenceless truth in the political domain. Politics, like science, should ideally focus on reality as a base for making policy. The environmental crisis is an existential crisis, and we can't afford to lose our leading minds in the process.

This implies, though, that we have to bite the bullet. We need to look the frightening reality of the environmental crisis in the eye and not shy away from feelings of shame and guilt. This is the hallmark of moral leadership. True authority takes up responsibility, especially when it is hard to do so. That is leading by example. Self-conscious feelings like shame and guilt have to be genuinely owned before an evolved sense of who we are can surface. Without taking up responsibility, we remain part of the problem instead of the solution. Without shame and guilt, there is no internal motive for giving back to nature at the expense of taking more.

Caring and understanding are crucial, but I am no proponent of the use of psychology to bypass feelings of shame and guilt when educating people on the human impact on the environment. I believe that *nudging* alone is not sufficient to convince people to restrain themselves, because it has to compete with a multi-billion-dollar advertising industry and digitally remastered political campaigns that try to persuade people to do otherwise. On top of that, effective climate action isn't compatible with business as usual: when we redirect our overconsumption to eco-products, it will still be overconsumption. In order to react to the environmental crisis effectively, we have to give up unsustainable luxuries and have to make strenuous efforts to let nature bounce back, for instance, with marine sanctuaries and rewilding projects. We need to curb our greed and lose the narcissistic fantasy that the world is our oyster. Without an internal emotional drive – without the affirmation of feelings of shame and guilt – there is not enough motivation to support reparative efforts. An unaffected cognitive grasp of the situation is just a too feeble gamble to bet our lives on.

In order to overcome our self-destructive ways, we have to acknowledge the full scope of our inner nature and carry it through to a sustainable conclusion. That is where psychology comes in: it helps us to understand our self, each other and our place in nature while we struggle to live well and keep on living well. It also helps to face reality once grandiose illusions are dispelled. As a matter of fact, it can be a relief to let that part go. It is the way to our natural home.

Notes

1 As opposed to some of the public reactions she got, ranging from disqualifying her arguments because of her Asperger's syndrome to hanging a doll with her name on the railing of a bridge in Rome.
2 In this state of affairs resounds the institutionalisation of the pleasure principle, liberated from the moderating dynamics with the reality principle.
3 Human overconsumption is so widespread in industrialised societies, that paradoxically many people at first feel ashamed if they want to break free from this unsustainable cycle.
4 The guidelines for making our personal lives more sustainable are clear-cut: house insulation, switch to renewable energy, eat less meat, fly less, repair more (among others). Industry and transport can only be regulated on governmental levels. The decision to "leave the oil in the soil" is a political one until the environmental obstacles become too great. Then the decision is made for us.
5 See for two informative books: Marshall, G. (2014). *Don't even think about it: Why our brains are wired to ignore climate change.* London: Bloomsbury; Stoknes, P.E. (2015). *What we think about when we try not to think about global warming: Toward a new psychology of climate action.* White River Junction, VA: Chelsea Green Publishing.
6 See Chapter 2.
7 Note that there is a form of sadness that prompt us to distance ourselves from nature, as an emotional means to leave an unattainable relationship. I will address these nuances later on in this chapter.
8 Though anger, like sadness, has a more versatile story to tell. Some forms of anger urge us to seek proximity, with the ulterior aim to turn the influence that nature has on us around. Further elaboration follows later in this chapter.
9 With Winnicott's famous phrase "There is no such thing as a baby" in mind, I say: "There is no such thing as humanity." What are we without "Mother Nature"?
10 A particular aggressive approach is fuelled by envy. Out of an emotional inability to stand that the other possesses qualities that you miss, those coveted qualities have to be destroyed. I can't completely discard the impression that the subjugation of nature in part is born out of envy.
11 Glenn Albrecht coined the term solastalgia to describe the distress caused by environmental change. See Albrecht, G. (2007). Solastalgia: The distress caused by environmental change. *Australasian Psychiatry*, 15, 95–98.
12 See Chapter 2.
13 The (somewhat hypomanic) motto on the website of SpaceX, founded by Elon Musk, is: "Making Life Multiplanetary". A lot of dreams and money are invested in the flight into space and the search for "planet B".
14 Shea, N. & Palu, L. (2019). A thawing Arctic is heating up a new Cold War. *National Geographic*, September.
15 And on top of that, for a considerable part it is imaginary. We claim our successes in small and isolated spheres of reality (also known as scientific experiments), but struggle our way through the intricacies of real life.
16 Likewise, apocalyptic convictions that the end time has come and that there is nothing that can be done are evenly illusory. They are the downside of narcissistic, grandiose fantasies.
17 The "overview effect" is known by astronauts viewing planet earth from outer space. Few things are better for putting our place in the world into perspective than to take a real look at our place in space. Seen from there all sorts of societal boundaries and divisions lose their importance, and the need to take care of this "pale blue dot" floating in an immeasurable dark universe lucidly comes into awareness.
18 Among them, some divisive ones like "They want to take away your hamburgers!"

19 Certainly I don't mean to idealise the UN and to devalue personal or national efforts; the UN owes its very existence to personal and national efforts. I only want to stress the importance of an encompassing mindset linked to some executive power.

20 An indispensable book for a better understanding of the psychodynamics involved in engaging with climate change is edited by Sally Weintrobe. An exemplary variety of scientists and practitioners zoom in on anxiety, the perversity in our culture, ecological debt, the myth of apathy and facing up to human nature (among others). See Weintrobe, S. (ed.) (2013). *Engaging with climate change: Psychoanalytic and interdisciplinary perspectives*. London: Routledge.

21 "Finally someone who speaks my mind!"

22 A transcending policy would be to strive for a just geopolitical power balance and for a cradle-to-cradle design of economy.

23 Some governments treat environmentalists as possible terrorists. Though this looks like hostile framing, it might well reflect a deeper truth: capitalism is truly frightened of environmentalism. The quintessential ideological issue is about our collective trust. Do we focus on securing a shared sustainable base in the natural world or do we focus on the maximisation of personal profit? Psychosocially it is about the dynamics between cooperation and competition.

24 Wilfred Bion has described this as the psychotic part of the personality. See Bion, W.R. (1957). Differentiation of the psychotic from the non-psychotic personalities. *International Journal of Psycho-Analysis*, 38(3–4), 266–275.

25 See, for an attentive example, the work of the Dutch photographer Kadir van Lohuizen.

26 See articles and editorials on Climategate in *Nature*, the science journal.

27 The absurdity here is that this alien force is supposed to be weak, evil and dangerous at the same time.

Outflow

Some books are written by writers; other books seem to write themselves. I believe that this book has written me.

When I closed my private practice two and a half years ago, I had no clear-cut plan. First I had to recover from this decision, which was as difficult as it was inevitable. Though I still was emotionally involved with the people who had come to me for psychotherapy, my ability to use my involvement professionally was tarnishing. I needed a break to clarify my own inner turbulence.

For months my mind had wandered, when suddenly an ambition surfaced to elucidate my ideas about emotions. I wanted to contribute to the understanding of our inner nature and link it to our relationship with outer nature, both human and non-human. Strengthened by the support of family, friends and colleagues, this ambition gradually solidified into the book that lies before you. And like I have learned things from teaching that I never learned from learning, my emotions and thoughts evolved while writing. In the process of writing, there is a delicate balance between intuitive association and logical argumentation. Somehow, it has been like learning to speak from within all over again. Hopefully, some of it resonates and serves you too.

And I find this to be the elusive gift of the deep: only when the mind floats lightly into the darkness of not-knowing, does the heart become clairvoyant. Then, all is now.

A truth beyond dream and disillusion might shine through.

References

Ainsworth, M., Blehar, M.C., Waters, E. & Wall, S. (1979). *Patterns of attachment: A psychological study of the strange situation.* Hillsdale, NJ: Lawrence Erlbaum.

Albrecht, G. (2007). Solastalgia: The distress caused by environmental change. *Australasian Psychiatry*, 15, 95–98.

Allen, J.G. & Fonagy, P. (eds.) (2006). *Handbook of mentalization-based treatment.* Hoboken, NJ: John Wiley & Sons Inc.

Alvarez, A. (2010). Levels of analytic work and levels of pathology: The work of calibration. *International Journal of Psychoanalysis*, 91(4), 859–878.

Alvarez, A. (2012). *The thinking heart: Three levels of psychoanalytic therapy with disturbed Children.* London: Routledge.

Anzieu, D. (1989). *The skin ego.* New Haven & London: Yale University Press.

Beebe, B. & Lachmann, F.M. (2002). *Infant research and adult treatment.* New York: The Analytic Press.

Bekoff, M. (2000). *The smile of a dolphin: Remarkable accounts of animal emotions.* New York: Discovery Books.

Berlin, H.A. (2011). The neural basis of the dynamic unconscious. *Neuropsychoanalysis*, 13(1), 5–31.

Bick, E. (1968). The experience of the skin in early object-relations. *International Journal of Psycho-Analysis*, 49, 484–486.

Bion, W.R. (1957). Differentiation of the psychotic from the non-psychotic. *International Journal of Psychoanalysis*, 38, 206–275.

Bion, W.R. (1959). Attacks on linking. *The International Journal of Psychoanalysis*, 40, 308–315.

Bion, W.R. (1962). *Learning from experience.* London: William Heinemann.

Bion, W.R. (1977). *Emotional turbulence in borderline personality disorders.* New York: International University Press.

Blatt, S.J. (1974). Levels of object representations in anaclitic and introjective depression. *Psychoanalytic Study of the Child*, 29, 107–157.

Blatt, S.J. & Blass, R.B. (1992). Relatedness and self-definition: Two primary dimensions in personality development, psychopathology and psychotherapy. In: Barron, J., Eagle, M. & Wolitsky, D. (eds.), *Interface of psychoanalysis and psychology* (399–428). Washington, DC: American Psychological Association.

Brewin, C.R. (2006). Understanding cognitive behaviour therapy: A retrieval competition account. *Behaviour Research and Therapy*, 44, 765–784.

Cannon, W.B. (1929). *Bodily changes in pain, hunger, fear and rage.* Boston: Branford.

Carver, C.S. & Harmon-Jones, E. (2009). Anger is an approach-related affect: Evidence and implications. *Psychological Bulletin*, 135, 183–204.

Coates, S. & Schecter, D. (2006). Preschoolers' traumatic stress post-9/11: Relational and developmental perspectives. In: Wachs, C. & Jacobs, L. (eds.), *Parent-focused child therapy: Attachment, identification and reflective functions* (93–110). Lanham, Boulder & New York: Rowman & Littlefield.

Crutzen, P. & Stoermer, E. (2000). The anthropocene, global change. *IGBP (International Geosphere-Biosphere Programme) Newsletter*, 41, 17–18.

Damasio, A. (2010). *Self comes to mind: Constructing the conscious brain*. New York, NY: Pantheon Books.

Darwin, C. (2009). *The expression of the emotions in man and animals*. London: Harper Perennial. (Originally published in 1872).

Dijksterhuis, A. (2007). *Het slimme onbewuste: Denken met gevoel*. Amsterdam: Uitgeverij Bert Bakker.

Dunn, B.D., Galton, H.C., Morgan, R., Evans, D., Oliver, C., Meyer, M., Cusack, R., Lawrence, A.D. & Dalgleish, T. (2010). Listening to your heart: How interoception shapes emotion experience and intuitive decision making. *Psychological Science*, 21, 1835–1844.

Fairbairn, W.R.D. (1963). Synopsis of an object-relations theory of the personality. *International Journal of Psychoanalysis*, 44, 224–225.

Fonagy, P., Gergely, G., Jurist, E. & Target, M. (2002). *Affect regulation, mentalization, and the development of the self*. New York: Other Press.

Fosha, D., Siegel, D.J. & Solomon, M. (eds.) (2009). *The healing power of emotion: Affective neuroscience, development, and clinical practice*. New York & London: W.W. Norton & Company.

Fotopoulou, A. (2015). The virtual bodily self: Mentalisation of the body as revealed in anosognosia for hemiplegia. *Consciousness and Cognition*, 33, 500–510.

Fotopoulou, A. & Tsakiris, M. (2017). Mentalizing homeostasis: The social origins of interoceptive inference. *Neuropsychoanalysis*, 19(1), 3–28.

Freed, P.J. & Mann, J.J. (2007). Sadness and Loss: Toward a neurobiopsychosocial model. *American Journal of Psychiatry*, 164, 28–34.

Freud, A. (1992). *The Ego and the mechanisms of defence*. London: Routledge. (Originally published in 1937).

Freud, S. (1911). *Formulations on the two principles of mental functioning*. Standard Edition, Vol. 12. London: Hogarth Press, 213–226.

Freud, S. (1914). *On narcissism: An introduction*. Standard Edition, Vol. 14. London: Hogarth Press, 67–104.

Freud, S. (1915). *The unconscious*. Standard Edition, Vol. 14. London: Hogarth Press, 166–204.

Freud, S. (1917a). *A difficulty in the path of psycho-analysis*. Standard Edition, Vol. 17. London: Hogarth Press.

Freud, S. (1917b). *Mourning and melancholia*. Standard Edition, Vol. 14. London: Hogarth Press, 239–258.

Freud, S. (1919). *The uncanny*. Standard Edition, Vol. 17. London: Hogarth Press, 217–256.

Freud, S. (1920). *Beyond the pleasure principle*. Standard Edition, Vol. 19. London: Hogarth Press, 7–64.

Freud, S. (1923). *The ego and the id*. Standard Edition, Vol. 19. London: Hogarth Press, 12–59.

Freud, S. (1930). *Civilization and its discontents*. Standard Edition, Vol. 21. London: Hogarth Press, 64–145.

Freud, S. (1950). *Project for a scientific psychology*. Standard Edition, Vol. 1. London: Hogarth Press, 281–397. (Originally published in 1895–96).

Frijda, N.H. (1986). *The emotions*. Cambridge: Cambridge University Press.

Frijda, N.H. (2016). The evolutionary emergence of what we call "emotions". *Cognition and Emotion*, 30(4), 609–620.

Friston, K. (2010). The free-energy principle: A unified brain theory? *Nature Reviews Neuroscience*, 11, 127–138.

Godfrey-Smith, P. (2016). *Other minds: The octopus and the evolution of intelligent life*. London: William Collins.

Gumley, A., Gillham, A., Taylor, K. & Schwannauer, M. (eds.) (2013). *Psychosis and emotion: The role of emotions in understanding psychosis, therapy and recovery*. New York & London: Routledge.

Hardy, A., Fowler, D., Freeman, D., Smith, B., Steel, C., Evans, J., Garety, P., Kuipers, E., Bebbington, P. & Dunn, G. (2005). Trauma and hallucinatory experience in psychosis. *The Journal of Nervous and Mental Disease*, 193(8), 501–507.

Harlow, H. (1959). Love in infant monkeys. *Scientific American*, 200(6), 68–74.

Hayes, S.C., Strosahl, K.D. & Wilson, K.G. (2012). *Acceptance and commitment therapy: The process and practice of mindful change*. 2nd Edition. New York, NY, US: Guilford Press.

Herbert, B.M. & Pollatos, O. (2012). The body in the mind: On the relationship between interoception and embodiment. *Topics in Cognitive Science*, 4(4), 692–704.

Horowitz, L.M. (2004). *Interpersonal foundations of psychopathology*. Washington, DC: American Psychological Association.

Jack, R.E., Sun, W., Delis, I., Garrod, O.G. & Schyns, P.G. (2016). Four not six: Revealing culturally common facial expressions of emotion. *Journal of Experimental Psychology: General*, 145(6), 708–730.

Jacobs Hendel, H. (2018). *It's not always depression: Working with the change triangle to listen to the body, discover core emotions, and connect to your authentic self*. New York: Spiegel & Grau.

James, W. (1983). *The principles of psychology*. Cambridge: Harvard University Press. (Originally published in 1890).

Kahneman, D. (2012). *Thinking, fast and slow*. London: Penguin Books Ltd.

Kernberg, O. (1967). Borderline personality organization. *Journal of the American Psychoanalytic Association*, 15(3), 641–685.

Klein, M. (1929). Personification in the play of children. *International Journal of Psycho-Analysis*, 10, 171–182.

Klein, M. (2002). Some theoretical conclusions regarding the emotional life of the infant. In: *Envy and gratitude and other works 1946–1963* (61–93). New York: The Free Press. (Originally published in 1952).

Klein, N. (2014). *This changes everything: Capitalism vs. the climate*. New York: Simon & Schuster.

Knafo, D. (2002). Revisiting Ernst Kris's concept of regression in the service of the Ego in art. *Psychoanalytic Psychology*, 19(1), 24–49.

Kohut, H. (2001). *The analysis of the self: A systematic approach to the psychoanalytic treatment of narcissistic personality disorders*. Madison, CT: International Universities Press, Inc. (Originally published in 1971).

Kris, A.O. (1985). Resistance in convergent and in divergent conflicts. *Psychoanalytic Quarterly*, 54, 537–568.

Ladan, A. (2014). *Dead certainties: On psychoanalysis, disillusion, and death.* London & New York: Routledge.

Leary, T.F. (1957). *The interpersonal diagnosis of personality.* New York: The Ronald Press Company.

LeDoux, J. (1996). *The emotional brain: The mysterious underpinnings of emotional life.* London: Phoenix.

Lensvelt-Mulder, G., Van der Hart, O., Van Ochten, J.M., Van Son, M.J.M., Steele, K. & Breeman, L. (2008). Relations among peritraumatic dissociation and posttraumatic stress: A meta-analysis. *Clinical Psychology Review,* 28, 1138–1151.

Lertzman, R. (2015). *Environmental Melancholia. Psychoanalytic dimensions of engagement.* London: Routledge.

Levin, K., Cashore, B., Bernstein, S. & Auld, G. (2012). Overcoming the tragedy of super wicked problems: Constraining our future selves to ameliorate global climate change. *Policy Sciences,* 45(2), 123–152.

Linehan, M.M. (1993). *Cognitive-behavioral treatment of borderline personality disorder.* New York: Guilford Press.

Litz, B.T., Stein, N., Delaney, E., Lebowitz, L., Nash, W.P., Silva, C. & Maguen, S. (2014). Moral injury and moral repair in war veterans: A preliminary model and intervention strategy. *Clinical Psychology Review,* 29, 695–706.

Llinás, R.R. (2001). *I of the vortex: From neurons to self.* Cambridge, MA: MIT Press.

Lousada, M. & Mazanti, L. (2017). *Real sex: Why everything you learned about sex is wrong.* London: Hayhouse.

Mahler, M.S., Pine, F. & Bergman, A. (1975). *The psychological birth of the human infant: Symbiosis and individuation.* New York: Basic Books.

Marshall, G. (2014). *Don't even think about it: Why our brains are wired to ignore climate change.* London: Bloomsbury.

Mommers, J. (2017). Shell made a film about climate change in 1991 (then neglected to heed its own warning). *The Correspondent,* 28 February.

Nathanson, D.L. (1994). *Shame and pride: Affect, sex and the birth of the self.* New York: Norton.

Nicolai, N.J. (1997). Over splitsen, splijten en dissociëren. *Tijdschrift voor Psychotherapie,* 23(2), 85–107.

Nicolaï, N.J. (2016). *Emotieregulatie als basis van het menselijk bestaan. De kunst van het evenwicht.* Leusden: Diagnosis Uitgevers.

O'Connell, M. (2018). Why Silicon Valley billionaires are prepping for the apocalypse in New Zealand. *The Guardian,* 15 February.

O'Shaughnessy, E. (1964). The absent object. *Journal of Child Psychotherapy,* 1(2), 34–43.

Ogden, P., Minton, K. & Pain, C. (2006). *Trauma and the body: A sensorimotor approach to psychotherapy.* New York: Norton.

Ogden, T.H. (1989). On the concept of an autistic-contiguous position. The International *Journal of Psychoanalysis,* 70(1), 127–140.

Panksepp, J. (1998). *Affective neuroscience: The foundations of human and animal emotions.* New York & Oxford: Oxford University Press.

Panksepp, J. & Biven, L. (2012). *The archaeology of mind: Neuroevolutionary origins of human emotions.* New York: W.W. Norton & Company.

Plutchick, R. (1980). *Emotion: A psychoevolutionary synthesis.* New York: Harper & Row.

Poe, E.A. (2018). *A descent into the Maelström.* Independently Published. (Originally published in 1841).

Posner, J., Russell, J.A. & Peterson, B.B. (2005). The circumplex model of affect: An integrative approach to affective neuroscience, cognitive development, and psychopathology. *Development and Psychopathology*, 17(3), 715–734.

Rotter, J.B. (1989). Internal versus external control of reinforcement: A case history of a variable. *American Psychologist*, 45, 489–493.

Russell, J.A. (1980). A circumplex model of affect. *Journal of Personality and Social Psychology*, 39, 1161–1178.

Schalkwijk, F. (2015). *The conscience and self-conscious emotions in adolescence: An integrative approach*. London: Routledge.

Schore, A.N. (1994). *Affect regulation and the origin of the self: The neurobiology of emotional development*. Mahwah, NJ: Erlbaum.

Shai, D. & Belsky, J. (2011). When words just won't do: Introducing parental embodied mentalizing. *Child Development Perspectives*, 5(3), 173–180.

Shapiro, F. (1995). *Eye movement desensitization and reprocessing: Basic principles, protocols, and procedures*. New York: Guilford Press.

Siegel, A. (2005). *The neurobiology of aggression and rage*. Boca Raton, FL: CRC Press.

Solms, M. (2018). Depression in neuropsychoanalysis: Why does depression feel bad? In: Spagnolo, R. (ed.), *Building bridges: The impact of neuropsychoanalysis on psychoanalytic clinical sessions* (39–54). London & New York: Routledge.

Solms, M. & Friston, K. (2018). How and why consciousness arises: Some considerations from physics and physiology. *Journal of Consciousness Studies*, 25(5–6), 202–238.

Solms, M. & Panksepp, J. (2015). The "id" knows more than the "ego" admits. In: *The feeling brain: Selected papers on neuropsychoanalysis* (143–181). London: Karnac Books.

Solms, M. & Turnbull, O. (2002). *The brain and the inner world: An introduction to the neuroscience of subjective experience*. New York: Other Press.

Solomon, M. (2009). Emotion in romantic partners: Intimacy found, intimacy lost, intimacy reclaimed. In: Fosha, D., Siegel, D.J. & Solomon, M. (eds.), *The healing power of emotion: Affective neuroscience, development, and clinical practice* (232–256). New York & London: W.W. Norton & Company.

Spagnolo, R. (ed.) (2018). *Building bridges: The impact of neuropsychoanalysis on psychoanalytic clinical sessions*. London & New York: Routledge.

Spiegel, D. (2008). Coming apart: Trauma and the fragmentation of the self. *Cerebrum*, 31 January. Website of the DANA Foundation.

Spitz, R.A. (1965). *The first year of life: A psychoanalytic study of normal and deviant development of object relations*. New York: International University Press.

Steele, K., Van der Hart, O. & Nijenhuis, E. (2005). Phase-oriented treatment of structural dissociation in complex traumatization: Overcoming trauma-related phobias. *Journal of Trauma & Dissociation*, 6(3), 11–53.

Stern, D.N. (1985). *The interpersonal world of the infant*. New York: Basic Books.

Stern, D.N. (2002). *The first relationship*. Cambridge: Harvard University Press.

Stoknes, P.E. (2015). *What we think about when we try not to think about global warming: Toward a new psychology of climate action*. White River Junction, VA: Chelsea Green Publishing.

Theriault, J.E., Young, L. & Barrett, L.F. (2019). The sense of should: A biologically-based model of social pressure. 9 January. https://doi.org/10.31234/osf.io/x5rbs

Thyson, P. & Thyson, R.L. (1990). *Psychoanalytic theories of development: An integration*. New Haven & London: Yale University Press.

Tronick, E. (1989). Emotions and emotional communication in infants. *American Psychologist*, 44(2), 112–119.

Tsakiris, M. (2017). The multisensory basis of the self: From body to identity to others. *The Quarterly Journal of Experimental Psychology*, 70(4), 597–609.

Van Os, J. (2009). A salience dysregulation syndrome. *The British Journal of Psychiatry: The Journal of Mental Science*, 194(2), 101–103.

Verhaeghe, P. (2012). *Identiteit*. Amsterdam: De Bezige Bij.

Verheugt-Pleijter, A. (2009). Denken over gevoelens en voelen over gedachtes: Over mentaliseren in ouderbegeleiding en kindertherapie. *Kinder- & Jeugdsychotherapie*, 36(3), 5–20.

Weintrobe, S. (ed.) (2013). *Engaging with climate change: Psychoanalytic and interdisciplinary perspectives*. London: Routledge.

Winnicott, D.W. (1960). The theory of the parent-infant relationship. *The International Journal of Psychoanalysis*, 41, 585–595.

Zachar, P. & Ellis, R.D. (2012). *Categorical versus dimensional models of affect: A seminar on the theories of Panksepp and Russell*. Amsterdam: John Benjamins Publishing Company.

Zellner, M. (2018). Foundations of addiction: Dysregulated SEEKING and PANIC processes. In: Spagnolo, R. (ed.), *Building bridges: The impact of neuropsychoanalysis on psychoanalytic clinical sessions* (23–38). London & New York: Routledge.

Index

Note: Page numbers in *italics* indicate a figure and page numbers in **bold** indicate a table on the corresponding page.

testing and 137–138; as self-conscious emotion 61; self-evaluation and 64–66
Shame and Pride (Nathanson) 71n6
social learning theory 21
solastalgia 145n11
Solms, Mark 16–17, 105
Solomon, Marion 100n3
SpaceX 145n13
spatial distance 19
Spitz, René 34
split-off 53
splitting 43–44, 110n12
status axis 23
Stern, D.N. 62
Still Face experiment 33–34, 62–63, 83
Strange Situation test 33
structural dissociation 130n29
structural model (Freud) 125
suicidal tendencies: in adolescents 101–102; as attempt to hide "not knowing how to live" 110n5; medication to suppress 101; multiple determinants for 101; psychological drive for separateness 101–102; *see also* depression
symptoms 53

Tas, Louis 71n7
terror, transformed into fear 93
therapeutic collaboration 50
Thunberg, Greta 131
top-down regulation 130n18
transference 45n3
transitional object 85
traumatisation 2, 53–54, 81; *see also* post-traumatic stress disorder (PTSD)
trust 50, 51; basic 21

unattainable fulfilment 29
unconsciousness 123, 127
United Nations Climate Summit 131
unwavering composure 119
uppers 107

vertical splitting 110n12
victimisation 71n7
visceral states 122

Winnicott, Donald 85

zone of human touch 18–19

Printed in Great Britain
by Amazon